THE ESSENTIAL
BOND

HarperEntertainment

A Division of HarperCollins*Publishers*

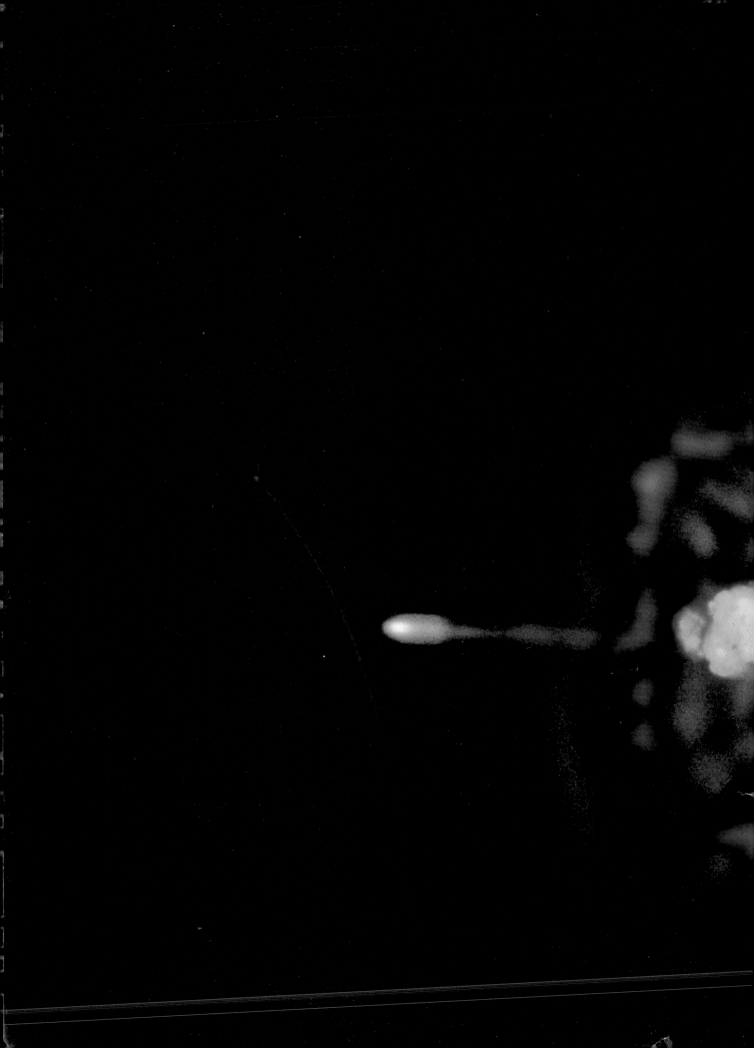

THE ESSENTIAL
BOND

The Authorized Guide to the World of 007

Lee Pfeiffer & Dave Worrall

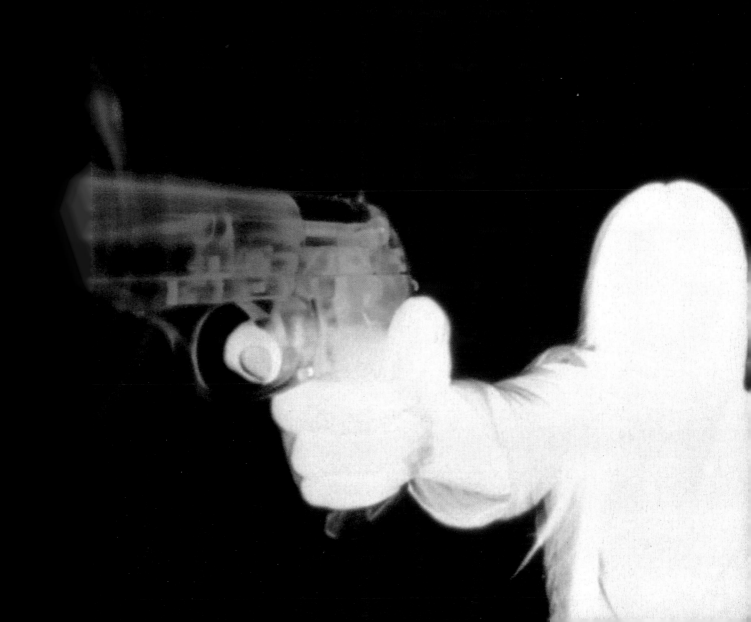

Originally published in the United Kingdom in 1998 by Boxtree, an imprint of Macmillan Publishers Ltd.

FIRST U.S. EDITION PUBLISHED 1999

Designed by Dan Newman

ISBN 0-06-107590-6

99 00 01 02 03 10 9 8 7 6 5 4 3 2 1

CONTENTS

To Dana Broccoli, for her enthusiasm and support for this book, and for Cubby, whose legacy made it possible.

FOREWORD

by Michael G Wilson

As JAMES BOND IS ABOUT TO ENTER THE NEW MILLENNIUM, EVEN those of us who have literally grown up with the series could not have predicted the lasting impact Agent 007 has had on popular culture. Even more surprising than Bond's durability is the extent of his universal appeal. Bond is not provincial – he belongs to people of all cultures and walks of life. He is also very much a survivor who has consistently proven wrong those who claimed that he would become outdated. Indeed, the post-Cold War years have brought the films their largest box-office grosses ever.

Most film series find it difficult to thrive in the wake of a popular actor leaving the leading role. However, Bond has continued to prosper not in spite of, but perhaps *because* of, the talents of the five actors who have brought him to life onscreen – each with his own unique interpretation of the role. With *The Essential Bond*, authors Lee Pfeiffer and Dave Worrall have provided an in-depth celebration of the series, but they have wisely refrained from calling this the definitive work about the James Bond films. There may never be a definitive work, because the series – like Bond himself – is constantly evolving.

When I'm asked to explain 007's international popularity, I can only surmise that there is a little part of each of us that emulates James Bond and his world. On a more obvious level, however, there is the inescapable fact that my stepfather Cubby Broccoli and his partner Harry Saltzman – then later, Cubby alone – made it possible for one to escape into an exotic world filled with larger-than-life characters, if only for a couple of hours. The success of the films is due to the legions of actors, writers, directors and technicians who have been very much part of the family for those of us at Eon Productions. They have always shared in Cubby's determination that every penny of the budget is reflected on the screen, and that the audience receives the best value for its money. It is a tradition that Barbara Broccoli and I and the other members of the Eon family are determined to carry on – as James Bond enters his second century.

M. Wilson

Acknowledgments

The authors would like to extend their sincere thanks to a number of individuals who have given their support and assistance to this volume. We are especially indebted to our good friends at Eon Productions in Los Angeles and London, without whom this project would not have been possible: Dana Broccoli, Michael G Wilson, Barbara Broccoli, David Pope, Amanda Schofield, Meg Simmonds, Michael Tavares and especially John Parkinson, whose continuing support of our projects has made it possible for two middle-aged men to avoid getting 'real jobs'! At Boxtree a very sincere thanks to our editor Emma Mann, as well as Adrian Sington and the designer of the book Dan Newman. Others who have earned our thanks by contributing facts and/or photographs are: Jeff Marshall, Andy Foley, Graham Rye, Bill Duelly, Hiroki Takeda, Makoto Wakmatsu, Bert Luxford, Oliver Rauw, Gary McGuire, Doug Redenius, Philip Nevitsky, Gary Giblin, David Oliver, Ron Plesnarski and Ray Donohue. We are also grateful to the following talented photographers for their generous permission to reprint their work:

Harry Myers, PIC Photo Agency, 280 Uxbridge Road, London W12 7JA.
George Martin, GHM Photographics, 11191 Westheimer #607, Houston, TX 77042, USA.
Tom Stroud, 52 Simon Block Avenue, Wilkes Barre, PA 18702, USA.

Many thanks also to Janet and Nicole Pfeiffer for tolerating the authors turning their home into a 'Bond Museum' during the course of researching and writing this book.

The authors invite readers to send their comments and corrections to: POB 1570 Christchurch, Dorset BH23 4XS, UK or POB 152 Dunellen, NJ 08812, USA. If requested, readers will receive further announcements about 007-related licensed products and events. E-mail address: spyguise@msn.com

REMEMBERING CUBBY

T HERE ARE MANY PEOPLE RESPONSIBLE FOR THE SUCCESS OF THE James Bond films. Certainly there would not have been a series to celebrate if it had not been for the remarkable talents of Ian Fleming, the literary 'father' of agent 007. However, if there is one man who was indisputably the driving force behind the amazing and enduring success of the films, it is Albert R Broccoli, known affectionately as 'Cubby' even to those who never met him personally. Through Cubby's early partnership on the series with Harry Saltzman the Bond films were turned into an international phenomenon. However, after Harry left the partnership, it was Cubby who revived the series in the wake of mounting speculation that 007 had outlived his era. Commencing with *The Spy Who Loved Me* in 1977, Cubby proved he had what it took to go it alone and re-energize the entire franchise. In later years he worked closely with his stepson Michael G Wilson and daughter Barbara Broccoli, taking comfort in the fact that he could count on them to continue his work.

It is our hope that this book commemorates Cubby's legacy by serving as a reference guide to the wonderful films he created. No book is definitive and we don't pretend this one is an exception. Omissions of certain minor characters, gadgets and vehicles had to be made because of considerations of space. However, we do hope it at least partially reminds fans of the excitement they continue to feel upon seeing a Bond movie for the first time. If it does, then we have succeeded in our goal of honouring Cubby and all the other enormously talented people who have brought the 007 movies to life.

Upon Cubby Broccoli's death in 1996, I asked my co-author Lee Pfeiffer to write his impressions of the man for a magazine I publish, *Collecting 007*. I believe there is no more fitting introduction to this book than the following tribute to a man who was loved and respected by all who came to know him.

Dave Worrall

It WAS EARLY MORNING WHEN I RECEIVED the phone call from Dave Worrall telling me, 'It's bad news. Cubby has passed away.' The news was hardly unexpected. The legendary producer, and last of the great showmen, had been ailing for some time and those of us who knew him knew the end could come at any time.

I thought back to the summer of 1989 when I first communicated with Cubby. He had gone to great trouble to contact me about a newspaper article I wrote praising *Licence To Kill*. Cubby had been dismayed by the lukewarm US box-office returns for the film. He told me he was grateful for my positive review, as well as some flattering comments I had made about his contributions to the cinema. I'm still a bit incredulous how such a small thing could mean so much to a man who has been honoured by royalty, but that was Cubby. He always said that pleasing one Bond fan meant more to him than any award.

Over time, we kept in touch. My friend Phil Lisa and I were grateful when Cubby authorized our book *The Incredible World of 007* in 1990. When it was published in 1992, my wife Janet and I were on holiday in Palm Springs, California. Cubby phoned the hotel to give this critique: 'I love it. Want to go to lunch and celebrate?' This was the definitive rhetorical question. Cubby took us to a favourite restaurant in Beverly Hills along with his lovely wife Dana, Michael G Wilson and

Danjaq executive John Parkinson. I'll never forget Cubby telling amusing stories about personally cooking pasta for the entire cast and crew of *The Spy Who Loved Me* when there was a problem with the caterer. ('Try finding a pasta strainer in the Egyptian desert!' he said.) I also recall this powerful man sheepishly cajoling everyone to try the chocolate soufflé because he didn't want to indulge in dessert alone. Although no one was hungry, when Cubby 'suggested' soufflé, everyone had soufflé!

I last saw Cubby in the summer of 1994 when he and Dana invited me to dinner in New York. I arrived at his townhouse off Park Avenue and we were driven to the restaurant in a British taxi. (Only Cubby had enough clout and class to find a British taxi in New York.) Although there were long queues for tables, upon seeing Cubby the restaurant staff parted the crowds like Moses did the Red Sea. Soon he was sitting comfortably and holding court with any number of people who knew him – or *claimed* to know him. Cubby was too polite to let on if he didn't recognize them. He was the only person I had ever met who could reminisce with people he didn't know! For hours over dinner, we talked of Bond and I was amazed at how much enthusiasm he still had for the series. Cubby had no doubt that Barbara and Michael would bring back the series in a big way. They were about to decide who would be the new 007 in *GoldenEye*, and I could tell from his sentiments that Pierce Brosnan would be Cubby's choice. After dinner, he offered me a lift in the British taxi. I politely declined, opting to walk in the summer night through the streets of Manhattan. As we parted, he said 'Keep in touch, kid.' I never saw him again. A routine operation later that week led to more serious problems from which he would never fully recover.

Fast forward to the summer of 1995. My partners and I are at Pinewood Studios in England filming documentaries for Eon Productions and MGM/UA Home Video about the making of the classic Bond movies. We are allowed to use Cubby's personal office to shoot interviews with alumni from the films. Cubby would have loved to have been present for this event. Here, once again, were people like Guy Hamilton, Eunice Gayson, Walter Gotell, Molly Peters, Desmond Llewelyn and so many other veterans of the films. Praising Cubby is a common link in their interviews. Over the course of several hectic days, filming is completed. America beckons with its impossibly fast pace of life, all-night editing

Cubby's office at Pinewood Studios.

sessions and other traumas for a group of novice film-makers. Yet, the whole project has been inspired by Cubby's long-term goal of getting the real story of the Bond productions on film.

As we prepare to leave Pinewood, I realize that this is the end of an era. It's obvious that this office will not be here for long and that Cubby will never return to it. Alone, I look around the understated office and take a moment to reflect. I try to imagine the giants who passed through this doorway. Giants with names like Shaw, Lenya, Pleasence, Young, Maibaum, Celi and so many others. Somehow, fate has chosen a group of people who were in grade school when the Bond legacy began to conduct the last official 007 project ever to take place in this office.

I try to make a permanent image in my mind of this place. There are a few posters from the Bond films, some scattered awards, a watercolour painting of his Rolls-Royce signed by the cast and crew of *A View To A Kill*, Cubby's crew jacket from *Octopussy* awaiting him on a coat rack, and , of course, his giant desk from behind which James Bond movies were created. Suddenly, I feel like an intruder. However, if there are spirits present, they are hopefully pleased that for one last time their co-workers have returned here to recall the classic films they made together. In leaving, I realize how privileged we have been to be in this place. I turn off the lights and close the door behind me, knowing that in doing so it closes an entire era in the history of the Bond films. The last intruder is gone. The ghosts of giants can walk here once more.

Thanks for the memories, Cubby – onscreen and off.

Lee Pfeiffer

DR. NO

(1962)

Director **TERENCE YOUNG** Producers **ALBERT R BROCCOLI & HARRY SALTZMAN**
Screenplay **RICHARD MAIBAUM, JOHANNA HARWOOD & BERKLEY MATHER**
Director of Photography **TED MOORE** Editor **PETER HUNT** Production Designer **KEN ADAM**
Music **MONTY NORMAN**
Release date: UK 5 October 1962, USA 8 May 1963. Running time: 105 minutes

ALTHOUGH IAN FLEMING'S NOVELS HAD BECOME literary sensations by 1961, producers Cubby Broccoli and Harry Saltzman found major studios less than enthusiastic about bringing Mr Bond to the screen. The most common objections? The subject was 'too British' and 'too blatantly sexual'. Eventually United Artists' chief Arthur Krim allocated a budget of $1 million for the first of what was hoped to be a modestly successful series of thrillers. The rest, as they say, is history. *Dr. No* was the surprise hit of 1962. Never before had audiences met an anti-hero quite like James Bond. Agent 007 was a connoisseur of fine food and drink. He attracted and bedded legions of beautiful women to satisfy his own healthy sexual appetites. He travelled the world in luxury with the most generous expense account ever granted a British civil servant. He was witty, charming, fearless and incorruptible. In one of those rare masterstrokes of casting, Sean Connery personified James Bond with such perfection that even Ian Fleming (initially critical of Connery for being too uncouth for the role) admitted that it was difficult imagining anyone else in the part.

Broccoli and Saltzman allocated their somewhat meagre budget wisely and fashioned a film which looked far more expensive than it actually was. With *Dr. No*, the producers established an informal 'stock company' of actors and technicians, many of whom would work on the Bond films for decades to come. The magnificent, hi-tech sets, unique main title sequences and editing style would all become hallmarks of the series and influence the entire

Previous spread: It's not always a tough life being a secret agent! Connery and Ursula Andress relax between takes in Jamaica.

Above and right: From conception to reality . . . Ken Adam's design for Dr No's laboratory.

action-film genre for decades to come. Fans often cite this film and its successor *From Russia With Love* as the 'purist' adaptations of Fleming's novels, primarily because – in this pre-gadget era – Bond remained very much a detective who relied on his wits to thwart his enemies. Despite the movie's surprise success, both Cubby Broccoli and Sean Connery would comment decades later that no one ever foresaw that Mr Bond would remain a cultural phenomenon at the start of a new century.

THE ASSIGNMENT

James Bond flies to Jamaica to investigate the disappearance of fellow agent John Strangways. Bond discovers the man has been murdered to prevent him from looking into the affairs of Dr No, a mysterious scientist who has established a virtual fortress on the nearby island of Crab Key. Bond and a local CIA contact named Quarrel arrive on Crab Key where they encounter Honey Ryder, a beautiful young woman who is reluctantly forced to flee with them after the group is discovered and hunted by Dr No's private army. Quarrel is killed in an ensuing battle and Bond and Honey are captured and brought to Dr No's magnificent lair. Here, Dr No informs 007 that he is an agent of SPECTRE, a secret international crime organization which is planning to demonstrate its power by destroying the American space programme. Bond matches wits with Dr No, and escapes numerous death traps before ensuring that his adversary falls victim to his own scheme. He and Honey escape the island immediately prior to a massive explosion which destroys the complex.

007'S WOMEN

HONEY RYDER (Ursula Andress)

The ultimate Bond woman. Intelligent (if undeniably naïve), resourceful and courageous, Honey set the standard for the girls who would follow in her footsteps. Bond first encounters the stunning beauty on the beaches of Crab Key where she is searching for valuable shells. An orphan from an early age, Honey is self-educated and quite capable of defending herself (as evidenced by her using a black widow spider to mortally wound a rapist). Her father was a marine biologist who had died in mysterious circumstances while exploring Crab Key. Honey almost shares her father's fate when she and 007 are captured by Dr No. Although Honey openly flirts with Bond, it is not until the end of his extraordinary mission that they finally become lovers.

Despite having her voiced dubbed for the film, Ursula Andress made such a striking appearance in *Dr. No* that she not only became an international star but also sent bikini sales soaring.

SYLVIA TRENCH (Eunice Gayson)

Although she appears only briefly in *Dr. No*, Sylvia Trench has the distinction of being the very first lady to have a romantic encounter with the cinematic James Bond when she flirts with him while

Sorry, Bond fans... this rare photograph proves Ursula was not naked during the radiation cleansing sequence.

playing Chemin de Fer at the posh London casino, Le Cercle. It is to Sylvia Trench that 007 first makes his immortal introduction, 'Bond . . . James Bond'. Despite losing a hefty sum to Mr Bond, Sylvia proves to be graceful in defeat by sneaking into Bond's apartment and greeting him wearing only one of his dress shirts. Her seductive tactics cause Bond to delay his departure for Jamaica from 'immediately' to 'almost immediately'.

007'S VILLAINS

DR NO (Joseph Wiseman)

The first in the infamous line of perverted geniuses who do battle with James Bond, Dr Julius No remains one of the cinema's most legendary villains. Superbly played by Joseph Wiseman, he is a truly unique character and his presence so dominates the film that it is almost a revelation to

TOP SECRET CAST & CREW DOSSIERS

❊ **Ursula Andress** returned to Jamaica in 1996 for the first time since filming *Dr. No* to appear as the guest of honour at an official James Bond Festival. Her appearance drew paparazzi from around the world, proving she remains the quintessential James Bond girl.

❊ **Lois Maxwell** was originally offered the role of Sylvia Trench, but opted instead for Moneypenny because she felt the Trench character was too blatantly sexual.

'You are nothing more than a stupid policeman … whose luck has run out!' Dr No challenges Agent 007.

TOP SECRET CAST & CREW DOSSIERS

❉ **Sean Connery** was first suggested for the role of Bond after Cubby Broccoli's wife Dana saw him in the Disney film *Darby O'Gill and the Little People*.

❉ **Ian Fleming** initially asked his friend and fellow Jamaica resident **Noel Coward** to play the part of Dr No. Coward's classic response was, 'No! No! No!'. **Christopher Lee**, a distant cousin of Fleming, also turned down the part, though he would later play Scaramanga in *The Man With The Golden Gun*.

realize that he is not seen until the final third of the movie. Setting the example for Bond bad guys to follow, Dr No may be a ruthless murderer with a Napoleon complex but he certainly gets top marks as a host, wining and dining the captive Bond while calmly explaining his unorthodox background. The son of a German missionary and a Chinese woman, No became the entrusted treasurer of the notorious oriental crime syndicate, The Tongs. He absconded with $10 million of their funds and became a member of the secret terrorist organization SPECTRE. From his atomic-powered fortress disguised as a bauxite mine on the private island of Crab Key off the Jamaican coast, No established his own mini-kingdom from which he sabotaged the American space pro-gramme. His wealth and success had a price, however – the loss of his hands in an experiment. Thus, he replaced them with metallic hands capable of

crushing stone. Ultimately, 007 manages to thwart his imminent plan to sabotage another US rocket. In the ensuing fight to the death, Dr No falls into a pool of boiling hot, radioactive water, a rather hideous death until one compares it to his demise in Fleming's novel where he was buried under a mountain of bird guano.

PROFESSOR DENT (Anthony Dawson)

In his role as a Jamaican geologist, Professor Dent is the very picture of respectability. He befriends Strangways, the British Intelligence agent who is investigating Dr No, and frequently plays bridge with him at the Queen's Club. In reality, Dent is a henchman for Dr No and plays a key role in the murder of Strangways. When 007 suspects Dent, the professor tries to assassinate him by placing a tarantula in 007's bed. When Bond emerges unscathed, Dent tries to do the job himself by ambushing 007 at the home of the seductive Miss Taro. Instead, he finds Bond waiting for him with Walther in hand. The sequence in which Bond calmly shoots Professor Dent was shortened after censors complained that Dent's death was cold-blooded murder.

'THE THREE BLIND MICE'

These are a trio of supposedly blind beggars in Kingston, Jamaica, who, in reality, are paid assassins working for Dr No. It is they who murder British agent Strangways and his secretary Miss Trueblood and set into motion the assignment which brings 007 to the island. The 'blind men' are first seen over the film's main titles accompanied by an orchestration of the song 'Three Blind Mice'. They make their final appearance in a chase sequence during which they use the hearse they are driving to try to force 007's car over a cliff. Bond turns the tables and the would-be assassins take the plunge, causing Bond to remark casually, 'I think they were on their way to a funeral.'

MISS TARO (Zena Marshall)

This exotic *femme fatale* works by day as the secretary to Pleydell-Smith, the British foreign secretary in Jamaica. However, she 'moonlights' as a spy for Dr No, and passes on top-secret information. Miss Taro invites James Bond to her house in the Blue Mountains for an erotic evening. In reality, it is a set-up for his assassination. After enjoying a sensuous session in Miss Taro's bed, Bond demonstrates the true meaning of coitus interruptus by having her promptly arrested. A short time later, his suspicions that he has been targeted are proven true when Professor Dent appears at the house in an unsuccessful attempt to murder him.

THE PHOTOGRAPHER
(Margaret LeWars)

This beautiful, mysterious Jamaican freelance photographer makes several attempts to snap 007's picture before Bond and Quarrel seize and interrogate her. Realizing the photographer is on the payroll of Dr No, Quarrel calmly asks 007 if he should break her arm. Bond, ever the gentleman, settles for destroying her film and releasing her.

MR JONES (Reggie Carter)

An agent of Dr No, Mr Jones disguises himself as a chauffeur sent to collect Bond from Kingston Airport. Agent 007 smells a rat and confronts Jones on an isolated road, using judo to disable him. Jones chooses to bite into a cyanide tablet rather than risk being interrogated. Stunt man Bob Simmons doubled for Carter in the fight with 007.

Professor Dent provides one of 007's few undesirable bedmates. Bob Simmons, doubling for Connery, reported this to be the most frightening stunt he had ever performed.

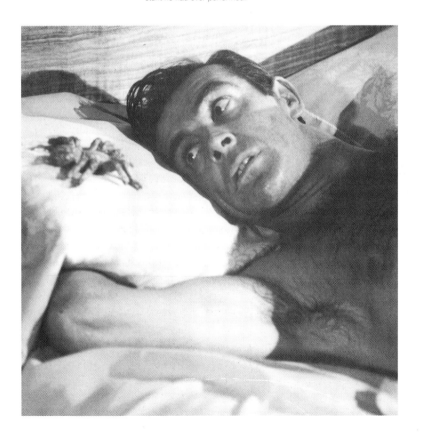

Bond meets Quarrel, the unlikely CIA agent who proves to be a valuable ally.

007'S ALLIES

QUARREL (John Kitzmiller)

Although viewed as condescending today, the character of Quarrel was something of a breakthrough in 1962 in that it presented a black man as tough and courageous. Played with immense charm and skill by John Kitzmiller, Quarrel is a seemingly lazy Jamaican fisherman. In reality, he works for the CIA and assists Felix Leiter with local operations. Quarrel is presented as a somewhat childlike individual who is terrified by superstitions and the much-fabled dragon which allegedly prowls Crab Key. However, this depiction cannot be attributed to racial stereotypes, as Honey Ryder is presented as equally naïve (although

the sequence in which Bond instructs Quarrel to 'fetch my shoes' is painful to watch today). On the positive side, Quarrel is a loyal and gallant ally to Bond and his fear of Crab Key turns out to be justified when he falls victim to the dragon (actually, a tank equipped with a flame-thrower). The death of Quarrel fills Bond with quiet rage and is one of the most sobering moments in the series. Quarrel's legacy continued to thrive a decade later, however, when his son Quarrel Jr assisted Bond in *Live And Let Die*.

FELIX LEITER (Jack Lord)

Leiter is the CIA agent assigned to Jamaica to work with James Bond to investigate the activities of Dr No. As in the novels, Bond and Leiter would go on to share numerous missions. Curiously, the producers of the films had the character played by a diverse group of actors over the years, with mixed

AROUND THE WORLD WITH 007

Dr. No was shot entirely on location in **Jamaica**, with interior scenes filmed at **Pinewood Studios** near London. Chris Blackwell (who went on to found Island Records) was employed at the age of fifteen to assist the location manager in finding suitable shooting sites for the production. Blackwell today is the owner of Ian Fleming's Jamaican home, Goldeneye.

results. Jack Lord's performance in *Dr No* is one of the most satisfying portrayals of Leiter. He is a soft-spoken, no-nonsense man of few words who exudes a cool but friendly demeanour. As in most of the films, Leiter plays only a peripheral role in the action, although he does show up in the finale to rescue Bond and Honey after their escape from Dr No's lair. Lord would go on to fame and fortune as the star of *Hawaii Five-0*.

M (Bernard Lee)

He is Bond's crusty superior at MI6. Despite his objections to Bond's lifestyle and womanizing, M holds his top agent in high regard – though rarely praises him. The Bond/M relationship is clearly defined in this film and remains relatively consistent even today, with several actors having played the role. As in the novels, M is a retired admiral in the Royal Navy who operates MI6 from the London HQ of Universal Exports, a corporate cover for the intelligence operation. Although Bond does not fear his exotic enemies, a simple glance of disapproval from M can reduce him to a chastised schoolboy. Bernard Lee plays the role with understated skill, making M a three-dimensional character and stealing every second of his often too brief time on screen. Lee would play the role in every Bond movie up to and including *Moonraker* (1979).

MISS MONEYPENNY (Lois Maxwell)

The loyal, workaholic secretary to M would have liked to have combined business with pleasure by seducing 007. The playful and flirtatious banter between the couple would become a staple of the series. Their relationship is defined in *Dr. No*: Moneypenny makes herself available and Bond proves to be evasive. Lois Maxwell remains the definitive Moneypenny in the minds of fans, probably because she would play the role in each Bond movie up to and including *A View To A Kill* (1985). Maxwell has theorized that Moneypenny and Bond spent one romantic weekend together but were afraid to continue the relationship because of the effect it would have on their respective careers. None of this is spelled out in the films, however, although in *GoldenEye* (1995) a more liberated Moneypenny implies that the couple never became lovers.

MAJOR BOOTHROYD (Peter Burton)

This is the role which would eventually evolve into that of Q, the gadgets genius, and it is played here for the first and only time by Peter Burton. In

Bernard Lee as the definitive M.

the first two films, Boothroyd is simply referred to as an armourer or equipment officer and the role is largely colourless. In *Dr. No*, Boothroyd warns Bond that he should carry a Walther PPK instead of a Beretta because the former has 'a delivery like a brick through a plate-glass window' whilst the latter is more appropriate for a lady's handbag.

PUSS-FELLER (Lester Pendergast)

This owner of a Kingston nightclub assists Bond, Leiter and Quarrel. In the novel, we are told that the character's bizarre name stems from his legendary battle against an octopus. In the film, he is known for wrestling alligators, thus leaving the origin of his name inconsistent.

JOHN STRANGWAYS
(Timothy Moxon)

The British MI6 agent in Jamaica investigating the activities of Dr No, Strangways makes a fatal mistake by informing his friend Professor Dent of his findings. Dent, a double agent for No, arranges to have Strangways assassinated by 'The Three Blind Mice'.

Original prop auctioned in London in the early 1990s.

VEHICLES

SUNBEAM ALPINE Bond's main mode of transport in his pre-Aston Martin days was his famed Bentley. However, as virtually all of the action in *Dr. No* takes place in Jamaica, not even 007's liberal expense account was ample enough to ship his car to the island from London. Therefore, he drives a Sunbeam convertible which has enough speed for him to outrace the villains. By swerving under a construction crane, Bond causes the pursuing hearse carrying 'The Three Blind Mice' assassins to veer off the road to an explosive death at the bottom of a ravine. The blue Sunbeam, a small British sports car, was actually hired by the production company from a local woman who was paid fifteen shillings per day.

Below: Bond's Sunbeam Alpine easily outmanoeuvers his deadly pursuers.

Bottom: No one escapes the clutches of Dr No's Dragon Tank.

DRAGON TANK The Dragon Tank is Dr No's main line of defence against trespassers on Crab Key. Disguised as a dragon to keep superstitious Jamaicans off the island, the armoured vehicle is equipped with a flamethrower. The two-man machine is used to deadly effect when Quarrel falls victim to its flame during a gun battle. In the novel, Bond and Honey hijack the tank and escape from Dr No's lair, but in the film version they flee by boat. A local swamp buggy, which was capable of being driven across the waterlogged marshes of the area, was used in the building of the Dragon Tank. The menacing-looking vehicle was, in fact, just a tubular framework clad with metal sheeting. At the end of the production, the producers agreed to return the tank to the company that built it on the understanding that it would be dismantled and used for scrap metal.

GADGETS & WEAPONS

WALTHER PPK 7.65MM Initially reluctant to part with a lighter-weight Beretta, Bond is forced by M to adopt this more powerful handgun. It would become his principal weapon in most of his cinematic missions. In this first Bond film, Q had yet to emerge as a significant character, hence 007's sole gadget is an ordinary Geiger counter.

MUSIC

The composer of record for the score of *Dr. No* is Monty Norman, although whether it was he or John Barry who actually wrote the famous 'James Bond Theme', which electrified audiences in this first 007 film, is still being debated. Norman maintains he composed the tune, but acknowledges that Barry reworked the orchestration. After many years of maintaining a silence on the issue, John Barry went to court in London in 1997 to seek being listed as the official composer of the work. As yet, the matter has not been decided. The Bond theme is used effectively throughout the film, primarily over the opening credits.

There are plenty of other memorable tunes, each with a Jamaican flavour, including 'Jamaican Jump Up' played by the Byron Lee Band and 'Underneath the Mango Tree', which Bond and

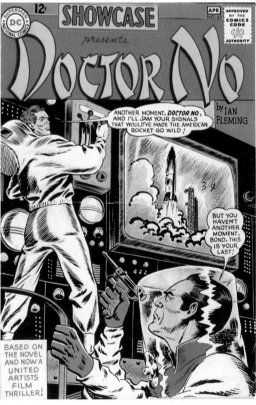

Honey sing briefly during their initial encounter on the beach.

MARKETING & MERCHANDISING

The advertising campaign for *Dr No* capitalized on the popularity of Ian Fleming's source novel, as well as elements of glamour, intrigue and sexuality. In the USA, President Kennedy's recent announcement that he was a Bond fan led the producers to include this line in the film's trailer, 'The favorite of millions from Hong Kong to Hyannisport' (the vacation home of the Kennedy clan). There was also a rather pedantic black-and-white featurette which gave the unintentional impression that *Dr No* was a low budget film.

In Britain, a unique trailer featured special narration by Sean Connery, who was shuttled around the world on a frenzied publicity tour always in the company of beautiful women. Eventually, the strategy of making Connery appear to be a real-life clone of 007 would cause the actor to become disgruntled. The only notable merchandise tie-ins to the film were a paperback edition of the novel featuring promotions for the film, a comic book adaptation of the screenplay, the soundtrack album and a 45rpm single of the Bond theme.

Below left: One of the first licensed 007 collectables: the 1962 DC Comics adaptation.

THE BOX OFFICE

Dr. No was the hit of the 1962/63 season, and eventually went on to gross £60 million worldwide. Helping matters, ironically, was the movie's condemnation by the Vatican as well as the Kremlin. The former cited Bond's cruelty and sexual aggressiveness, while the latter said that Bond was the personification of everything evil about capitalism. Naturally, the controversy only increased public awareness and made for greater earnings. The film would eventually be successfully re-released over the years, often paired with subsequent Bond movies as a double feature. ∎

WELCOME TO SPECTRE

The Special Executive for Counter-Intelligence, Terrorism, Revenge and Extortion is a secret organization headed by mankind's greatest criminals. The group's founder, evil genius Ernst Stavro Blofeld, has ambitious goals to blackmail major political powers into paying exorbitant sums to avert worldwide catastrophes. (Exactly what incentive money would hold for an organization that can afford to have its Japanese headquarters located in a dormant volcano remains a mystery.) SPECTRE is largely apolitical. However, in the days of the Cold War, there were alliances with Communist nations who would pay Blofeld to wreak havoc on the free world.

There are many benefits in working for SPECTRE. You get to work with glamorous and equally sinister men and women, travel the world on large expense accounts and find an equal opportunity environment which welcomes people of all races and tolerates those with handicaps. For example, Dr No had metallic hands and Largo was blind in one eye. However, there are a few drawbacks. The 'retirement' plan is rather dubious. Inevitably, agents end up falling victim to James Bond or being dealt with harshly by Blofeld, who may opt to send them for a dip in his piranha pool. SPECTRE figured prominently in *Dr. No, From Russia With Love, Thunderball, You Only Live Twice, On Her Majesty's Secret Service* and *Diamonds Are Forever*.

FROM RUSSIA WITH LOVE

(1963)

Director **TERENCE YOUNG** Producers **ALBERT R BROCCOLI & HARRY SALTZMAN**
Screenplay **RICHARD MAIBAUM & JOHANNA HARWOOD** Director of Photography **TED MOORE**
Editor **PETER HUNT** Art Director **SYD CAIN** Music **JOHN BARRY**

Release date: UK 10 October 1963, USA 8 April 1964. Running time: 116 minutes

As PRESIDENT KENNEDY HAD NAMED *FROM RUSSIA, With Love* among his ten favourite books of all time, producers Broccoli and Saltzman chose this as the follow-up to the smash-hit cinematic debut of James Bond, *Dr. No*. Ian Fleming's novel was the quintessential Cold War thriller, but the producers had the foresight to envision a period of détente and made the villains SPECTRE instead of the Soviet undercover agency SMERSH. Armed with a significantly higher budget, Broccoli and Saltzman created what many fans feel is the best entry in the series. Certainly, it boasts one of the most inspired casts, with even minor character roles being superbly played by a brilliant ensemble of international actors.

From Russia With Love is significant in that – with the exception of *On Her Majesty's Secret Service* – it represents the last time that Bond would be seen without the hi-tech gadgetry which became a hallmark of the later films. (The attaché case he is given by Q in *From Russia With Love* is innovative but very believable.) Bond remains a down-to-earth detective who faces admittedly exotic foes in even more exotic locations, but remains in the real world. The film boasts any number of outstanding elements. Among them, the introduction of the now standard pre-credits sequence, the inspired main title credits being shown over the undulating body of a belly dancer, and the use of a popular singer to croon a hit title song. *From Russia With Love* also demonstrates editor Peter Hunt at his best.

Previous spread: Bond
interrogates Tatiana about
the Lektor. (Note the
microphone cord on her
leg.)

Right: The mission
begins. Bond en-route to
meet Kerim Bey in
Istanbul.

His work on the train fight sequence between Bond and Grant aboard the Orient Express makes the scene one of cinema's classic action set pieces.

THE ASSIGNMENT

James Bond is informed by M that a beautiful Soviet agent has fallen in love with him and wishes to defect. She promises to steal a valued decoding machine called the Lektor which MI6 desperately wants. Bond is warned the scenario may be a trap, and indeed it is. Unbeknown to the 'defector', Tatiana Romanova, the Soviets and British are being used as pawns in an inspired scheme masterminded by SPECTRE. Tatiana is unaware that her immediate superior, Colonel Rosa Klebb, is actually working for SPECTRE. The plan is for Bond and Tatiana to steal the Lektor then be executed by assassin Red Grant. SPECTRE will then recover the machine and sell it back to the Soviets, embarrassing MI6 in the process and murdering Bond in revenge for his killing of Dr No.

Bond flies to Turkey to rendezvous with Tatiana and, with the assistance of local intelligence chief Kerim Bey, steals the Lektor and escapes aboard the Orient Express. On board, however, is Red Grant. Grant kills Kerim, but is in turn strangled by 007 in a fierce hand-to-hand battle. Bond and Tatiana escape to Venice, destroying a SPECTRE motorboat fleet in the process. There, they are menaced by Rosa Klebb who makes a last-ditch attempt to recover the Lektor. Instead, she is killed by Tatiana, who now professes her genuine love for James Bond.

007'S WOMEN

TATIANA ROMANOVA (Daniela Bianchi)
A corporal in Soviet Army Intelligence, Tatiana – assigned to the Soviet embassy in Istanbul – is used as a pawn in a murderous double-cross

orchestrated by SPECTRE and Colonel Rosa Klebb. The innocent and naïve Tatiana is ordered to seduce Bond, unaware of the extent to which she is being manipulated. Indeed, Klebb has their lovemaking secretly filmed as part of a planned murder and sex scandal – a rather daring concept for a 1963 film.

Daniela Bianchi, a novice actress and former Miss Rome, gives a sincere and totally credible performance and remains one of the more memorable of the Bond women. Surprisingly, she retired from acting only a few years after her success in *From Russia With Love*. She did, however, appear with other Bond alumni in the low-budget 007 spoof *Operation Kid Brother* in 1967.

SYLVIA TRENCH (Eunice Gayson)
James Bond's *Dr. No* paramour makes her second and final appearance in a 007 film. As in the previous film, her romantic encounter with Bond (this time on the banks of a river) is interrupted by his assignment. Still, Bond makes time to 'entertain' her in the back seat of his Bentley before reporting to HQ. Director Terence Young envisioned that the character of Sylvia would

appear in every Bond film. However, when Guy Hamilton took the director's chair for *Goldfinger*, the idea was permanently shelved. Perhaps there was concern that even Bond's libido could be overtaxed by the aggressive Sylvia.

VIDA AND ZORA, THE GYPSY FIGHTING GIRLS
(Martine Beswick and Aliza Gur)
Decades before female wrestling became an accepted spectator sport, 007 was already benefiting from an early incarnation of the ritual. While visiting a gypsy camp with Kerim Bey, Bond witnesses a rather brutal way of settling problems caused by a love triangle. Two gypsy women vying for the same man fight a fierce hand-to-hand battle to see who will claim him as her lover. The wrestling sequence was considered quite shocking for its time and still has considerable impact because it is masterfully choreographed and edited.

KERIM'S GIRL (Nadja Regin)
Although seen only briefly, the sensual mistress of Kerim Bey inadvertently saves his life when she lures him away from his desk for an

Above left: Martine Beswick and Aliza Gur rehearsed the classic gypsy girl fight at Pinewood Studios.

Above: The onscreen result.

Right: A SPECTRE family portrait: Rosa Klebb, Morzeny and Kronsteen are called before an irate Blofeld.

Opposite: The superbly directed and edited fight with Red Grant aboard the Orient Express.

erotic interlude only seconds before a limpet mine explodes. Kerim's mistress is portrayed by Nadja Regin, whose sultry good looks impressed the producers enough to cast her as the traitorous cabaret dancer who almost lures Bond to his death in the next 007 film, *Goldfinger*. Regin therefore has the distinction of being the first actress to appear in a different role in another Bond movie.

007'S VILLAINS

ROSA KLEBB (Lotte Lenya)

Described in Ian Fleming's novel as a repulsive, 'toad-like' woman, SMERSH Colonel Rosa Klebb is one of the cinema's greatest villainesses. Unbeknown to her superiors, Klebb is SPECTRE agent number three, reporting directly to Ernst Stavro Blofeld and entrusted to carry out the theft of the Lektor and the execution of 007. Klebb is humourless and quite masculine in behaviour and appearance. On the surface she appears to be asexual, but her brief and intimidating flirtations with Tatiana hint at lesbianism (whereas in Fleming's novel this is blatantly obvious). At the climax of the film, Klebb tries personally to

murder 007 with the now famous shoe containing a poison-tipped knife but falls victim to Tatiana's gun.

The casting of Lotte Lenya as Klebb is truly inspirational. In reality a gentle, cultured woman who gained in popularity by teaming up with her husband composer Kurt Weill for memorable stage productions (including *The Threepenny Opera*), Lenya is absolutely riveting as Klebb. The actress always found it amusing that, despite her significant accomplishments dating back to the 1930s, she was best remembered for the mad woman of SPECTRE who, in the words of Bond, 'had her kicks'.

DONALD 'RED' GRANT (Robert Shaw)

Arguably the most realistic and frightening of all the Bond villains, Grant was described as a 'homicidal paranoiac'. In other words, a perfect candidate for SPECTRE. Grant had escaped from Dartmoor prison in England at the height of the Cold War and joined the organization as an assassin. His total ruthlessness and superior skills make him both feared and respected by his superiors. Grant is also in peak physical condition, having completed SPECTRE's training courses with impressive results. He is chosen by Colonel Klebb to assassinate James Bond and Tatiana.

After killing Bond's contact, Captain Nash, in Zagreb, Yugoslavia, Grant assumes the man's identity and lures Bond into his confidence aboard the Orient Express. Here, he disarms 007 and promises him a torturous death. Grant makes a fatal mistake by opening Bond's attaché case, which results in a tear gas cartridge exploding in his face. In the brutal hand-to-hand battle which follows, Bond succeeds in strangling Grant with his own garrotte.

Robert Shaw gives a brilliant performance as Grant, successfully alternating between a talkative, obnoxiously friendly type in his guise as Nash and a cunning and ruthless killer. Shaw, an award-winning playwright, would eventually become a popular leading man in such films as *Jaws* and *The Deep* before his premature death from a heart attack in 1978.

KRONSTEEN (Vladek Sheybal)

SPECTRE agent number five and director of planning, Kronsteen is also an internationally recognized chess champion. 'Moonlighting' in his criminal capacity, it is Kronsteen – reporting directly to Blofeld – who concocts the elaborate mission to lure James Bond into stealing the Soviet Lektor decoding machine. Warned that Bond is a worthy adversary, the egotistical Kronsteen replies, 'Who is Bond compared to Kronsteen?' Unfortunately, Kronsteen finds out when Bond thwarts his foolproof scheme – leading to his falling victim to the latest in SPECTRE fashion, a shoe with a poison-tipped knife.

Vladek Sheybal, who played Kronsteen, was a respected Polish actor and theatre director who was initially reluctant to appear in *From Russia With Love*. However, his friend Sean Connery convinced him to take the role, and Sheybal later professed to being amazed at the impact it had on his career. He also appeared as a villain in the 1967 Bond spoof *Casino Royale* and later starred as Sean Connery's brother in the 1975 epic *The Wind and The Lion*.

KRILENCU (Fred Haggerty)

This Bulgarian master of murder is employed by the Soviets to assassinate Western agents in Turkey. The arch enemy of Kerim Bey, Krilencu is ordered by SMERSH to interrupt an uneasy truce and kill Kerim, who they mistakenly believe has murdered several of their agents. In fact, both Krilencu and Kerim are unknowingly being pitted against each other by SPECTRE.

Plotting to steal the Lektor, Bond and Kerim examine blueprints of the Soviet embassy.

After Krilencu makes two unsuccessful attempts on Kerim's life, Kerim shoots him with a sniper's rifle as the Bulgarian attempts to climb out of the window of his hide-out. This sequence contains an in-joke, as the wall of Krilencu's apartment carries a billboard of Anita Ekberg in the Bob Hope comedy *Call Me Bwana*, which was produced by Broccoli and Saltzman. (In the novel, the actress with the 'big mouth' was Marilyn Monroe.)

MORZENY (Walter Gotell)

Head of the training school for agents on SPECTRE island, Morzeny proudly escorts Rosa Klebb around the facility and introduces her to assassin Red Grant. Alas, Morzeny's career is cut short when he leads a flotilla of SPECTRE speedboats to intercept James Bond, who is escaping to Venice with Tatiana. In a superbly staged sequence, Bond dumps fuel tanks into the ocean and ignites them by firing a flare into the petrol-soaked water. Morzeny and his men perish in the resulting inferno, as Bond racks up yet another large entry in Blofeld's seemingly inexhaustible capital expenditures budget. Walter Gotell, who is silently menacing as Morzeny, would later appear as the charismatic KGB General Gogol in future Bond films.

ERNST STAVRO BLOFELD

(Anthony Dawson)

In his first screen appearance, the SPECTRE mastermind's face is unseen as he develops a murderous plot in conjunction with Rosa Klebb and Kronsteen. Blofeld is given no background in his screen debut, but traits which would become his hallmark are already established. For example, he has a habit of stroking his white Persian cat whilst planning diabolical schemes. He is devoid of any overt emotions and discusses matters of life and death as though he were commenting on the weather. He strikes fear into the hearts of even the most cold-blooded killers, and makes analogies about SPECTRE and the Japanese fighting fish he keeps in his office (both let their intended victims do battle with each other until they are too weak to defend themselves). After warning his underlings about the price of failure, he orders the assassination of the person who feels he is immune to the threat. (Blofeld would repeat this novel exercise in irony in *Thunderball* and *You Only Live Twice*.) Anthony Dawson, who portrayed Professor Dent in *Dr. No*, played Blofeld in *From Russia With Love*, though his voice was dubbed by actor Eric Pohlman.

007'S ALLIES

KERIM BEY (Pedro Armendariz)

A former circus strongman, Kerim is a key member of MI6 and head of Station T in Istanbul. His headquarters are hidden amidst a carpet shop located in a busy bazaar. From here Kerim directs activities designed to spy on the Soviets and their Bulgarian henchmen. Controlling a large network of spies, his key employees comprise his sons (of whom he seemingly has a never-ending supply). Kerim's tactics are so effective that he has been able to install a naval periscope underneath the Soviet embassy's boardroom, thus allowing him to spy on meetings. He and Bond fast become friends and allies, possibly because neither is immune to enjoying a good drink and a willing woman. Kerim plays a vital role in 007's theft of the Lektor and his knowledge of the ancient sewer system allows them to escape the enemy and flee aboard the Orient Express. Tragically, it is onboard the train that he is murdered at the hands of Red Grant.

Pedro Armendariz gave a wonderfully charismatic portrayal of Kerim, making him one of the most memorable characters to appear in a Bond film. The veteran actor, a one-time member of John Ford's famous 'stock company', was battling terminal cancer during the filming of *From Russia With Love*. He barely managed to finish the film before he was hospitalized. Wracked with pain, he had a gun smuggled into his room and used it to commit suicide just weeks after completing his work on the 007 film.

His son Pedro Armendariz Jr appeared as a corrupt dictator in *Licence To Kill* (1989).

M (Bernard Lee)

In his second screen appearance, Bernard Lee hones the role of M to perfection, with a slightly more benign attitude towards Bond than had been shown in *Dr. No*. Amusingly, M – who disapproves of Bond's womanizing – has no choice but to order 007 to bed Soviet agent Tatiana Romanova in the hope that the seduction will allow British intelligence to gain access to a Lektor decoding machine. We almost get a rare glimpse into M's personal life later in the film. The MI6 chief is surrounded by his top staff members as he plays a tape recording of Bond interrogating Tatiana, who is more interested in discussing 007's love life. When she asks Bond if he has had any experiences with oriental women, he begins to relate a story about when he and M

Special-effects technician Bert Luxford prepares the model of the SPECTRE helicopter for its spectacular demise.

were in Tokyo. A red-faced M instantly shuts off the tape. While we don't hear the details, the very idea that he and Bond may have shared any type of sexual experience with Japanese women is too hilarious to contemplate.

MISS MONEYPENNY (Lois Maxwell)

By Lois Maxwell's second screen appearance in *From Russia With Love*, the audience already had a picture of the Bond/Moneypenny relationship and fans would debate henceforth about whether they had ever been lovers. In this film, Moneypenny was still overt in her attempts to seduce 007. (She would become increasingly aloof as the series progressed.)

BOOTHROYD (Desmond Llewelyn)

After actor Peter Burton became unavailable to repeat the role of the MI6 armourer he played in *Dr. No*, Desmond Llewelyn accepted the part in *From Russia With Love*. He went on to become the person who would appear in more Bond films than any other actor. Although Q (not referred to by name yet) is still very much a peripheral character devoid of any memorable personality traits at this early stage, he does provide Bond with his first hi-tech gadget, the lethal attaché case that will save Bond's life in his fight against Red Grant.

VEHICLES

BENTLEY MARK IV For the first and only time in an Eon-produced Bond film, we see James

TOP SECRET CAST & CREW DOSSIERS

✳ Director **Terence Young**'s wife makes her big screen debut – and farewell – in *From Russia With Love*. She is the lady who appears on a bridge in Venice filming Bond and Tatiana as they pass beneath in a gondola.

✳ Location manager **Bill Hill** was pressed into making his screen debut in Turkey when the actor chosen to play the ill-fated MI6 agent Captain Nash proved unavailable at the last minute. Hill suddenly found himself in Nash's clothes for his tragic encounter with Red Grant.

World premiere night at the Odeon Theatre in Leicester Square, London.

Bond's Bentley Mark IV convertible. (Different Bentleys were used in the 1967 Bond spoof *Casino Royale* and in 1983's *Never Say Never Again*.) The car is devoid of any hi-tech gadgetry except for a telephone (quite remarkable in 1963). Although Bond is not seen behind the wheel of the classic vehicle, he does find a novel use for it when he invites Sylvia Trench into the back seat to enjoy some 'lunch'. We don't know precisely what's on the menu, but we get a pretty good idea when Bond raises the convertible's top.

GADGETS & WEAPONS

ATTACHÉ CASE This 'nasty little Christmas present', as Bond describes it, represents his first state-of-the-art gadget from Q. Issued as standard field equipment to all 'Double-0' agents, the leather case contained a number of unorthodox items: a magnetized tin of talcum powder concealing a tear gas cartridge, a hidden knife, fifty gold sovereigns and ample room to contain a folding sniper's rifle. The case had unique locks which had to be turned horizontally prior to opening. Failure to do so would result in the tear gas bomb exploding. The case, which saves Bond's life in his battle with Red Grant, remains intact in the archives of Eon Productions in London and Desmond Llewelyn often takes it on publicity tours.

FOLDING SNIPER'S RIFLE This is an innovative weapon from Q Branch. The rifle was contained within the stock, into which the barrel, infrared scope and gun could be fitted. The entire package snapped together quickly and proved to be quite useful. Kerim 'borrows' the weapon to kill Krilencu, and Bond used the rifle to destroy a SPECTRE helicopter.

POISON-TIPPED SHOE Those who are snobbish about fashion had better stay clear of SPECTRE. Blofeld – whose sense of style is even less evident than his sense of humour – had his agents don these basic black shoes which contained a razor-sharp, poison-tipped blade that could be activated by clicking the shoes together. After being stabbed, a victim would succumb within twelve seconds, though Blofeld – ever the perfectionist – insists upon finding a faster-working venom.

WRISTWATCH/PIANO WIRE GARROTTE Used with lethal effect by Red Grant, this device is a wristwatch which conceals a retractable piano wire that can be used to strangle victims. Grant kills Bond's double at the SPECTRE training school using the wire and attempts to murder the real 007 in a brutal fight aboard the Orient Express. Alas, Bond turns the tables and kills Grant with his own device.

CAMERA/TAPE RECORDER Disguised as an ordinary box camera, this device conceals a reel-to-reel tape recorder which Bond uses whilst interrogating Tatiana about the Lektor.

THE LEKTOR This is a typewriter-sized Soviet decoding machine desperately desired by MI6. Housed in the Soviet embassy in Istanbul, the Lektor is the bait used by SPECTRE to lure Bond into a deadly trap. Curiously, the device is called the Spektor in Fleming's novel, wherein the villains are SMERSH agents. Because Bond's adversaries onscreen were from SPECTRE, the device would be confused with the criminal organization. Thus, the screenwriters changed the decoder's name to Lektor.

MUSIC

Starting with *From Russia With Love*, John Barry would become the premier musical contributor to the series. The film introduces Barry's memorable theme '007' which would feature prominently in several of the future Bond movies. His score is truly sensational, seamlessly blending the 'James Bond Theme' into the title track. The main titles feature the instrumental version of the song and Matt Monro's vocal version is heard over the end credits.

MARKETING & MERCHANDISING

With *Dr. No* a box-office smash, the marketing budget for *From Russia With Love* was far more generous. The film-makers promoted this as a true 'event' movie and several different advertising campaigns were designed. One of the two styles of American one-sheet posters depicted Bond with four scantily clad women whilst another poster focused on the action and Bond's 'incredible' new women and villains. At this point in time, there were few merchandising tie-ins. A paperback version of the novel featured stills from the film, and the prerequisite soundtrack album was a hit. There were also numerous 'cover' versions of the title song recorded, some of dubious quality. After the release of *Goldfinger*, however, manufacturers retroactively released merchandise based on *From Russia With Love*. Most prominent was an elaborate children's version of Bond's lethal attaché case. This one did not contain a tear gas mechanism, although if the case was opened incorrectly some harmless caps exploded. Created by Multiple Toys in the USA, a boxed attaché case can today command up to £600. In Britain, a few other toys made it to the market including *From Russia With Love* jigsaw puzzles and a slide-viewer set. Each of these items is considered highly desirable by collectors.

Eon Productions' stationery illustrates pre-production artwork.

THE BOX OFFICE

Whilst the success of *Dr. No* caught the motion picture industry by surprise, there had been high expectations for *From Russia With Love*. The producers and studio were not to be disappointed, as the film went on to gross a (then) magnificent $78.9 million worldwide. Of significance to the film-makers was the increasingly apparent fact that Bond's appeal was truly universal and not limited to British audiences. Fans in every corner of the world responded with enthusiasm, making the producers even more determined to ensure that James Bond would become the ultimate international icon of the 1960s. ∎

These Italian commemorative stickers are extremely rare examples of licensed merchandise for *From Russia With Love*.

AROUND THE WORLD WITH 007

From Russia With Love was filmed on location in **Turkey**, with second unit work shot in **Venice** (although the principal actors were never actually there). The helicopter chase sequence was actually shot in the hills of northern **Scotland**, whilst interiors and the sequences at SPECTRE island were re-created at **Pinewood Studios** in England. (The SPECTRE mansion is in fact the Pinewood administrative office and looks virtually identical today.)

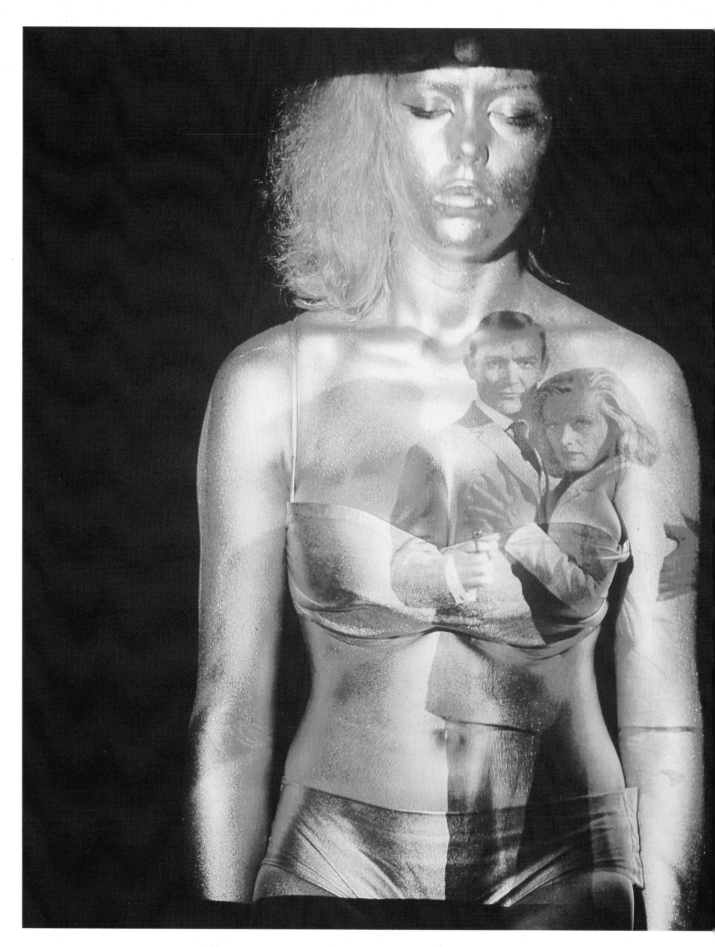

GOLDFINGER

(1964)

Director **GUY HAMILTON** Producers **ALBERT R BROCCOLI & HARRY SALTZMAN**
Screenplay **RICHARD MAIBAUM & PAUL DEHN** Director of Photography **TED MOORE**
Editor **PETER HUNT** Production Designer **KEN ADAM** Music **JOHN BARRY**

Release date: UK 17 September 1964, USA 22 December 1964. Running time: 111 minutes

*G*OLDFINGER REPRESENTED A TURNING POINT for the James Bond films both artistically and in terms of the series' impact on popular culture. This was the first one to emphasize the hi-tech elements that would become a staple of the series. Likewise, *Goldfinger* reflected director Guy Hamilton's determination to bring a more tongue-in-cheek approach to the films, and thus introduced much more overt humour than had been seen previously. While some still argue that with *Goldfinger* the Bond movies abandoned all attempts to reflect real-life espionage stories, it can also be argued that this film presented the image of Bond that has made him an enduring phenomenon: a cool-under-fire hero with a propensity to make witticisms even when faced with certain death.

Goldfinger was the first of the larger-than-life Bond films and the producers ensured that the (relatively) hefty $3.5 million budget was apparent onscreen. Whilst Sean Connery seemed to have found a comfortable style in which to play 007, with this film the technicians increasingly became the behind-the-scenes stars. Certainly, there can be no overstating the contribution of production designer Ken Adam, who – denied access to the real Fort Knox – let his imagination run wild and carried out Cubby Broccoli's order to create 'a cathedral of gold' at Pinewood Studios spectacularly well. Equally impressive is special-effects master John Stears' adaptation of the now legendary gadget-laden Aston Martin DB5, which has since earned the name 'The Most Famous Car in the World'.

Above: Goldfinger's men attack Fort Knox.

Previous spread: Model Margaret Nolan provided the background image in the main title sequence.

Goldfinger was the first of the Bond films to be classified as a box-office blockbuster. In those less cynical times, even critics were generally unanimous in their praise of the innovative style of the films. For many, the series reached an artistic high with this film, and it is certainly almost impossible to find much fault with it. Except for some back-screen projection work (which looked somewhat shoddy even in 1964), virtually every other element of the film gels perfectly. Along with *From Russia With Love*, *Goldfinger* also presents the most memorable cast of characters to be found in any Bond film. Gert Frobe's title villain and Harold Sakata's Oddjob are truly unforgettable and Honor Blackman's Pussy Galore (yes, we really did blush at the name way back then) was one of the first of the liberated screen heroines.

THE ASSIGNMENT

James Bond is assigned to track the movements of billionaire Auric Goldfinger, whom MI6 suspects of smuggling large quantities of gold in and out of England. In Miami, Bond seduces Goldfinger's gorgeous confederate Jill Masterson, who helps 007 humiliate her boss by exposing him as a cheat at cards. For her betrayal, Jill dies a horrifying death: she is coated from head to toe in gold paint – a grisly warning sign to Bond to stay out of Goldfinger's affairs. In a high-stakes golf game, Bond – posing as a shady character with access to a fortune in Nazi gold – again humiliates Goldfinger after finding him cheating. Goldfinger issues one more warning to Bond to keep away by having his manservant Oddjob decapitate a statue with a razor-brimmed bowler hat.

Bond follows Goldfinger to his Swiss headquarters and encounters Tilly Masterson, the vengeful sister of Jill who is determined to assassinate Goldfinger. Like her sister, she also dies at the hands of Oddjob. Bond is captured and brought to Goldfinger's Kentucky estate where he discovers that his adversary is planning an outrageous scheme to increase the value of his own gold by using an atomic bomb to contaminate Fort Knox. With time running out, Bond manages to seduce Pussy Galore, the personal pilot of Goldfinger, who alerts the US government. Goldfinger's forces are defeated in an intense battle during which Bond manages to electrocute Oddjob and deactivate the atomic bomb with only seconds to spare. Bond later confronts Goldfinger aboard a plane which the defeated megalomaniac has hijacked. In the ensuing mêlée, Goldfinger is sucked out of the window to his death, while Bond and Pussy manage to parachute to safety.

007'S WOMEN

PUSSY GALORE (Honor Blackman)
Pussy Galore does not appear until well into the story. However, the audience's introduction to her is memorable. Bond is awakened from a drug-induced sleep and finds himself staring into the face of a gorgeous blonde. 'Who are you?' asks Bond groggily. 'My name is Pussy Galore,' is the reply. 'I must be dreaming,' says Bond with understandable incredulity. With the casting of sexy *Avengers* star Honor Blackman, the lesbian tendencies of the literary Pussy Galore were only insinuated in the film version. ('I'm immune,' she informs Bond, referring to his obvious attempts to charm her.) Pussy and her Flying Circus of female stunt pilots are to spray a lethal nerve gas over Fort Knox to immobilize the troops prior to Goldfinger's invasion. However, she falls for Bond after he finally succeeds in seducing her. His prowess is enough not only to ensure that she becomes an instant heterosexual but also to turn her allegiance to his cause. She secretly

replaces the gas with a harmless substance which helps to thwart Goldfinger. The mature presence of Honor Blackman (at thirty-seven, the oldest Bond girl) added immeasurably to ensuring that Pussy Galore became one of the most memorable of all 007's lovers. Additionally, the name became part of the international lexicon and remains so today.

JILL MASTERSON (Shirley Eaton)

This beautiful, free-spirited young woman aids and abets Auric Goldfinger in his obsession with cheating at cards by using binoculars to spy on the other man's deck. Bond discovers the scheme and persuades Jill to help him humiliate Goldfinger, forcing him to lose thousands of dollars to his opponent. In the process of seducing Jill, Bond is knocked unconscious by Oddjob and awakens to a shocking sight – the body of Jill on his bed, dead from skin suffocation after having been gilded in gold paint. The resulting image caused a sensation when Shirley Eaton re-created the scene for

Above: Honor Blackman as Pussy Galore with her Flying Circus of female pilots.

Left: Model Margaret Nolan not only appeared as Dink but was also the golden girl seen in the main title sequence and on the movie poster.

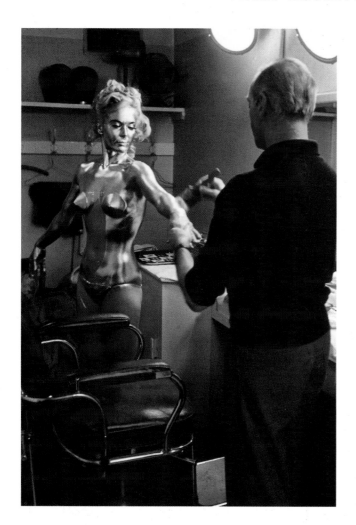

Above: Shirley Eaton gets the brush-off (literally) and becomes one of the most photographed actresses of the decade.

Above right: Tania Mallet poses for a publicity shot on the Fort Knox set at Pinewood Studios.

the cover of *Life* magazine. The image was so unforgettable that she became one of the most photographed actresses of the 1960s – despite the fact that she appears in the film for less than five minutes. Indeed, her brief sequence in *Goldfinger* remains one of the most enduring images in cinematic history.

TILLY MASTERSON (Tania Mallet)
Equally as beautiful as her ill-fated sister Jill, Tilly embarks on a one-woman mission of revenge to kill Auric Goldfinger. She follows her prey to Switzerland, where she has a chance encounter with 007, who tries without success to persuade her not to interfere with his mission. Later, Bond encounters Tilly in the grounds of Goldfinger's headquarters where they are pursued in a high-speed car chase. Ultimately, Tilly – like her sister – dies at the hands of Oddjob.

Tania Mallet was a well-known British fashion model when she was cast in the brief but pivotal role of Tilly Masterson. Although without previous acting experience, she acquitted herself quite well in *Goldfinger.* She retired from the

screen shortly afterwards but remains in demand by top fashion magazines today. In 1996, she was reunited with her cinematic 'sister' Shirley Eaton at a James Bond Fan Club convention at Pinewood Studios.

007'S VILLAINS

AURIC GOLDFINGER (Gert Frobe)
'The man with the Midas touch', Auric Goldfinger is one of the world's richest men. The British billionaire has it all: an exotic lifestyle, private jet, ownership of a posh British country club, a private army of henchmen and the services of Oddjob, the mute muscle-man who serves as a lethal major-domo for the megalomaniac. Goldfinger has an obsession with increasing his hoard of personal gold – by any means necessary, including smuggling, cheating and murdering. He melts gold down and disguises it as parts of his Rolls-Royce, thus allowing him to move the precious metal internationally without arousing suspicion. A corpulent, extremely intelligent man, Goldfinger is actually a ruthless killer. Though apolitical, he

had eagerly accepted the 'gift' of an atomic bomb from the Red Chinese in order to carry out his most inspired scheme, 'Operation Grand Slam', the radioactive contamination of the gold supply at Fort Knox. This would ensure that the value of his own gold would multiply many times. He perishes after a hand-to-hand battle with Bond aboard an aircraft – he is sucked out of the window when the cabin depressurizes.

Goldfinger was so magnificently played by German actor Gert Frobe that many Bond fans don't realize he was dubbed entirely by actor Michael Collins because he could not speak a word of English.

ODDJOB (Harold Sakata)

He is the fanatically loyal, muscle-bound Korean manservant to Goldfinger. At first glance, Oddjob's appearance seems amusing: the stocky, moustached oriental, clad in a formal manservant's outfit complete with bowler hat. As a skilled murderer, his primary weapons are karate and his steel-rimmed bowler hat, which is capable of decapitating a statue. He is almost invulnerable in hand-to-hand combat as Bond discovers in the superbly directed showdown with Oddjob in the vaults of Fort Knox. During this classic scene 007 manages to use the bowler hat as a means to electrocute his opponent.

Although Oddjob has been immortalized as one of the cinema's greatest villains, actor Harold Sakata who portrayed him was a gentle, soft-spoken man. A native of Hawaii, he won a silver medal in the 1948 Olympics for weightlifting. Sakata, who also wrestled as Tosh Togo, used his wildly popular role to launch an entire career as a character actor, appearing in many films and television advertisements in his Oddjob persona.

MR SOLO (Martin Benson)

The arrogant Mafia don accepts a $1 million payment from Goldfinger in return for smuggling an atomic bomb into the USA from Red China. When Solo refuses to forego his payment and become a partner in 'Operation Grand Slam', Goldfinger has him crushed to death in a Lincoln

Cubby Broccoli on the Miami set at Pinewood Studios with Gert Frobe and Austin Willis.

One of cinema's classic fight sequences . . . Bond versus Oddjob in the vaults of Fort Knox. This sequence does not appear in the final cut of the film.

KISCH (Michael Mellinger)

A valuable henchman to Goldfinger, Kisch carries out distasteful assignments including the execution of the Mafia dons at Auric Stud. However, when 'Operation Grand Slam' goes awry, Kisch is locked in the vaults of Fort Knox with Oddjob as the nuclear bomb ticks away. When Kisch attempts to stop the device, Oddjob tosses him over a railing to his death.

CAPUNGO (Alf Joint)

Capungo's (Spanish for thug) brief but memorable appearance occurs in the pre-credits sequence where he tangles with Bond and ends up electrocuted in a bath. 'Shocking' is Bond's analysis of the situation. Alf Joint, the stunt man who portrayed Capungo, got the part when the actor originally cast was arrested as a cat burglar. In the electrocution sequence, Joint was severely burned when a hot coil wrapped around his leg. The screams you hear are not entirely due to his acting abilities.

BONITA (Nadja Regin)

Bonita is the beautiful, but traitorous, cabaret dancer Bond romances in the pre-credits sequence. He narrowly escapes falling victim to Capungo by seeing the approaching thug's reflection in Bonita's eye. He twirls her around and she receives the blow meant for him. Nadja Regin also appeared as Kerim Bey's nymphomaniac mistress in *From Russia With Love*. Alas, her treatment in that film was not much better, as she was almost blown up by a limpet mine during a love-making session.

007'S ALLIES

M (Bernard Lee)

Bond has a particularly strained relationship with his superior during the early stages of the mission. M admonishes his top agent for failing to carry out orders to observe Goldfinger's actions discreetly in Miami Beach. Later, M orders Bond to join him for dinner with Colonel Smithers of the Bank of England. Bond exacts a small measure of revenge against M during the course of the meal by showing off his superior knowledge of brandy.

MISS MONEYPENNY (Lois Maxwell)

This time round, the ever-optimistic Moneypenny attempts to persuade Bond to drop in at her place by promising to bake him an angel cake. Bond politely declines, blaming a conflicting business

Continental at a car scrapyard – a sequence that proved to be upsetting to many Americans, according to production designer Ken Adam. It wasn't because of objections to Solo's horrendous fate; rather, people could not bear to see the wholesale destruction of a new Lincoln Continental, which at that time represented the American 'dream car'.

MR LING (Burt Kwouk)

Mr Ling is a Red Chinese expert in nuclear fission who is sent to the USA to oversee Goldfinger's use of the atomic bomb. It is during Goldfinger's secret conversation with Mr Ling that James Bond overhears the billionaire describe his plans for 'Operation Grand Slam'. Ling is eventually double-crossed and murdered by Goldfinger during the battle inside Fort Knox.

Actor Burt Kwouk made another appearance in a Bond film, *You Only Live Twice*, playing one of Blofeld's henchmen. However, he is best known for playing Cato, the wacky manservant to Peter Sellers' Inspector Clouseau in *The Pink Panther* films.

Mr Solo prepares to embark on his 'pressing' engagement as Bond slips the 'homer' into his pocket.

appointment. Moneypenny is certain she is being snubbed again until M's voice comes through her intercom and cynically warns her to 'omit the customary by-play with 007' because he has a dinner appointment with him. 'Moneypenny, won't you ever believe me?' Bond asks rhetorically as he retrieves his hat from the rack.

COLONEL SMITHERS (Richard Vernon)

He is the distinguished representative of the Bank of England who informs Bond and M about the dangers of Goldfinger's international gold-smuggling operations. As bait for Goldfinger, Smithers lends 007 a rare gold bar which originated from a lost hoard of Nazi bullion. The dining sequence with Smithers is wonderfully written and acted. Even Bond looks out of his element amid the ridiculously over-the-top decor of the dining room. Dressed in dinner jackets, the trio eat at an enormous table. It is moments like these that define the Bond films by providing many subtle pleasures.

FELIX LEITER (Cec Linder)

Bond's CIA counterpart makes his second appearance in a 007 film. Initially played by Jack Lord in *Dr. No*, the role is assumed by Cec Linder in *Goldfinger*. The casting is not nearly as successful this time. While Linder is a perfectly capable actor, he is not the cool, slick character defined by Lord. Linder's Leiter appears to be much older

than Bond and it is difficult to imagine both men having shared numerous death-defying adventures. Nevertheless, Leiter appears onscreen a good deal of the time and plays a pivotal role in arranging the surprise attack on Goldfinger's forces at Fort Knox.

Linder was the only prominent member of the cast actually to fly to Miami for the opening sequence at the Fontainebleau Hotel. The rest of the scene was shot at Pinewood Studios.

Q (Desmond Llewelyn)

Until *Goldfinger*, the character of Q was primarily that of an uninteresting bureaucrat. With this film, however, director Guy Hamilton instructed Desmond Llewelyn to have some fun with his sequence by showing antagonism towards Bond. After all, it is 007 who routinely destroys all those marvellous gadgets which Q and his team have spent countless days inventing. The edge this puts on the Q/Bond relationship is one that endures to this day and has become a hallmark of the series.

With *Goldfinger* we also get the first glimpse of the eccentric inventor's workshop and such gadgets as gas-spewing parking meters, a Thermos flask containing

Desmond Llewelyn's Q takes a cynical approach to outfitting 007.

James Bond's gadget-laden Aston Martin DB5, known to this day as 'The Most Famous Car in the World'.

Martin DB5. After he has given 007 a guided tour of its many devices, Bond accuses him of joking about the inclusion of an ejector seat in the car. 'I never joke about my work, 007,' Q replies with deadpan humour, thereby generating one of the biggest laughs in the series.

VEHICLES

ASTON MARTIN DB5 The introduction of the gadget-laden Aston Martin DB5 resulted in this remarkable vehicle gaining the name 'The Most Famous Car in the World'. Special-effects expert John Stears approached the Aston Martin car company with a view to using one of their cars for *Goldfinger*, but explained that the film company couldn't afford to actually buy one. Aston Martin decided to lend them the car on the condition that it was returned at the end of filming and could be used for their own promotional purposes. A deal was struck and Stears and his team went about the task of turning this highly desirable British sports car into a deadly, death-defying arsenal on wheels. Its features were:

- hydraulic overriders, front and back, which could be used as rams (although this function is not used in the film)

a bomb and a man being sprayed with machine-gun fire to test a bullet-proof coat. ('It hasn't been perfected yet,' observes Q dryly.) Seconds later, Q introduces Bond to what would become the most famous car in the world . . . the Aston

The laser beam in this famous sequence was added optically in post-production.

- front-mounted machine guns concealed behind the indicator lights
- a bullet-proof shield that emerged to protect the rear window
- revolving licence plates valid in England, France and Switzerland
- concealed in the rear light clusters, a high-powered oil jet and a device that dispensed nails to foil pursuing cars (although this was never shown in the film for fear of imitation by over-zealous children)
- rear smoke screen
- revolving tyre slasher that emerged from the hub of the nearside rear wheel
- mobile phone concealed within the driver's door panel (not seen in the film)
- a weapons tray underneath the driver's seat (again, not seen in the film)
- an onboard radar display screen for tracking enemy vehicles (assuming a homing device has been placed in the target car)
- a weapons control panel concealed within the centre arm rest
- an ejector seat for the removal of unwanted passengers (the control button for this was hidden in the top of the gear stick)

The car features prominently in a stunning and highly amusing chase sequence in which Bond evades his pursuers while using most of the gadgetry described by Q. In reality two cars were used during filming, one of which did not feature any of the working gadgets. Shortly after the film was completed, the second vehicle was furnished with identical gadgetry to that of the original. It was used for publicity purposes and appeared in the follow-up movie *Thunderball*.

1937 ROLLS-ROYCE III SEDANCE De VILLE Goldfinger's pristine vehicle from the 1930s, the yellow-and-black Rolls serves a dual function. Goldfinger routinely melts down gold and recasts it as parts of the car, thus allowing him to smuggle the bullion internationally from his metallurgical facility in Kent, England. Bond succeeds in placing a homing device in the boot of the car, making it possible to trail the billionaire throughout Switzerland. Weighing in at over 7,000 pounds, the twelve-cylinder engine was more than capable of cruising at over a hundred miles an hour. Originally custom-built for the Rt Hon. Lord Fairhaven of Anglesey Abbey, Cambridgeshire, it was auctioned in 1986 at Sothebys of New York and bought for $121,000.

LOCKHEED JET STAR PLANE This is the private jet of Auric Goldfinger, lavishly furnished with every luxury imaginable. The plane is piloted by Pussy Galore and it is here that a drugged Bond awakens and meets her for the first time. The plane transports 007 from Switzerland to Auric Stud, Goldfinger's estate in Kentucky. The model work of the distance shots of the Jet Star are among the least convincing special effects in the film. The model also doubled as the presidential jet seen at the end of the film.

GADGETS & WEAPONS

GOLDEN PISTOL In an attempt to deceive US troops during their counterattack on his forces at Fort Knox, Goldfinger changes into a general's uniform and carries a gold-plated revolver which he uses to murder Red Chinese nuclear expert, Mr Ling.

GOLDFINGER'S LASER Incredible as it may seem, back in 1964 the idea of an industrial laser was considered to be the stuff of science fiction. Therefore, Goldfinger has to launch into an explanation of the tool which will be used to dissect 007, who is spread-eagled on a metal table. As the beam slowly works its way up to his manhood, 007 tries frantically to talk his way out of the predicament. (He eventually does, but not before understandably sweating off a few pounds in a classic sequence that makes all male viewers squirm.) The laser effect was achieved by having technician Burt Luxford hide under the table with a blowtorch and cut through the metal from below. (The laser beam was added optically later.)

Small wonder that Sean Connery's fear looks so realistic. The laser also plays a pivotal role in the break-in of Fort Knox when Goldfinger mounts it atop a military ambulance and uses it to cut through the metal doors of the gold depository.

ODDJOB'S BOWLER HAT When Goldfinger's mute henchman doffs his hat to a lady, it's generally not because he has good manners. The unique item, which features a metallic brim, is used to deadly effect when Oddjob kills Tilly Masterson with it. Fittingly, the hat eventually proves to be the instrument of Oddjob's own destruction. Incidentally, the original hat is still displayed at various Bond events and was exhibited for several years at Planet Hollywood in London.

HOMER Bond receives one of the earliest prototypes of a homing device from Q. The small, metallic 'bug' is placed inside Goldfinger's Rolls-Royce by 007, thus allowing him to follow the billionaire through Switzerland. As Bond's Aston Martin features a hidden monitor which displays a map indicating Goldfinger's whereabouts up to a range of 150 miles, he rationalizes that the device would 'allow a man to stop off for a quick one en route'. Q also gives 007 a smaller version of the homer which Bond hides in a hollowed-out space in the heel of his shoe, thus allowing Felix Leiter to trace him.

SEAGULL SNORKEL This device signals to the audience that the Bond of *Goldfinger* will be far more humorous than the 007 of the first two films. The pre-credits sequence opens with a shot of a seagull gliding through murky waters near an industrial complex. The 'bird' suddenly rises up and we see it is a decoy attached to the top of James Bond's scuba mask. Bond soon discards the phoney fowl as well as his drysuit, under which he reveals a sparkling white dinner jacket – complete with carnation. The joke is absurd, but it is also hilarious and more than any other scene to date personifies the essence of the Bond character. Incidentally, the scene is replayed almost verbatim by Arnold Schwarzenegger in *True Lies*.

MUSIC

With *Goldfinger*, the tradition of Bond theme songs becoming pop hits began. The brassy title song by John Barry (with unforgettable lyrics by

Corgi's version of the Aston Martin. Introduced in 1965, the car is still being produced today.

Leslie Bricusse and Anthony Newley) became an instant smash hit, reaching the top ten chart in the USA. The soundtrack album went gold, a phenomenal achievement for a non-musical. Barry also crafted many other memorable themes in the film, including 'Into Miami', which follows the main titles, and the thrilling 'Dawn Raid on Fort Knox'. In a frustrating occurrence that would become all too common, neither Barry's title theme nor his score was nominated for an Oscar.

MARKETING & MERCHANDISING

By the time he completed filming *Goldfinger*, the bloom was beginning to come off the rose when it came to Sean Connery's enthusiasm for playing 007. Besieged by an army of journalists and paparazzi during production, he became understandably intolerant of being asked inane questions by uninformed reporters who continued to try to make him indistinguishable from the role he played. Thus, the producers created innovative methods for other cast members to promote the film. Honor Blackman was fitted with an actual gold finger which she wore on publicity tours. The absurd bauble required security guards to accompany her everywhere, including the lavatory. Blackman found a mixed reception in the media to discussing her character's name. Whenever she sensed an interviewer's embarrassment, she took wicked pleasure in mentioning Pussy Galore repeatedly. Shirley Eaton embarked on an international tour designed to promote her image as the much-photographed 'Golden Girl'.

Even the Aston Martin DB5 did its duty. The vehicle proved so popular that the producers had to commission another two cars simply to tour the world on publicity junkets (including the 1964 World's Fair, where it caused a sensation with the public). Following the film's release, Corgi Toys of England produced its first incarnation of the DB5 – and it quickly became the best-selling toy of the year. Meticulously made, it was to launch the longest, uninterrupted licensing agreement in the history of the industry, as Corgi continue to produce them to this day. Long after *Goldfinger* premiered, products were still being introduced to capitalize on the film's success. Jigsaw puzzles and the pre-requisite board games were available, as well as an action doll of Oddjob (which actually tossed a bowler hat). A series of bubble-gum cards in Britain caused a scandal when they were

withdrawn because of the abundance of bikini-clad women. (Their value today is put at about £300.)

THE BOX OFFICE

With *Goldfinger*, the Bond success story became a true phenomenon. Even Broccoli and Saltzman could not anticipate the public's wild reaction to the film. At the London premiere, the police had to use force to restrain the crowds from storming the cinema. In Paris, an obsessive female fan threw herself through the window of the Aston Martin which Sean Connery was driving to the premiere.

Goldfinger quickly made back its production costs and worldwide grosses eventually exceeded $125 million – a truly incredible sum for its day. For a time, the *Guinness Book of World Records* cited the film as the fastest grossing motion picture in history. ∎

This original 1965 marketing photograph illustrates licensed Bond collectables. Many items did not appear until months after the film had premiered.

THUNDERBALL

(1965)

Director **TERENCE YOUNG** Presenters **ALBERT R BROCCOLI & HARRY SALTZMAN**
Producer **KEVIN McCLORY** Screenplay **RICHARD MAIBAUM & JOHN HOPKINS based on an**
original story by **KEVIN McCLORY, JACK WHITTINGHAM & IAN FLEMING**
Director of Photography **TED MOORE** Editor **PETER HUNT** Production Designer **KEN ADAM**
Music **JOHN BARRY**

Release date: UK and USA 29 December 1965. Running time: 130 minutes

ORIGINALLY INTENDED TO BE THE FIRST JAMES BOND film, *Thunderball* became the centre of complicated legal battles extending from the early 1960s to the present. Former Ian Fleming collaborators Kevin McClory and Jack Whittingham had sued the author following the 1961 publication of *Thunderball*, claiming Fleming had based the novel on elements of a screenplay the trio had created years before in an unsuccessful attempt to bring 007 to the big screen. Eventually, the lawsuit was settled out of court and McClory retained certain screen rights to the novel. By now, James Bond was a box-office sensation, and Broccoli and Saltzman did not envy the thought of McClory making a rival production over which they had no control. Thus, an agreement was made in which McClory would receive producer's credit for a screen version of *Thunderball*, and Broccoli and Saltzman would act as executive producers.

Thunderball was granted a $5.6 million budget by United Artists, the same studio which originally was reluctant to spend $1 million on *Dr. No*. Times had changed, however, and Bond was the leading pop culture icon. By early 1965, when principal photography began, the 007 films had already spawned legions of imitators both on television and on the big screen. The producers knew they had to demonstrate that a genuine Bond movie had scope and spectacle which could never be replicated by the impersonators. With *Thunderball*, the Bond films became truly epic.

Above: Largo's henchmen Vargas and Janni kidnap Paula in this rehearsal shot. (Vargas does not wear a cap in the final cut.)

Previous spread: Roles reversed: Bond massages Patricia, the masseur at the Shrublands health clinic.

AROUND THE WORLD WITH 007

Thunderball was shot primarily in the **Bahamas**, where producer Kevin McClory resided. Consequently, McClory was able to suggest suitable locations for many key sequences of the film. Principal photography centred on **Nassau** (where the local government staged a special out-of-season carnival – the 'Junkanoo' parade) and adjoining **Paradise Island**. The home of a local millionaire couple – the Sullivans – served as Largo's estate, Palmyra, and the SPECTRE underwater assault begins in the grounds of the home of another millionaire, Huntington Hartford. Paradise Island so enchanted Sean Connery that he now maintains a permanent residence there. The pre-credits jet pack sequence was filmed at the **Château d'Anet** near Paris, while interiors were shot at **Pinewood Studios** in England.

The film is somewhat controversial among Bond scholars. Some feel it is too long and even director Terence Young complained that the abundance of underwater sequences slowed the pace. For most fans, however, *Thunderball* is top-flight entertainment filled with eye-popping locales, exotic women and exceptional photography, music and special effects. If there is a negative element in the film, it is the increasing reliance on hardware and technology. Sean Connery was correct in noting that Bond was becoming less interesting as a character and falling victim to the emphasis on gadgets and stunts. He complained that he was tiring of Bond mania and looked forward to leaving the series to stretch his acting skills in other types of films. Nevertheless, *Thunderball* emerged as one of the top-grossing films of all time. Although critics were starting to take a dim view of the emphasis on hi-tech hardware, even the normally staid *New York Times* found the film's merits so impressive that it chose *Thunderball* as one of the year's ten best movies.

THE ASSIGNMENT

Under the guidance of its number two operative, Emilio Largo, SPECTRE hijacks two atomic bombs from a British Vulcan aircraft during a NATO training exercise off the coast of Nassau. An ultimatum is delivered to the prime minister of England threatening to use the bombs to destroy a major city in Britain or the USA unless an exorbitant ransom is paid. In a desperate race against time, M assigns 007 to the Bahamas to thwart SPECTRE. Bond makes the acquaintance of Largo, who poses as a wealthy legitimate businessman, and seduces his mistress, Domino Derval, who ultimately plays a key role in helping Bond discover the bombs.

Agent 007 learns that Largo and an underwater army are transporting the atomic bombs to Miami Beach, the intended target of their attack. He and a group of US Navy Aquaparas defeat the SPECTRE armada in a spectacular underwater battle. Largo escapes on his hydrofoil yacht, the *Disco Volante* and in a pitched fight with Bond gains the upper hand before ultimately being assassinated by Domino. The disarmed bombs are finally destroyed when the *Disco Volante* crashes, leaving Bond and Domino to be rescued at sea.

007'S WOMEN

DOMINO DERVAL (Claudine Auger)
Dominique, or 'Domino' to her friends, is a beautiful, but somewhat morose young woman who serves as the mistress to SPECTRE's number two agent, Emilio Largo. While her lifestyle with Largo allows her to indulge in many luxuries, she is kept a virtual prisoner by him. The bored French beauty is a willing lover to James Bond, who reluctantly informs her that her brother, a NATO pilot, has been murdered under the orders of Largo. Emotionally shattered by the news, Domino risks her life to help Bond and it is she who gains ultimate revenge by personally killing Largo.

Claudine Auger, a former Miss France, was an inspired choice for the role of Domino, one of the more complex of the 007 heroines. Auger is not only a stunning beauty, but she satisfactorily conveys the inner sadness of a pampered, but unloved, young woman caught in a seemingly inescapable web of deceit and danger. (Like several other Bond actresses from the earlier films, Auger was dubbed for the final cut.)

PAULA CAPLAN (Martine Beswick)
This beautiful native Bahamian works with Bond and fellow MI6 agent Pinder in Nassau. Unique among the women in Bond's life in that there is no indication she was his lover, Paula is captured by

Fiona Volpe. Rather than risk divulging classified information, she heroically takes a cyanide pill.

Martine Beswick, who provides a stunning screen presence as Paula, had appeared as one of the gypsy fighting girls in *From Russia With Love*. Beswick relished her role, particularly when director Terence Young ordered her to sunbathe extensively to darken her tan. 'What a job!' she exclaimed years later, recalling the fun she had filming *Thunderball*.

PATRICIA FEARING (Molly Peters)

This lady is a sexually liberated physiotherapist who 'nurses' Bond back to health at the Shrublands clinic. A vivacious blonde, Pat willingly succumbs to the temptations of a mink glove which Bond employs liberally in their lovemaking. Patricia appears onscreen only briefly, but her scenes with Bond are among the most memorable in the film. Molly Peters conveys a convincing combination of naïveté and sensuality.

The scene in which Bond seduces her in a steam room was considered so provocative that the set was cleared, although by today's standards it's pretty tame. An in-joke occurs when Bond leaves Shrublands and promises to reunite with Pat 'another time, another place'. The line is a sly reference to Connery's earlier film *Another Time, Another Place* in which he starred with Lana Turner.

007'S VILLAINS

EMILIO LARGO (Adolfo Celi)

A brilliant number two agent for SPECTRE, Largo leads a lavish lifestyle, posing as a millionaire playboy in Nassau. He resides in an opulent waterfront estate called Palmyra as well as on his hydrofoil yacht, the *Disco Volante*. Largo is entrusted by Blofeld to hijack two NATO atomic bombs and hold England and the USA to ransom. He is a ruthless killer who is also charming and

Below, left to right:

Martine Beswick, Luciana Paluzzi and Claudine Auger between takes on Paradise Island.

Luciana Paluzzi and Adolfo Celi on the set on Paradise Island in the Bahamas.

FIONA VOLPE (Luciana Paluzzi)

A smoulderingly sensual SPECTRE 'black widow' assassin, Fiona uses her perfect body as a weapon to seduce and then murder her prey. She derives genuine pleasure from sex, despite the fact that she is inevitably preparing to kill her lover. A key figure in Largo's scheme to hijack atomic bombs, Fiona becomes the mistress of NATO pilot Major Derval, whose murder she orchestrates. Fiona seduces 007 as well . . . though he was on to her actual identity. Eventually, Fiona falls victim to one of her own murderous schemes, taking a fatal bullet intended for Bond.

Luciana Paluzzi is nothing less than mesmerizing as a classic 007 villainess. She initially auditioned for the role of Domino, but the producers had the good sense to see she would make a much more interesting 'bad girl' than heroine.

COUNT LIPPE (Guy Doleman)

This is the SPECTRE agent whom Bond encounters while undergoing physiotherapy at the Shrublands health spa. He tries to kill Bond when 007 is strapped to a traction table. Bond reciprocates by locking him in a steam bath cabinet. When Bond discovers Lippe transporting NATO pilot Major Derval's body into Shrublands, Lippe makes another attempt on 007's life in a manner most unbecoming for a villain (he mundanely fires a few pot shots at Bond's Aston Martin). Marked for death by Blofeld because of his bumbling, Lippe is assassinated by Fiona Volpe who uses a rocket-firing motorcycle to terminate her former colleague. (In this sequence, stunt man Bob Simmons was almost killed in the spectacular demolition of the car.)

Guy Doleman makes Lippe a tragic figure even by SPECTRE standards. (You just know that when you blow an assignment for Blofeld, your punishment will not be a reprimand in your personnel file.) He would later appear as Harry Palmer's humourless boss in *The Ipcress File* and *Funeral in Berlin*.

LADISLAV KUTZE (George Pravda)

Kutze is a noted Polish atomic scientist who secretly defects to SPECTRE and oversees the arming of the two stolen NATO atomic bombs. Following the defeat of Largo, Kutze has a change of allegiance and disarms the bombs, in the process rescuing Domino from certain death by Largo. Ironically, the luckless Kutze is left at sea after the destruction of the *Disco Volante*. Although he warns Bond he cannot swim, 007 is

polite, and he relishes the attentions of his love-starved mistress, Domino. His interaction with Bond provides those trademark, highly enjoyable sequences wherein 007 and the villain socialize while dropping *double entrendres* designed to show that neither man is successfully bluffing the other. Naturally, Largo is undone at the moment of his greatest triumph by his failure to respect 007's capabilities. In an ironic twist, he is eventually killed by a spear shot by Domino – the woman for whom he planned a torturous death.

Adolfo Celi makes a visually striking villain. With his snow-white hair and black eye-patch, he is an imposing presence and a worthy successor to the Bond villains who preceded him.

understandably more preoccupied with being rescued with Domino in his arms. Kutze simply vanishes and we never discover his fate.

ANGELO PALAZZI (Paul Stassino)

This SPECTRE agent spends two years undergoing extensive plastic surgery to make him an identical twin of NATO pilot Francois Derval. The elaborate scheme calls for Palazzi to assume the pilot's identity and murder the crew of the Vulcan jet carrying two live atomic bombs. The plan succeeds and he ditches the plane in the ocean off the coast of Nassau where Largo and his men recover the bombs. Unfortunately, Palazzi doesn't live to enjoy the fruits of the SPECTRE retirement plan. Because of his attempt to blackmail Blofeld into increasing his fee, he is left to drown in the submerged Vulcan after Largo slices through his air hose.

VARGAS (Philip Locke)

One of the original 'Men in Black', this silent SPECTRE assassin, with a penchant for dark clothes, operates as Largo's right-hand man. The mysterious Vargas seems content to carry out kidnappings and murders, and even Largo appears repulsed by his preoccupation with violence. He tells Bond, 'Vargas does not drink. Vargas does not smoke. Vargas does not make love. What do you do, Vargas?' At which, the SPECTRE killer looks shyly away. Vargas falls victim to Bond's spear gun when he attempts to assassinate 007 on Love Beach. Observing Vargas impaled on a palm tree, Bond wryly notes to Domino, 'I think he got the point.'

QUIST (Bill Cummings)

The bumbling Quist of SPECTRE is assigned by Largo to break into Bond's Nassau hotel room and assassinate him. Instead, Bond discovers his uninvited guest hiding in the shower, scalds him with hot water, disarms him and sends him back to Largo. Needless to say, Largo's response is extreme. He has the would-be killer tossed into his shark pool, where he is the main entrée for lunch. Stunt man Bill Cummings was given a £250 bonus for literally falling into the sharks. Fortunately, the shot required only one take.

JACQUES BOITIER

(Bob Simmons and Rose Alba)
This French SPECTRE assassin is responsible for the deaths of numerous MI6 agents. Bond attends the man's funeral in France, filled with regret that

Bath time – 007 style. Rare photographs of Luciana Paluzzi, Sean Connery and director Terence Young on the set.

Rik Van Nutter was the third actor to portray Felix Leiter.

listens attentively to Largo's scheme. Prior to this, however, he becomes convinced he has been cheated by one of his men, and – showing true Machiavellian tactics – electrocutes the man in his seat. The latest model of SPECTRE electric chairs lowers into the floor, where the body conveniently disappears, then re-emerges as part of the room's furniture.

The part of Blofeld was played by Anthony Dawson (Professor Dent in *Dr. No*) and was dubbed by Eric Pohlmann.

007'S ALLIES

FELIX LEITER (Rik Van Nutter)

James Bond's friend and CIA colleague has a much more proactive role in *Thunderball*. Leiter is initially seen as a mysterious figure stalking Bond in Nassau (although for a professional agent, he is somewhat conspicuous as he wears sunglasses with his formal wear *inside* the casino). The audience doesn't recognize him because Rik Van Nutter is the third actor to portray Leiter and he bears no resemblance to his predecessors – though he is an inspired choice for the role. After he joins up with 007, he helps search for the missing atomic bombs and actually can be credited for saving Miami Beach from destruction by rescuing James Bond in time to alert the armed forces.

Van Nutter was surprised to be chosen for the role. At the time he was married to actress Anita Ekberg (who appeared in the 1963 Broccoli–Saltzman comedy *Call Me Bwana*). Dining with the Broccolis one evening, Van Nutter and Ekberg were shocked when Cubby offered him the part of Leiter. Despite being well accepted by Bond fans, for reasons still unknown Van Nutter was never asked to play the part again.

PINDER (Earl Cameron)

A native Bahamian, Pinder is an MI6 agent who operates out of a secret headquarters behind a shop in the marketplace of Nassau. Here, Pinder has a modest operation consisting of hi-frequency radio equipment and a darkroom to develop secret photographs. Pinder's HQ also serves as the place where Bond is given his latest arsenal by the ill-tempered Q. Pinder helps Bond gain access to Largo's estate at Palmyra by arranging for a blackout to take place. A curious error occurs in the film as we see Bond and Leiter in a helicopter searching the ocean for signs of the Vulcan bomber. Leiter refers to sighting a manta ray swimming beneath them, but the voice

he was allowed to die peacefully in his sleep. Agent 007 smells a rat, however, when he suspects all is not right with Boitier's statuesque widow. He greets the grieving woman with a right hook, exposing the 'widow' as Boitier himself. The ensuing hand-to-hand battle is typical of the Bond fights from the early films: lightning-fast editing accompanied by a terrifically exciting score by John Barry. Stunt man Bob Simmons, who co-ordinated the fight, also portrayed the widow during the action sequence. Prior to that, actress Rose Alba played the part, accounting for how Simmons' legs could have looked so attractive in a dress!

ERNST STAVRO BLOFELD
(Anthony Dawson)

With his second appearance in a Bond film, Blofeld still remains shrouded in mystery. As with *From Russia With Love*, the audience does not see the SPECTRE chief's face, although his omnipresent white cat is very much in evidence. This time round, Blofeld holds court in the hi-tech Parisian HQ of the criminal organization, where he

inexplicably belongs to Robert Rietty, who played Pinder.

Q (Desmond Llewelyn)

Although most of the British population would welcome a trip to sunny Nassau, the prospect of leaving London only serves to aggravate Q, who pays a surprise visit to 007 in order to equip him with the latest state-of-the-art gadgetry. Bond irritates the weapons genius by fidgeting with the hi-tech devices, a practice Desmond Llewelyn says Sean Connery would do in real life. Llewelyn also reports that the role of Q was initially longer in *Thunderball*, and included a sequence in which Q admonishes Bond for walking away to play cards with Felix Leiter. Much to Llewelyn's chagrin, the sequence was cut from the final print.

M (Bernard Lee)

The by-play between Bond and M is particularly insightful in *Thunderball*. Although M chastises Bond in front of the home secretary and his fellow '00' agents for being late for an emergency meeting, he defends him shortly afterwards to Group Captain Pritchard, who doubts that Bond could have seen NATO pilot Derval dead at Shrublands. M quickly explains that if 007 says he saw the man dead, that is enough reason to make enquiries, thus putting Pritchard in his place. In these subtle ways, the writers demonstrate that M has respect and feeling for Bond, despite disapproving of his lifestyle.

MISS MONEYPENNY (Lois Maxwell)

The standard office flirtation between Bond and Moneypenny is very amusing this time, when M overhears Moneypenny refer to him as 'the old man'. M delivers an admonishment that reduces 007 and Moneypenny to looking like embarrassed children. Bond also can't resist teasing the jealous Moneypenny by informing her he will be able to recognize the beautiful Domino by two moles on her thigh.

VEHICLES

ASTON MARTIN DB5 Although the majority of the onscreen action in *Thunderball* takes place either on the sea or under water, vehicles still figure prominently. Due to the popularity of the Aston Martin DB5 in *Goldfinger*, it was brought back for an encore in this film. Although not deploying the gadgets seen previously, the car was given a new weapon, a water cannon concealed in the rear of its bodywork. This aided Bond's escape by literally

Largo's floating fortress, the *Disco Volante*. Ken Adam modified an actual hydrofoil called *The Flying Fish* and added the detachable 50-foot 'cocoon'.

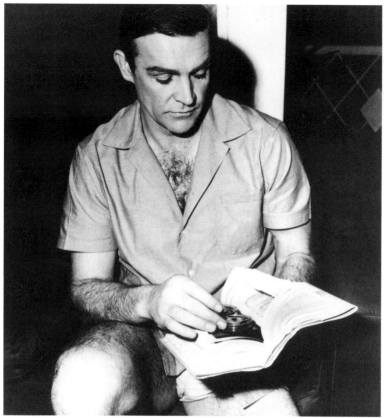

Above: Did Q invent the first audio book? Bond uses this tape recorder to catch an intruder in his hotel room.

Right: Hell on wheels – Fiona's deadly, rocket-firing BSA motorcycle.

featured a machine gun and deck cannon) plays an integral part in the climax of the film. Largo left the cocoon behind and his loyal crew were forced to fight the US fleet while he attempted to escape with the NATO bombs. Special-effects expert John Stears remembers that when a model of the boat was dynamited during the climax of the film, the explosion was so great that it broke all of the windows on Bay Street in Nassau, many miles away.

GADGETS & WEAPONS

MINI-BREATHING DEVICE This small apparatus is designed to be used in the event that a rebreather is not available. Bond is given the device by Q, who cautions him that it will only provide up to four minutes of air. (Despite this, Bond miraculously uses it throughout the underwater battle.) The device, which saves Bond's life in Largo's shark pool, retracts into a 'convenient pocket size' according to Q. 'Assuming one has a convenient pocket,' responds the cynical

washing the pursuing villains away during the pre-credits sequence. Later in the film, the DB5 is seen briefly in the chase scene in which Count Lippe's car is destroyed by Fiona's rocket-firing BSA motorcycle.

BSA LIGHTNING MOTORCYCLE The aforementioned motorcyle was adapted by special effects supervisor Bert Luxford at Pinewood Studios. The missiles, although not armed, did actually fire. However, the explosion which destroyed Lippe's car was detonated by stunt driver Bob Simmons who was doubling for actor Guy Doleman.

THE *DISCO VOLANTE* Largo's hi-tech yacht was, in reality, an old Italian hydrofoil called *The Flying Fish*. The production company purchased the vessel in Puerto Rico and had it refurbished in Miami. In the film, the underside of the hull features a secret door through which SPECTRE frogmen secretly load the NATO atomic bombs aboard. The rear portion of the craft is actually a fifty-foot cocoon which could be separated from the main structure, thus enabling the *Disco Volante* to become a high-powered hydrofoil. The heavily armed cocoon (it

Connery rehearses the jet pack sequence at the Château d'Anet near Paris. Pilot Bill Suitor actually flew the device.

007. The British military was so impressed by this gadget that they approached the film-makers for the technical data – only to be told that the unit did not actually work and was only as effective as the user's capability to hold his breath.

GEIGER WATCH Q gives Bond an expensive Breitling watch which houses a geiger counter, thus enabling Bond to detect the bombs concealed behind the secret doors hidden within the hull of Largo's yacht, the *Disco Volante*.

BELL JET PACK Bond's spectacular escape from assassin Jacques Boitier's château in the pre-

credits sequence provides one of the most enduring sequences in any 007 epic: his use of the famed Bell jet pack. Developed for the US military, the device was employed by the producers for the scene in which Bond soars above the château, leaving his SPECTRE pursuers far behind. The one-man unit soars up to 600 feet in the air and could keep the user airborne for up to four minutes.

UNDERWATER CAMERA Allegedly one of the world's first underwater cameras, Bond is presented with this device which he uses to photograph the hidden doors in the hull of the *Disco*

The atom bomb sled displayed in London to promote the film in 1965.

One of countless collectables released in 1965, fans could get a 'shot' of 007 vodka.

Volante. The camera has infrared film which allows Bond to photograph in the absence of natural lighting, and can take eight photographs in rapid succession.

UNDERWATER PROPULSION UNIT

This specially designed unit straps to Bond's oxygen tanks, propelling him under water at a rapid pace. It is used extensively in the climactic battle with Largo. The unit also features high-velocity spear guns and a searchlight.

RADIOACTIVE PILL AND MINI FLARE DEVICE

When hopelessly trapped in a cave, Bond swallows the pill which omits a radioactive signal. This alerts Leiter, who rescues 007 after seeing the flare, thus thwarting Largo's plan to bomb Miami Beach.

MUSIC

John Barry's genius for producing superb motion picture scores was never more apparent than in his work on *Thunderball*. Initially, the theme song was to be entitled 'Mr Kiss Kiss Bang Bang' and the track was recorded alternately by Shirley Bassey and Dionne Warwick. At literally the last

moment, it was decided that a new title theme would be needed – one that mentioned *Thunderball*. Aided by lyrics by Don Black, Barry composed the new song virtually overnight and Tom Jones recorded it (initially fainting when he belted out the sustained, high-decibel closing note). Additionally, Barry was under such pressure to produce the background score that much of the music was not completed when the soundtrack album was released in November 1965. Thus, the record features music from only the first half of the film. Barry's magnificent score makes the extensive – and potentially slow-moving under-water sequences – seem vibrant and thrilling. His work on *Thunderball* remains one of his most impressive achievements.

MARKETING & MERCHANDISING

Following the worldwide success of *Goldfinger*, the public's appetite for all things relating to Bond became insatiable, with sales of the Fleming novels during the mid-Sixties hitting over 6 million in the USA alone. Suddenly, 007's licence to kill was also a licence to print money as manufacturers around the world sought to tie in their products with the screen's most famous secret agent. By the time *Thunderball* was released in late 1965, it was virtually impossible to go into a shop without seeing the now-famous '007 gun logo' emblazoned on products of every description. Fans could wear 007 shoes, raincoats, aftershave and even underwear.

The Gilbert company of the USA was probably the most prolific manufacturer of James Bond toys. Their extensive range included a series of miniature figurines, twelve-inch dolls, watches and cars. The Gilbert 007 Road Race Set, an elaborate slot car layout, was sold exclusively through Sears catalogue in 1965. However, it was discovered that a large majority of these sets had a manufacturer's defect which prevented them from working. The ensuing returns eventually bankrupted Gilbert. (Ironically, the set today sells for up to £1,000 on the collectors' circuit.) In England, Lone Star Toys produced an array of toy guns, gadgets and accessory sets.

'And the kitchen sink', says 007 as he is about to enter the underwater battle wearing a virtual arsenal of hi-tech gadgetry. The same 'kitchen sink' philosophy applied to the marketing campaign for *Thunderball*. Virtually all the stops were pulled out to ensure that the public recognized this as 'The Biggest Bond of all'. In the USA, the television documentary *The Incredible World of James Bond* was aired four weeks prior to the film's release and was the highest-rated programme of the week. Ford Motor Company produced a tongue-in-cheek look at the destruction of Count Lippe's car with the short film *A Child's Guide to Blowing Up a Motorcar*. Three of the most prominent US publications – *Playboy*, *Life* and *Popular Science* – devoted cover stories to the movie, whilst nearly every magazine across Europe featured a *Thunderball*–007 article. The film was even too big for one advertising campaign. Artists Robert McGinnis and Frank McCarthy were employed to create the now classic series of film posters which alerted fans to 'Look Up! Look Down! Look Out!'.

THE BOX OFFICE

Without a doubt, *Thunderball* was the *Star Wars* of its day. Long before George Lucas could even define an Ewok, the Bond films had established themselves as the most successful series of all time. That fanaticism – which began with *Goldfinger* – reached monumental proportions with *Thunderball*. In New York, the Paramount

Theater tried in vain to accommodate crowds by showing the film twenty-four hours a day. (The theatre manager was threatened with divorce because he was unable to leave his cinema for days at a time.) In London, demand for world premiere tickets was so extensive that two premieres had to be held. The Bond phenomenon was worldwide and led *Thunderball* to become one of the top grossing films of all time. (In terms of the number of admissions, it still beats many of the blockbusters released in recent years.) The film went on to gross an incredible $141 million worldwide – a respectable sum even by today's standards, but a remarkable achievement in 1965. ■

Above: The elaborate but ill-fated Gilbert 007 Road Race toy.

Below: An extremely rare version of the 1965 Gilbert 007 action figure.

YOU ONLY LIVE TWICE

(1967)

Director **LEWIS GILBERT** Producers **ALBERT R BROCCOLI & HARRY SALTZMAN**
Screenplay **ROALD DAHL** Director of Photography **FREDDIE YOUNG** Editor **THELMA CONNELL**
Production Designer **KEN ADAM** Music **JOHN BARRY**
Release date: UK 12 June 1967, USA 13 June 1967. Running time: 116 minutes

WITH THE HI-TECH, GADGET-LADEN *THUNDERBALL* raking in record-breaking international grosses, Broccoli and Saltzman had every reason to follow a similar strategy in planning the next 007 production *You Only Live Twice*. Originally, *On Her Majesty's Secret Service* had been scheduled to follow *Thunderball*, but the decision was made to delay that film and bring Bond to the Far East in the screen adaptation of Ian Fleming's penultimate full-length 007 novel. For the first time, however, virtually every element of a Fleming novel was ignored in place of an original screenplay by the noted writer Roald Dahl. Dahl's script retained only two aspects of the book: the Japanese location and the Bond/Blofeld conflict. Instead of Fleming's moody tale set in the SPECTRE chief's castle and 'Garden of Death', Dahl created a space-age adventure complete with rocket ships, expensive special effects and large-scale action set-pieces.

You Only Live Twice has been criticized for carrying the reliance on gadgetry to the extreme. As in *Thunderball*, the character of James Bond becomes less a flesh-and-blood person than a catalyst for increasingly outlandish events. Nevertheless, *Twice* is a truly spectacular film boasting sets by Ken Adam which one reviewer aptly described as being worthy of exhibition at a World's Fair. Indeed, Adam's magnificent volcano set is one of the cinema's major achievements in production design. Equally impressive is Oscar-winning director of photography Freddie Young's gorgeous cinematography, John Barry's lush musical score and some of the

Above: Ken Adam's magnificent volcano set – scene of the spectacular climactic battle – at Pinewood Studios.

Previous spread: Aki, Tiger and Bond prepare for their encounter with Blofeld.

best editing in the series. (Although credited to Thelma Connell, Peter Hunt – now second unit director – did a great deal of uncredited editing at the request of the producers.) Lewis Gilbert, recently acclaimed for his work on *Alfie*, directed (and would go on to direct two more 007 adventures). From an acting standpoint, Sean Connery appears relatively uninterested in the proceedings, perhaps due to his well-publicized complaints about his frustration with the increasingly long production schedules of the Bond films and the fanaticism of the international press. (A furious

Connery complained that reporters followed him into the toilet for an interview.) By the time production had been completed, Connery publicly announced that *You Only Live Twice* would be his last appearance as James Bond.

THE ASSIGNMENT

American and Soviet space craft are mysteriously vanishing and both nations are blaming each other. Aware that the next incident will cause a nuclear war, M assigns James Bond to Japan, where he suspects a third party might be orchestrating the conflict. Arriving in Tokyo, 007 teams with the head of the Japanese Secret Service, Tiger Tanaka, and one of his top agents, the beautiful Aki. Bond uncovers evidence that SPECTRE is causing the friction between East and West. He disguises himself as a Japanese and trains in Tanaka's school for Ninjas. When Aki is killed in the line of duty, Bond is assigned to 'marry' another agent, the comely Kissy Suzuki, and the two mingle with the population of a remote fishing village. They discover that SPECTRE is launching rockets which capture the US and Soviet space craft and returning them to a magnificent lair inside a dormant volcano. Bond infiltrates the volcano and comes face to face with SPECTRE chief Ernst Stavro

Blofeld, who informs him that he has just launched another rocket in the hopes of causing a third world war from which he will emerge as the leader of the remaining civilization. With only minutes until Armageddon, Bond and his allies launch a full assault on the volcano and, in a spectacular battle, thwart the nuclear threat. Although Blofeld escapes, Bond has saved the world from an atomic holocaust.

007's WOMEN

AKI (Akiko Wakabayashi)

A 'new generation' Japanese Secret Service agent, Aki is soft-spoken, polite and gentle. However, she is also extremely courageous and resourceful, as 007 discovers when working closely with her in and around Tokyo. Aki works directly for Secret Service chief Tiger Tanaka and is assigned to Tanaka's Ninja training school to assist Bond in disguising himself as a Japanese. She does not hesitate to mix business with pleasure and becomes 007's lover. While at the Ninja school, however, she is murdered by an assassin with poison intended for Bond.

Akiko Wakabayashi plays the role of Aki with infectious charm. Initially, she was to play the role of Kissy Suzuki, but convinced director Lewis Gilbert that she would be more suitable for the ill-fated Aki.

KISSY SUZUKI (Mie Hama)

A top agent of Tiger Tanaka, Kissy is assigned to marry James Bond, thus allowing the couple to pose as peasants in a fishing village where they can investigate SPECTRE activities. She weds Bond using an assumed name in an elaborate and traditional Japanese ceremony which is one of the more unusual and fascinating sequences to appear in a 007 film. Eventually, Kissy and Bond locate the volcano lair of Blofeld. In the massive battle that follows, Kissy distinguishes herself in the midst of the action. Unlike Aki, Kissy refuses to bed 007 while the mission is in progress but is eager to succumb in its aftermath.

Bond 'marries' Kissy Suzuki in the beautifully filmed wedding sequence.

Bob Simmons rehearses the fight sequence in Blofeld's lair, with actor Ronald Rich as Hans, Blofeld's bodyguard.

Mie Hama plays the role of Kissy with considerable charm and the fact that she appears primarily in a bikini provided the publicity department with ample opportunity to capitalize on her stunning figure. Bond purists note the strange fact that her character's name is not mentioned once in the film.

007'S VILLAINS

ERNST STAVRO BLOFELD
(Donald Pleasence)

For the first time, 007 meets the SPECTRE mastermind face to face. The sequence lives up to expectations, as Blofeld is played with eerie, low-key menace by the distinguished British character actor Donald Pleasence. The repartee between Bond and Blofeld is brief but very well written and Pleasence's appearance – complete with a distinctive scar over his eye – is bizarre enough to have launched a seemingly endless array of bald-headed villains who continue to populate spy films even today. Like all great 007 villains, Blofeld possesses a dry wit and never displays his temper, even when Bond destroys his latest home away from home, the hollowed-out volcano rocket site. (Just how he managed to hollow out a volcano then populate it with a full army and space rocket without arousing suspicion is never fully explained.)

Both Telly Savalas and Charles Gray would portray Blofeld in the next two Bond films, but Pleasence

remains the most memorable of the trio.

MR OSATO (Teru Shimada)

One of Japan's leading industrialists and owner of Osato Chemicals and Engineering, the high-powered executive is actually on the SPECTRE payroll. Osato provides liquid oxygen to the criminal organization to fuel Blofeld's rocket ship. When Bond discovers Osato's involvement with Blofeld, the industrialist is ordered to kill him. When he does not succeed, Blofeld personally murders him to demonstrate 'the price of failure' to 007.

Actor Teru Shimada is impressive as the dignified, yet ruthless, Osato. During the 1960s, he seemed to corner the market in roles requiring distinguished, older Japanese actors. He was previously seen in a heroic part in the *Man From UNCLE* feature film *One Spy Too Many*.

HELGA BRANDT (Karin Dor)

This ravishing redhead works as the 'confidential secretary' to Mr Osato. Like her boss, however, she is a SPECTRE agent. When Bond is captured by Osato, she allows Bond to seduce her and – in a completely nonsensical plot twist – pretends to defect to his side only to try to kill him by stranding him in a Cessna aircraft destined to crash. When Bond survives the wreck, Brandt pays with her life in a harrowing sequence in which she is plunged into Blofeld's piranha pool.

Played effectively by the German actress Karin Dor, Helga Brandt is a sultry villainess, somewhat reminiscent of Fiona Volpe. However, the role is only sketchily written and the character is never fully developed.

007'S ALLIES

TIGER TANAKA (Tetsuro Tamba)
The charismatic head of the Japanese Secret Service forms a close alliance with 007. Tanaka is a legendary figure in Japan and rarely makes public appearances. Bond literally drops in on his secret HQ, located under the streets of Tokyo. Here, Tanaka maintains a luxurious private train which boasts a screening room, full service bar and staff. He also has another headquarters located in a magnificent ancient castle, as well as a Ninja school where top agents are trained in the art of surprise and concealment.

Tetsuro Tamba was criticized in some quarters for being too young to play the head of the Japanese Secret Service. However, because of their similar ages, Tamba's Tanaka shares an excellent onscreen chemistry with Connery's Bond. Both are total professionals, but are not above making witticisms and indulging in the attentions of beautiful women. In recent years, Tetsuro Tamba has emerged as a significant religious leader in Japan.

HENDERSON (Charles Gray)
Henderson, an MI6 agent, is Bond's contact in Tokyo. His brief appearance in *You Only Live Twice* is a well-written sequence which alternates between subtle humour and sudden tragedy. Henderson is a fascinating character, having lived since the end of the Second World War in Japan.

He loves the culture but refuses to go entirely native. Thus, his house is an amusing combination of oriental and occidental furnishings. Bond recognizes Henderson by the fact that he has a wooden leg, the result of a wound in the battle for Singapore. In the midst of informing Bond about his theories concerning the US/Soviet space crisis, Henderson is stabbed to death by an assassin.

Charles Gray's performance is truly a gem and impressed the producers enough for them to cast him – less successfully – as Blofeld in *Diamonds Are Forever*.

M (Bernard Lee)
Following his staged 'death' designed to deceive his enemies, Bond meets with M to discuss the disappearance of Soviet and US space craft. M warns 007 that this is 'the big one', and he is not overstating the case. If Bond does not resolve the crisis, a nuclear war is imminent. The scenes between 007 and his superior are far too brief this time, leaving the viewer desiring more of the expected by-play. However, we do get to see M in his naval uniform for the first and only time in the series.

MISS MONEYPENNY (Lois Maxwell)
Moneypenny almost gets Bond finally to say 'I love you', but not in the context desired: it's 007's

Above: The alluring assassin Helga Brandt was played by German actress Karin Dor.

Far left: 'Allow me to introduce myself. I am Ernst Stavro Blofeld.' Donald Pleasence as the SPECTRE chief.

Left: Czech actor Jan Werich in a rare pre-production pose as the original Blofeld. When Werich became ill, Donald Pleasence took over.

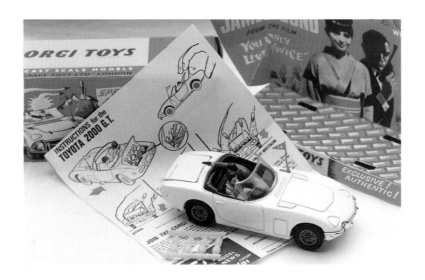

Aki's 2000 GT sports car did not exist as a convertible. It was specially adapted for the film by Toyota, and afterwards became another classic Corgi toy.

code word for greeting Tiger Tanaka. Frustratingly for Moneypenny, Bond denies her even this concession. She also tosses him a book called *Instant Japanese* to help him in his assignment, but Bond reminds her that he took 'a first in oriental languages at Cambridge'.

Moneypenny does get the last laugh, however: at the completion of the mission, she goes on the submarine's deck where Bond and Kissy's raft has washed up, thus ruining the couple's romantic encounter.

Q (Desmond Llewelyn)
The grumpy gadgets master arrives in Japan in a foul mood. He quickly gets down to business by presenting Bond with the 'Little Nellie' autogyro. Clad in khaki shorts he at least looks like a tourist but there is no evidence that Q is enjoying this field assignment any more than he did equipping Bond in Nassau for *Thunderball*.

VEHICLES

TOYOTA 2000 GT *You Only Live Twice* is unique among the Bond films because it remains the only one to date in which 007 does not drive. During his escape from Osato's office Bond is rescued by Aki, who makes their getaway in a white Toyota 2000 GT sports car. Later in the film, when Bond and Aki are being pursued by gun-toting villains, Aki uses the onboard closed-circuit television system to request help from Tanaka. In reality, Toyota never built the 2000 GT as a convertible. Two

cars were specially modified for the film. After principal photography in Japan was completed, the cars were shipped to Pinewood Studios where John Stears and his team installed one of the world's first portable video recorders in the glove compartment and a monitor and transmitter behind the bucket seats. Insert photography of these gadgets was filmed entirely at the studio. Today, Toyota have one of the cars in their Japanese museum; the other is owned by a private collector.

LITTLE NELLIE Perhaps the second most famous of all Bond's vehicles (next to the Aston Martin DB5) is the portable mini-helicopter, affectionately known as Little Nellie. In reality, Nellie is an autogyro built and flown by Wing Commander Ken Wallis. Production designer Ken Adam first heard about it whilst listening to a radio interview. Simultaneously, Harry Saltzman saw photographs of it in an aviation magazine. Once the commander had given the producers a test flight over the backlot of Pinewood Studios, it was decided to include this remarkable machine in the screenplay for *You Only Live Twice*. In the film, Bond uses Little Nellie (which arrives in Japan packed in four large suitcases) to fly a reconnaissance mission over remote volcanoes in search of the missing US and Soviet space ships. Whilst in the air, Bond is surrounded by four SPECTRE machine-gun firing helicopters. In a spectacularly filmed dog fight, 007 deploys all of Nellie's gadgets to destroy the enemy. The special-effects team constructed the now famous yellow cowling and installed the following armaments:
• two front-mounted machine guns
• two rocket launchers
• two heat-seeking air-to-air missiles
• two rear flame guns
• smoke ejectors
• aerial mines launched on tiny parachutes
Towards the end of 1966, Ken Wallis made some eighty-five flights (which kept him in the air for forty-six hours) to capture Little Nellie's battle onscreen. All of the sequences with Sean Connery were filmed against a blue screen at Pinewood Studios. The opening sequences were initially shot in Japan but, because local laws prevented any firing of guns in mid-air, production was completed over a mountain range in Spain. During filming, aerial cameraman Johnny Jordan, who was suspended on a rig under a helicopter, was caught in an updraft, which drew him into the

AROUND THE WORLD WITH 007

Filmed entirely on location in **Japan** (with the exception of second unit photography done in **Hong Kong**, **Nassau** and **Spain**), *Twice* utilized the exotic backdrops of **Tokyo**, **Kobe** and the world-famous **Himeji** castle. The remote fishing village of **Akime**, known for its hot springs, served as the fishing village where Bond and Kissy 'honeymoon', while the volcano on **Kyushu** led to complications because much of the production equipment had to be transported by foot and packhorse. Because of fans' hysteria at the presence of Sean Connery in Tokyo, director Lewis Gilbert had to hide the cameras for some of the sequences to minimize the attention drawn to the production. As in previous films, **Pinewood Studios** played host to all the interior set sequences.

blades of another helicopter beneath him, severing the lower part of one of his legs.

Such is the enduring fame of Little Nellie that Ken Wallis built an exact replica which is proudly displayed today at Planet Hollywood in London.

TANAKA'S HELICOPTER When Bond and Aki are pursued by a car-load of gunmen, Tiger Tanaka deploys a unique helicopter to rescue them. The large, two-rotor chopper features a gigantic electro-magnet which is lowered on to the villains' car, lifting them off the ground and eventually dropping them into the sea. The sequence is admittedly amusing, but rather absurd. Surely Tanaka cannot routinely use this as a method of discouraging enemies. Bond and Aki watch the wonderfully photographed close-ups of the action on a television monitor in the Toyota 2000 GT but who is filming it all is never explained.

BIRD 1 This is the name of the SPECTRE rocket which is responsible for capturing the missing US and Soviet space craft. Launched from Blofeld's volcano lair, Bird 1 has the capability of opening up its front section and literally swallowing another space capsule. Following the capture of the other space craft, Bird 1 returns to the volcano where the US and Soviet crews are imprisoned. Production designer Ken Adam constructed a full-scale rocket that was actually capable of performing a limited launch. Incredibly, he did not receive an Oscar nomination for his work.

M 1 SUBMARINE The threat of nuclear war is drastic enough for M personally to get involved in a field operation. The MI6 chief travels to the Sea of Japan to await James Bond's clandestine arrival on board his personal submarine, M 1. Once aboard, 007 is briefed on the mission in M's opulent wood-panelled office. The submarine makes an ironic reappearance at the end of the film when it surfaces directly under the raft on which Bond and Kissy are attempting to make love. This gives Moneypenny the satisfaction of heeding M's command to go on deck and order Bond to report immediately.

GADGETS & WEAPONS

NINJA WEAPONS When Bond visits Tanaka's training school for Ninjas, he is shown a variety of innovative weaponry. For example, there are rocket pistols and rifles that fire jet-propelled bullets which explode on impact; metallic

Bond's cigarettes are a hazard to other people's health.

throwing stars, an ancient martial arts' weapon with razor-sharp blades that Tanaka ultimately uses to save Bond from being killed by Blofeld; and a rocket-firing cigarette, that conceals a small exploding missile (this device is integral in Bond's efforts to thwart SPECTRE). When Tanaka advises him that 'this can save your life, this cigarette', Bond jokes that he sounds like an advertisement.

SAFE DECODER After breaking into Osato's headquarters, Bond uses a state-of-the-art device to crack his safe and retrieve important documents. The safe decoder, which is a compact unit, runs through every possible code variation at lightning-fast speed until the proper code is found.

UNDERWATER BREATHING UNIT & SHROUD Following his feigned assassination in Hong Kong, Bond is buried at sea as a Royal Navy commander. His body is wrapped like a mummy in a shroud and dropped into

This poster of Bond in Little Nellie was rarely seen. In the final version, Sean Connery's face was repainted and the exploding bodies in the background were removed.

the ocean, where frogmen recover him and bring him aboard the M 1 submarine. Bond is cut out of the shroud, revealing a full breathing unit he has used to survive the ordeal. He emerges from the shroud in his commander's uniform, and – in keeping with strict naval protocol – says, 'Request permission to come aboard, sir.'

HELGA'S LIPSTICK BOMB Whilst he is on board Helga Brandt's Cessna plane, Bond's deceitful lover double-crosses him and uses a small stun bomb concealed in her lipstick to send the plane into a rapid descent. Helga parachutes to safety, leaving 007 to face (almost) certain death.

MUSIC

John Barry's score for *You Only Live Twice* is a profound and beautiful work of art. Combining familiar Bond themes with strains of oriental music, Barry created a unique blend which – along with that of *On Her Majesty's Secret Service* – remains his most impressive contribution to a 007 film. The lovely title song has poetic lyrics by Leslie Bricusse which, along with Nancy Sinatra's vocals, add immeasurably to its impact. Barry also provides any number of other outstanding themes which complement both the action and love

sequences magnificently. Much of the edge-of-the-seat suspense found in the climax of the film can be attributed to Barry's work.

MARKETING & MERCHANDISING

To ensure that the public knew this would be an even bigger epic than *Thunderball*, the producers devised a massive advertising campaign. Alas, it would be the most controversial one, at least from Sean Connery's point of view. Long before the film opened, the teaser poster featured scenes from previous Bond films along with a depiction of Connery holding a space helmet. 'This man IS James Bond', screamed the narrative. The producers – concerned about the almost simultaneous release of the big budget Bond spoof *Casino Royale* – were trying to remind fans that this was the true cinematic 007. However, the campaign annoyed Connery, since his name did not even appear on the poster. Having already decided to resign from the role because of fears of typecasting, Connery resented the continued implication that he and his onscreen alter ego were inseparable. (Ultimately, it was too late to modify the advertisements, but in Britain certain campaigns made last-minute changes to read 'Sean Connery AS James Bond'.) The marketing department created not one but three magnificent poster designs by artists Frank McCarthy and Robert McGinnis – each of which has become highly sought after by collectors today. Lois Maxwell was sent on a seventeen-city tour of the USA and was an honoured guest at Expo 67 in Canada.

Product tie-ins included a series of collectors' slides which were sold and packaged with bubble gum and allowed the buyer to purchase a small viewer via a mail-order promotion. The soundtrack album was part of a massive promotion in the UK which included life-size models of Connery for shop windows. Airfix, one of the most prolific manufacturers of construction kits of the era, manufactured what is probably the most detailed model of Little Nellie. Such was its popularity on the collectors' market (with original kits commanding a price over £300) that Airfix reissued this kit in 1996. Additionally, Airfix produced a 1:24 scale model of the Toyota 2000 GT, as did Doyusha of Japan almost thirty years later. Continuing their relationship with the Bond marketplace, Corgi Toys of England released a magnificent die-cast replica of the Toyota 2000 GT. Complete with hand-painted figures of Bond and Aki, the car featured an option not seen in the film: a rocket launcher in the boot. One of the rarest pieces of *You Only Live Twice* memorabilia is a children's playset based on the SPECTRE volcano lair. Sold only in France, the toy is among the most expensive and sought-after of all Bond collectables.

THE BOX OFFICE

With a budget of $9.5 million, the cost of bringing *You Only Live Twice* to completion was $3 million more than that expended on *Thunderball*. The reasons are very apparent. *Twice* fulfilled the producers' promise always to ensure that every penny was reflected on the screen. This *looks* like an epic film, with stupendous sets and exotic Far Eastern locales. Yet *You Only Live Twice* had to contend with a rival Bond spectacular, Columbia's big-budget 007 satire *Casino Royale* (the one Fleming novel to which Broccoli and Saltzman did not own the rights). That film's producer, Charles K Feldman, assumed he could not compete with Eon in making a 'serious' Bond movie, so opted instead for an all-star spoof which cost more than $12 million. Broccoli and Saltzman were clearly concerned that the rival 007 film would confuse the audience, especially since both would be in cinemas at the same time. There is indeed evidence that the producers' concerns were

Original props and products are displayed in a window of Selfridge's department store in London.

well-founded, as box-office receipts for *You Only Live Twice* were significantly lower than those for *Thunderball* in the USA, at $68.5 million versus $77.6 million. Worldwide grosses were $111.6 million compared with $141.2 million for the preceding film. Still, *You Only Live Twice* was considered an enormous hit by any definition, a rather remarkable achievement considering that since the release of *Thunderball*, the spy mania boom had peaked and begun to subside. Yet, Bond outlived his cinematic rivals and continued to prosper. However, the resignation of Sean Connery as 007 left many wondering if the character would indeed be able to live twice with another star in the role. ■

Sean Connery's wife Diane Cilento (left, with black wig) doubled for actress Mie Hama in the sequence in which Kissy dives into the water.

ON HER MAJESTY'S SECRET SERVICE

(1969)

Director **PETER HUNT** Producers **ALBERT R BROCCOLI & HARRY SALTZMAN**
Screenplay **RICHARD MAIBAUM** Director of Photography **MICHAEL REED** Editor **JOHN GLEN**
Production Designer **SYD CAIN** Music **JOHN BARRY**

Release date: UK and USA 18 December 1969. Running time: 140 minutes

FOR ANY NUMBER OF REASONS, *ON HER MAJESTY'S Secret Service* is an anomaly among the Bond films. The most obvious difference is the presence of George Lazenby in the role of 007. Lazenby, a model with no prior acting experience, convinced the film-makers that he was the man for the role following Sean Connery's departure from the series with *You Only Live Twice*. Known primarily in the UK for his 'beefcake' presence in a *Fry's* chocolate television advertisement, Lazenby, an Australian, suitably impressed the producers with his good looks and physical prowess during a fight sequence staged as a screen test. Another notable difference in this Bond film is the directorial debut of long-time Bond editor Peter Hunt, who willingly took on the massive task of overseeing the logistics of this epic production.

Screenwriter Richard Maibaum makes a bold departure from the established formula, sticking closely to Ian Fleming's source novel (one of his best) and downplaying the hardware and gadgetry. It was Peter Hunt's vision to bring the basics back to Bond and develop his character as well as the characters of those surrounding him. Artistically, he made the correct choice as the 007 of *OHMSS* is a complex, sometimes haunted, soul who finds his life revitalized

Right: Saved from death's embrace. Bond rescues Tracy after her suicide attempt on a Portuguese beach.

Previous spread: Bond with two of Blofeld's 'Angels of Death'.

007 contemplates escaping Blofeld's mountain-top headquarters.

through a love affair with Tracy di Vicenzo, whom he later marries. Although the audience is fully prepared for the tragic consequences of the wedding (Bond cannot continue his sleuthing with a wife in tow, à la *The Thin Man* series), the sequence in which Tracy is murdered is a profound and devastating moment. In essence, the Bond films fully matured with this movie, even if future entries would return to the reliable formula of gadgetry and spectacle.

Although *OHMSS* was routinely dismissed by critics who cited Lazenby as a brave but disappointing successor to Connery, the intervening years have been notably kinder to both the film and its star. Indeed, due in no small part to Peter Hunt's inspired direction, *OHMSS* generally ranks among the top films with the fans. Likewise, Lazenby has emerged as a very popular contributor to the series and has enjoyed large enthusiastic audiences during his public appearances at Bond-related events. In summary, *OHMSS* is a brilliant thriller in its own right and justifiably ranks among the best Bond films ever made.

THE ASSIGNMENT

In the course of his obsessive mission to locate Blofeld, James Bond rescues the beautiful but bored Countess Tracy di Vicenzo from suicide. Agent 007 later learns that she is the rebellious daughter of Marc Ange Draco, the most powerful organized-crime kingpin in Europe. Draco makes Bond a proposition: if 007 marries his wayward daughter and tames her wild ways, Draco will use the enormous resources of his organization to locate Blofeld. Bond declines to marry Tracy but does agree to date her. Eventually, a genuine romance blossoms.

Bond learns that Blofeld has a massive headquarters called Piz Gloria located in the Swiss Alps. Posing as Sir Hilary Bray, a representative of the College of Arms in London, Bond arrives at Piz Gloria ostensibly to trace Blofeld's family tree. Agent 007 is exposed and captured by Blofeld, who informs him he intends to hold the United

Nations to ransom under threat of biological warfare. Blofeld has sent numerous beautiful women throughout the world, all of them hypnotized to unleash deadly germs upon receiving his command. Bond, assisted by the daring Tracy, makes a dramatic escape but his lover is captured by Blofeld. Bond and Draco lead a massive raid on Piz Gloria during which they succeed in rescuing Tracy and thwarting Blofeld's scheme. After a hand-to-hand battle aboard a racing bobsled, Bond presumes his enemy has been killed.

Agent 007 and Tracy marry and set off on a much-deserved honeymoon, as they debate the number of children they will have. Suddenly, tragedy strikes when Blofeld and his henchwoman Irma Bunt speed by and spray the couple's car with machine-gun fire, mortally wounding Tracy. A heartbroken Bond is left to cradle in his arms the only woman he has ever truly loved.

007'S WOMEN

TRACY DI VICENZO (Diana Rigg)
Those who criticize the Bond women as being bimbos have obviously not seen *On Her Majesty's Secret Service*. The character of Tracy is wonderfully written, allowing Bond to become involved with an interesting, three-dimensional woman who is intelligent, courageous and humorous. The producers also had the wisdom to cast a well-known actress in this extremely important role. Diana Rigg, already a star from her years on *The Avengers*, gave a wonderful performance and it is difficult to imagine anyone else in the part. Tracy is a truly complex character, alternating between a suicidal, love-starved, spoiled rich girl and a daring and vivacious adventurer. For once, Bond has truly met his equal in every way imaginable. Agent 007 first rescues her from committing suicide on a Portuguese beach. She later rejects Bond's romantic overtures, assuming that he is trying to buy her father's favour. However, a very believable romance develops and the love scenes between Bond and Tracy (which could have been embarrassing) are quite moving and add emotional impact to the daring, down-beat climax.

BLOFELD'S 'ANGELS OF DEATH'
Upon his arrival at Piz Gloria (in disguise as Sir Hilary Bray), 007 is introduced to a bevy of beautiful young women from around the world. They believe they have been summoned for experimental treatment of their allergies. In reality, Blofeld

Mr and Mrs James Bond. Tracy proudly displays her wedding ring.

has hypnotized them and returns them to their respective nations with a 'gift': a perfume atomizer with a hidden radio transmitter installed. Upon hearing his command, the 'angels' are to unleash the deadly Virus Omega from the atomizer, thus endangering entire strains of livestock around the world. Bond is delighted to be in the presence of these girls, especially since each of them takes pleasure in attempting to seduce the virginal Sir Hilary, but his liaisons prove to be his undoing.

A number of the 'angels' went on to rather prominent careers. Most notably, Julie Ege, a former Miss Norway, starred in several Hammer horror films. Anouska Hempel retired from acting and is now the successful owner of the highly fashionable Blakes Hotel in London. Joanna Lumley found fame in other feature films and as Patrick Macnee's co-star in *The New Avengers*. In recent years,

Above: Tracy's Mercury Cougar aids Bond's escape during a snowstorm.

Right: Telly Savalas relaxes between takes on the set at Pinewood Studios.

she starred in the wildly successful television comedy series *Absolutely Fabulous*. Interestingly, she has also narrated a number of audio tapes of the Bond novels.

RUBY BARTLETT (Angela Scoular)
The first of Bond's 'conquests' of the 'Angels of Death'. While Bond is giving a boring recitation on genealogy in his guise as Sir Hilary Bray, Ruby takes advantage of his Scottish attire by secretly placing her hand underneath his kilt and writing her room number in lipstick on his thigh. Bond explains his momentary discomfort by saying he feels 'a slight stiffness coming on'. Later, his erotic encounter is interrupted in a rather bizarre fashion as he witnesses a portion of Ruby's 'cure for my allergy' caused by an aversion to chicken. She is suddenly hypnotized by a kaleidoscope of lights above her bed as the soothing voice of Blofeld instructs her to love chickens. Bond will later discover that this 'treatment' has far more sinister implications.

007'S VILLAINS

ERNST STAVRO BLOFELD (Telly Savalas)
The character of Blofeld in *On Her Majesty's Secret Service* was required to be more of a physical threat to 007 than the SPECTRE chief of the previous films. Consequently, actor Telly Savalas was chosen for the role, despite the fact that he had been typecast as unsophisticated gangster types in dozens of previous films. Savalas is competent enough in the scenes in which he must be

refined or charming, but he is much better suited to the climactic action sequences. Donald Pleasence had presented a far more menacing and intriguing Blofeld in the preceding film, but the thought of him battling with Bond in hand-to-hand combat would have been ludicrous. If Savalas presents a slightly less inspired Blofeld, the evil genius's scheme is also rather mundane: he threatens to unleash biological warfare unless he is issued a full pardon for past crimes and his dubious claim to the title of Count is recognized. Somehow, it is difficult to fathom that the United Nations would risk the annihilation of the human race rather than agree to these rather modest demands. Still, the inevitable clash of Bond's and Blofeld's egos provides the film with some very memorable sequences and Lazenby and Savalas display a good deal of chemistry together. This Blofeld also shares one character trait with 007: an overactive libido. Just as Bond's preoccupation with seducing the girls of Piz Gloria leads to disastrous consequences, so too does Blofeld's attempts to woo Tracy. Again, Telly Savalas is a more plausible presence in these scenes than Donald Pleasence would have been. Indeed, it would be difficult to imagine Pleasence's Blofeld swooning like a lovestruck schoolboy as Tracy waxes lyrical with lines like 'Thy dawn, O Master of the World, thy dawn ...'

IRMA BUNT (Ilse Steppat)
A villainess of Rosa Klebb's calibre, Bunt serves as Blofeld's omnipresent henchwoman and it is she

who acts as a grotesque mother hen over the 'Angels of Death' to ensure they do not stray from Piz Gloria. Bunt is a short, stocky, humourless woman who incites derisive comments from the girls at Piz Gloria, but who instills a sense of fear and trepidation. Bunt greets Bond, in his guise as Sir Hilary, at Murren train station in Switzerland and escorts him by helicopter to Piz Gloria. Her instincts tell her that Sir Hilary is not who he appears to be and she plans an ambush for Bond by hiding under the covers of Ruby Bartlett's bed when 007 makes his nocturnal visit. Although she is not seen during the battle at Piz Gloria, it is Bunt who wields the machine gun which kills Tracy in the film's tragic climax. Excellently played by German actress Ilse Steppat (who died shortly after filming was completed), Bunt is one of the more memorable Bond villainesses. The fact that she escapes apparently unscathed from her murder of Tracy Bond only adds to her notoriety.

GRUNTHER (Yuri Borienko)

Grunther is the stony-faced head of security at Piz Gloria and henchman to Blofeld and Irma Bunt. He seems to be on hand during every devious deed committed by the duo. Despite his imposing physical presence, Grunther is roundly beaten in the exciting hand-to-hand fight with Tracy during the assault on Piz Gloria. Yuri Borienko, who played Grunther, was initially selected as Bond's opponent in a fight sequence staged as George Lazenby's screen test. Unlike Borienko, however, Lazenby was unskilled in the art of make-believe fighting and ended up breaking Borienko's nose. Perhaps as consolation, Borienko was rewarded with the role of Grunther.

007'S ALLIES

MARC ANGE DRACO (Gabriele Ferzetti)

Draco is the head of the Union Corse, one of the most powerful organized-crime syndicates in

Europe. As Tracy di Vicenzo's father, Draco is sick with worry concerning his wayward daughter whom he has raised alone since his wife's death when Tracy was twelve. Draco, who began his crime career as a bandit hiding in the hills, has evolved into a feared Mafia don as well as the head of an empire of legitimate businesses, chief among which is Draco Construction located in Portugal, where he maintains a large estate. Draco, a charismatic and likable fellow despite his reputation as an international criminal, is grateful to Bond for saving Tracy's life. He offers 007 a £1 million dowry if he agrees to marry her, in the hope that such a union will reawaken his daughter's interest in life. Bond declines but ends up falling in love with Tracy and marrying her anyway. Draco is also a man of action who is able to mobilize a small private army to accompany Bond in the assault on Piz Gloria – an attack Draco personally leads. At Bond and Tracy's wedding, there is a wonderful sequence in which Draco chats amicably with his enemy

Irma Bunt and Grunther await the arrival of Sir Hilary Bray in Switzerland.

TOP SECRET CAST & CREW DOSSIERS

✳ While filming a chase sequence through the back streets and over the rooftops of London (below) **George Lazenby** injured his arm scaling a wall. In the scene, Bond discovers one of Blofeld's men spying on his meeting with Hilary Bray at the College of Arms and gives chase. The whole sequence was deleted from the final cut.

Unlikely allies: M and Draco share a drink at the wedding of Bond and Tracy.

M about past operations. Gabriele Ferzetti, the winner of two Italian Oscars, delivers an endearing performance and remains – like Pedro Armendariz in *From Russia With Love* – one of Bond's most impressive onscreen allies.

CAMPBELL (Bernard Horsfall)

This MI6 agent is assigned to assist 007 in a clandestine fashion. In Bern, Campbell arranges to deliver a safe-cracking/photocopier machine to the offices of Blofeld's lawyer Gumbold so that Bond can photograph secret documents. At Piz Gloria, however, he attempts to gain access to Blofeld's institute by posing as a mountain climber. He is discovered and murdered and his body strung up by its heels as a grisly warning to Bond. This sequence was achieved through the use of a matte painting by artist Cliff Culley. Actor Bernard Horsfall was hanging from a studio ceiling and the Alps were painted in behind him. Alas, Horsfall's luck was not much better than his onscreen character's. For reasons unknown, British television and early video prints of *On Her Majesty's Secret Service* for many years eliminated the safe-cracking sequence and part of his attempt to bluff his way on to Piz Gloria. The scenes were only recently restored on video.

SIR HILARY BRAY (George Baker)

Genealogist at the College of Arms, Bray, a soft-spoken baronet, is approached by Blofeld to travel to Piz Gloria to verify his claim to the title Count de Bleuchamp. Bond intervenes and convinces Bray to let him take his place. Bray relents only as a matter of national importance, but insists that Bond gain at least a cursory knowledge of genealogy. Actor George Baker provided the voice of Bond for the scenes in which he impersonates Sir Hilary. Additionally, Baker dubbed the character of Bond in an ill-fated US television showing of *On Her Majesty's Secret Service* in the 1970s which included a re-edited version of the film and a superfluous prologue with a voice-over by 007. (After objections from Cubby Broccoli, this version was never shown again.) Baker, an early candidate for the role of Bond, also played Captain Benson in *The Spy Who Loved Me*.

M (Bernard Lee)

We get a brief, but fascinating, glimpse into the private life of Bond's crusty superior in *On Her Majesty's Secret Service* when 007 visits M's home, known as Quarterdeck. Here, we see the MI6 chief relaxing by engaging in his favourite (unlikely) pastime lepidopterology, the study of moths and butterflies. (Bond can't resist showing off his knowledge of the subject by correctly identifying a rare species.) Back at the office, we get one of the best-written sequences between the two characters ever to appear in a Bond film. M, frustrated by 007's inability to track down Blofeld, removes him from the case. In anger, Bond promptly resigns. Through the efforts of Moneypenny, the men both calm down and resolve their differences with their pride intact. It's a wonderful sequence superbly acted by both Bernard Lee and George Lazenby, and it is made all the more rewarding by the subtle and unspoken way in which the affection between the two men is depicted.

MISS MONEYPENNY (Lois Maxwell)

For once, Moneypenny plays a pivotal role in the storyline. Following the sequence in which Bond resigns in anger, he dictates his formal resignation to Moneypenny and instructs her to present it to M. Bond is greatly hurt when his boss accepts it without comment – until Moneypenny advises him that she altered the memo and made it a request for a leave of absence. Bond, already regretting his temper tantrum, thanks Moneypenny . . . and in a very moving scene, so does M (albeit over his intercom). The scene demonstrates that Moneypenny is far more valuable than her role as secretary might indicate. She knows the psyches of the two most important men in her life, and she is able to resolve a crisis without either man losing face. Alas, for all her troubles, Moneypenny must suffer the pain of witnessing Bond's wedding. In a very touching sequence, Bond almost shyly acknowledges her presence by tossing her his hat one last time before embarking on his honeymoon. Moneypenny explains the tears in her eyes by saying, 'I always cry at weddings,' but even M seems sympathetic to her plight. It's refreshing to see Lois Maxwell's considerable skills as an actress given the opportunity to shine. Her scenes in *On Her Majesty's Secret Service* are her most impressive in the series.

Q (Desmond Llewelyn)

With the virtual elimination of gadgetry in the script, the role of Q is reduced to little more than two cameo appearances. He is seen briefly in the pre-credits scene unsuccessfully trying to impress M with his newest invention, radioactive lint. He later makes a short, but amusing, appearance at Bond's wedding where 007 informs him, 'This time I've got the gadgets and I know how to use them!'.

VEHICLES

ASTON MARTIN DBS

To inject some much-needed action into *On Her Majesty's Secret Service* to counter the fact that this is basically a melancholy story, Bond is given a sleek new Aston Martin – the 1969 DBS. This sports car has none of the gadgetry of the DB5 but it does feature a telescopic rifle built into the glove compartment. The DBS is featured in the opening sequence of the film in which 007 rescues Tracy. Ironically, it is seen again at the tragic climax in which Bond is powerless to prevent his wife's murder. Two DBS models were used during filming, and are today both in private collections, one in Australia and the other in England.

TRACY'S COUGAR

Tracy's Ford Cougar was given the most time onscreen in *On Her Majesty's Secret Service*, even though Bond was not behind the wheel. Pursued by SPECTRE agents through the hazardous mountain terrain, Tracy veers off the road and on to a race track. Here, she and Bond and the villains weave in and out of the rally cars taking part in a spectacular road race on ice. Eventually, and after much destruction, Tracy and Bond escape, leaving the villains' car

George Lazenby and director Peter Hunt on location at Piz Gloria.

A rare moment of relaxation in an otherwise gruelling production schedule.

Artist's prototype for the British quad poster.

For Your Ice Only: George Lazenby and Diana Rigg at a press show in London prior to departing for location shooting in Switzerland.

in flames. This sequence took over a week to film, with the Ford Motor Company supplying the cars – the majority being British Escort models. Four Mercury Cougars were provided for the filming but miraculously, the main car survived most of the ordeal.

BOBSLEDS One of Bond's most unusual modes of transport, the bobsleds were used in the chase between 007 and Blofeld during the film's climax. Blofeld makes his escape from the destroyed Piz Gloria, pursued by Bond in another sled. A thrilling and spectacular chase ensues, which was filmed not only by Willy Bogner Jr (who skied backwards down the bobsled run) but also by Johnny Jordan, who was suspended by a rig from a helicopter speeding down the mountainside.

GADGETS & WEAPONS

MINOX B CAMERA This small pocket-

sized camera is used by 007 to photograph a map indicating the locations of Blofeld's 'Angels of Death'. This was standard equipment used by real-life spies after the Second World War.

SAFE-CRACKING MACHINE During the sequence where Bond breaks into the offices of Blofeld's lawyer, Gumbold, he uses this gadget, which is also a portable photocopier. Agent 007 copies important documents which lead him to Blofeld's mountain-top lair at Piz Gloria.

RADIOACTIVE LINT At the very beginning of the film, Q demonstrates this new invention to a clearly uninterested M. However, it does not feature in the film's main plot.

MUSIC

John Barry composed what is, to the majority of fans, his greatest 007 score ever with *On Her Majesty's Secret Service*. Blending the romantic overtones of Bond's relationship with Tracy, the almost epic overtures which accompany the spectacular Swiss scenery and the inevitable James Bond theme in the action sequences, this is without doubt a masterpiece of film composing. It was also the first James Bond film since *Dr. No* to feature an instrumental track for the main title sequence, rather than the now-familiar song by a famous performer. Hal David's lyrics, combined with the triumphant use of Louis Armstrong on vocals, for the song 'We Have All The Time In The World' (heard later in the film) provided not only one of the most romantic songs in the series, but an instantly recognizable tune which to this day captivates audiences around the world.

MARKETING & MERCHANDISING

Before production had been completed on *On Her Majesty's Secret Service*, George Lazenby stunned the producers by announcing that this would be his one and only Bond film. Influenced by bad advice from radicals who convinced him that 007 would never survive into the 1970s, Lazenby gambled that playing Bond just once would ensure a future as a leading man. Ignoring Cubby Broccoli's warning that he needed to establish a track record first, he refused to sign a multi-picture deal, leaving the producers to promote *OHMSS* with a 'one-shot' star. This was a nightmare to the marketing departments, who opted to emphasize

the character of James Bond at the expense of Lazenby the actor.

Consequently, the American teaser poster omitted Lazenby's face and replaced it with a silhouette. His name was also moved below the titles, with 'James Bond 007' receiving the star billing. Lazenby did appear on the magnificent regular release cinema poster, which was beautifully designed by Frank McCarthy and Robert McGinnis. Three featurettes were also produced showing the behind-the-scenes production of the movie: *Shot on Ice* covered the car chase in the stock-car race, *Above it All* showed cameraman Johnny Jordan's daring methods of filming the ski sequence whilst suspended from a harness beneath a helicopter and *Swiss Movement* concentrated on interviews with the cast.

The fallout from the Lazenby debacle seemed to affect the merchandising, as few collectables were produced beyond the standard soundtrack album and film edition of the book. For this reason, *OHMSS* tie-ins are highly treasured by collectors and command big money on the fan circuit. Among the more interesting items to be produced was a line of vehicles from Corgi Toys, which included Tracy's Cougar, Campbell's Volkswagon, two bobsleds (one bearing Blofeld's Piz Gloria emblem, the other featuring a '007' logo) and two gift sets which today are among the rarest of all collectables. Rumour has it that a replica of Tracy's wedding ring bearing the words 'We Have All the

Time in the World' was reproduced by Arts Galore of London. To this day, no one can verify if the product was actually made, as one has yet to appear on the international collectors' market. (Its value would be such that it could be exchanged for the real wedding ring.)

THE BOX OFFICE

One of the great injustices concerning *On Her Majesty's Secret Service* is the widely held belief that the film was a box-office failure. In fact, with over $80 million grossed worldwide it was a considerable hit for a film budgeted at $7 million. What is true is that *OHMSS* performed weakly in relation to the previous Bond films. Mixed critical reaction was partly responsible, but another factor was the film's running time of two hours and twenty minutes, which reduced the number of daily showings in cinemas. The US market proved to be particularly soft and the film's status was further hampered by many cinemas pairing it with another film. However, the enthusiasm of fans for *OHMSS* has been amply demonstrated by the film's ultimate success in the home video market. ■

AROUND THE WORLD WITH 007

Location filming was truly international in scope, with sequences shot in **London**, **Switzerland** and **Portugal**. Most striking, of course, are the scenes shot in the **Swiss Alps** in and around the small villages of **Murren** and **Lauterbrunnen**. The **Schilthorn** mountain played host to Blofeld's Piz Gloria. In reality, his lair was an uncompleted restaurant situated at its peak. The producers, having been frustrated in their search for a suitable location, were jubilant at the picture-perfect setting of the restaurant. They immediately offered to furnish the interior and also to build a permanent helipad as part of the deal. Today, in commemoration of the film, the restaurant (which is accessible only by cable car) bears the name Piz Gloria and remains one of Switzerland's most exotic tourist attractions (above).

DIAMONDS ARE FOREVER

(1971)

Director **GUY HAMILTON** Producers **ALBERT R BROCCOLI & HARRY SALTZMAN**
Screenplay **RICHARD MAIBAUM & TOM MANKIEWICZ** Director of Photography **TED MOORE**
Editors **BERT BATES & JOHN W HOLMES** Production Designer **KEN ADAM** Music **JOHN BARRY**
Release date: UK 30 December 1971, USA 17 December 1971. Running time: 119 minutes

ALTHOUGH IT IS WIDELY BELIEVED THAT THE
emphasis on overt humour and sight gags began with Roger Moore's
introduction as James Bond in *Live And Let Die*, the truth is that
the trend actually started with *Diamonds Are Forever*. Because
the noble experiment to make a humanistic 007 epic with *On Her
Majesty's Secret Service* had resulted in disappointing box-office
grosses, there was real concern that Bond was outdated in the era of
anti-heroes seen in films such as *Easy Rider*, *The Wild Bunch* and
Shaft. Broccoli and Saltzman realized they had to do something
dramatic to reawaken interest in the 007 franchise. Although
American actor John Gavin had been signed as the new Bond for
Diamonds Are Forever, studio brass insisted that all attempts possible be made to entice Sean Connery to return to the role.

The idea of Connery playing Bond again was considered a pipe-
dream. His well-known aversion to 'Bond mania' and the paparazzi,
combined with his increasingly strained relationship with Broccoli
and Saltzman, seemed permanently to preclude him from consid-
eration. However, in the film world success – or the lack of it –
breeds strange bedfellows and Connery's recent non-Bond films had
not distinguished themselves at the box office. Moreover, he was
attempting to find funding for the Scottish International Educational
Trust, a charity he had recently started in his native country. After
repeated overtures, Connery stunned the film industry by agreeing

Above: Jill St John as Tiffany Case. Raquel Welch had been strongly considered for the role.

Previous spread: Director Guy Hamilton rehearsing Sean Connery and Denise Perrier in the pre-credits sequence.

to return as Bond once more: for a then record salary of $1,250,000 plus a percentage of the profits. (Connery donated the entire sum to his charity.)

For all the hype and anticipation, *Diamonds Are Forever* failed to live up to expectations – at least artistically. The decision to introduce over-the-top humour and characters was a step in the wrong direction and, for the first time, the screenplay is weak and not particularly involving. Despite the fact that *Goldfinger* director Guy Hamilton was back, the film suffered from a tendency not to take itself seriously enough and the climactic battle, usually the highlight of a Bond film, is a rather uninspired affair that skimps on spectacular action.

Still, *Diamonds* proves to have many entertaining aspects. The pre-credits sequence in which Bond relentlessly hunts Blofeld (presumably because of the murder of his wife) is extremely effective, Ken Adam's sets are up to par, and John Barry's score adds immeasurably to the atmosphere. The film's strength is the reassuring presence of Sean Connery, who – despite the fact that his weight seems to fluctuate noticeably throughout the movie – manages to recapture the same wry wit and charisma he injected into 007 years before. In summary, *Diamonds Are Forever*

is an entertaining film, but its parts are more impressive than the whole.

THE ASSIGNMENT

Someone is hoarding large quantities of diamonds from the international black market. James Bond is assigned to find out who the thieves are and why the diamonds have not been turning up for sale. Posing as a diamond smuggler, Bond travels to Holland to meet a key player in the pipeline, the beautiful Tiffany Case. The trail leads to Las Vegas, where Bond discovers that his arch enemy Blofeld is behind the scheme. Blofeld has captured reclusive billionaire and magnate Willard Whyte and assumed control of his empire. From here, he has overseen the launch of a diamond-encrusted satellite which has the ability to use a deadly laser to destroy major cities from outer space. Blofeld moves his operations to an oil rig off the California coast, where he issues a demand to the United Nations for an extravagant ransom or the satellite will be used to destroy Washington DC. Bond confronts his old enemy on the rig amidst a pitched battle between Blofeld's army and US armed forces helicopters. During the mêlée, Bond succeeds in destroying Blofeld's control room, thus rendering the satellite harmless, although the question remains as to how to recover the diamonds from space.

007'S WOMEN

TIFFANY CASE (Jill St John)
Tiffany Case helped create the unjustified impression that Bond's women's IQs measured less than their bra sizes. When Bond first meets her, she is hard-edged and intriguing, as befitting a professional smuggler. Unfortunately, this aspect of her personality disappears later in the film, when she inexplicably becomes naïve and easily manipulated by Bond and others. It's difficult to fault Jill St John's performance, as she is playing the role as written. To her credit, she still maintains periodic moments of sensuality. Yet, Tiffany Case (she was named after the diamond store where her unwed mother gave birth to her) is a weak leading lady when compared to her predecessors, and her exaggerated ineptitude makes it difficult to accept her as a worthy adversary or lover for James Bond.

PLENTY O'TOOLE (Lana Wood)
Although onscreen for only a few moments, Plenty O'Toole represents the traditional Bond

girl. She is voluptuous, sexually aggressive and, while somewhat naïve, street-wise enough to use the men around her to her own advantage. Bond encounters her at the craps table at The Whyte House Casino in Las Vegas. Her introduction to him – 'Hi, I'm Plenty' – leads to a classic witticism as 007 eyes her ample bosom and says, 'But of course you are.' Although Plenty has nothing to do with the diamond-smuggling case, the topless beauty is tossed from Bond's hotel suite by a squad of goons working for Morton Slumber. The hapless Plenty is later found drowned in a pool after being mistaken for Tiffany Case. In the final cut, her death is meaningless because she is not involved with the diamond caper. In the original script, however, she spies Bond and Tiffany making love. A jealous Plenty arrives at Tiffany's house to berate her, but is mistaken for Tiffany and killed by Wint and Kidd. Lana Wood, whose bubbly presence is a highlight of the film, is the younger sister of the late Natalie Wood.

007'S VILLAINS

ERNST STAVRO BLOFELD
(Charles Gray)
James Bond's arch enemy makes his last appearance to date, and it's his least effective. The character of Blofeld, as played previously by Donald Pleasence and Telly Savalas, was a genuine megalomaniac with sadistic tendencies. Charles Gray does not resemble the previous incarnations of Blofeld in any way – he isn't even bald. Gray is a fine actor and he is charming and witty in the role. However, that is the problem. No one expects Blofeld, the bloodthirsty menace, to be charming. He and Bond enjoy a rather civil relationship devoid of all tension – rather remarkable considering he murdered 007's beloved wife. Gray also had another obstacle to overcome. His brief but memorable role as Henderson in *You Only Live Twice* was still fresh in audience's minds when he assumed the part of Blofeld. For the record, this Blofeld not only lacks menace but also resorts to dressing in drag. His fate remains unclear at the end of the film and he has yet to reappear in a Bond movie.

KIDD & WINT (Bruce Glover, Putter Smith)
At first glance, the bizarre appearance of this pair causes amusement. However, in reality, they are cold-blooded killers employed by Blofeld who pride themselves on devising inventive methods for murder. Among their victims are Mrs Whistler, Dr

Tynan and Shady Tree. Wint and Kidd are cultured, overly polite and seemingly charming. Like Bond, they have a penchant for making a witticism following the demise of an opponent, although this pair's quips are more lethal than their weaponry and make Bond's one-liners seem Shakespearean in their inspiration. Additionally, they are also lovers and the abundance of jokes at the expense of their sexuality make these the most politically incorrect Bond villains ever. Wint and Kidd make several attempts on Bond's life but they instill little sense of fear because they are used primarily for comedic effect. Ultimately, the pair attempt to kill Bond in the film's climax, only to have Kidd turned into a human shish kebab and Wint tossed over the side of a ship attached to a bomb. The parts are wonderfully played by Bruce Glover and Putter Smith. Smith, who was a jazz musician with no previous acting experience, is particularly memorable due to his innocent, hangdog appearance which makes him the most unlikely of murderers.

Blofeld...or is it? Charles Gray as the infamous villain's double in the pre-credits sequence.

Mr Wint and Mr Kidd – the most politically incorrect Bond villains ever.

PETER FRANKS (Joe Robinson)

Bond impersonates this British diamond smuggler to win the confidence of Tiffany Case. When the real Franks shows up at her apartment in Amsterdam, Bond must eliminate the man or his cover will be blown. The fight in the lift between 007 and Franks is one of the best sequences in the film because it is reminiscent of the classic battles in previous films. The fact that stunt co-ordinator Bob Simmons had to stage the action in a confined space makes the scene all the more unique and exciting. Actor Joe Robinson was reunited with Guy Hamilton in 1996 at Pinewood Studios and the two recounted the filming of the fight sequence for a videotaped interview.

BAMBI & THUMPER

(Trina Parks, Donna Garrett)

In an inspired action sequence, Bond attempts to rescue Willard Whyte from captivity but finds he is guarded by unlikely security officers, Bambi and Thumper, two attractive, scantily clad gymnasts who give Bond a rather humiliating beating by springing about the room and using their athletic abilities to bash him soundly. When the battle continues into a swimming pool, Bond gains the upper hand by simply holding these two powerful women under the water until they surrender. Surely, the writers could have come up with a more believable method for Bond to beat his two seemingly indestructible opponents.

BERT SAXBY (Bruce Cabot)

A henchman to Blofeld, Saxby acts as the pit boss at the Whyte House Casino. He is eventually killed in an ill-fated attempt to assassinate Willard Whyte. The role was played by noted character actor Bruce Cabot, who died shortly after filming was complete. Saxby does provide one good inside joke. The name plate on his desk reads 'Albert R Saxby', an obvious reference to Albert R Broccoli.

SHADY TREE (Leonard Barr)

Shady Tree is an over-the-hill old-time stand-up comedian who remains popular on the nightclub circuit in Las Vegas. By night, he entertains audiences with a barrage of corny jokes. ('People say I have the body of Rock Hudson. If he ever sees what I've been doing to it, he'll be madder than hell!') By day, he acts as a courier for the diamond-smuggling syndicate. Tree is eventually murdered by Wint and Kidd, although the sequence showing his actual death was deleted from the movie. Leonard Barr's brief appearances as Tree are comedic gems.

PROFESSOR DR METZ (Joseph Furst)

This ill-tempered but brilliant scientist sides with Blofeld in the naïve belief that the SPECTRE chief is committed to universal nuclear disarmament. Metz builds the deadly diamond-powered laser satellite which Blofeld uses to hold the world to ransom. He believes the device will be used to threaten major destruction unless the superpowers destroy all their nuclear weapons. In fact, Metz is opposed to using the laser and hopes merely to bluff the world into complying with his demands for peace. By the time he discovers that Blofeld's real aim is to extort money, the damage has been done and he is powerless to stop his 'partner's' plan to destroy Washington DC.

AROUND THE WORLD WITH 007

Although largely filmed in the USA with key sequences in **Las Vegas**, **Nevada** and **California**, the production also made use of locations in the south of **France** and in **Amsterdam**, Holland. Sean Connery was on the set of the latter locations for a very limited time, although much was made of this footage to give the film an international flavour. Studio shots, as usual, were done at **Pinewood Studios** in England.

MORTON SLUMBER (David Bauer)

The owner–operator of the Slumber Funeral Home in Las Vegas, Slumber is also a member of the diamond-smuggling pipeline who uses his crematorium for illicit purposes. In an amusing sequence Bond, posing as Peter Franks, arrives at the Slumber Funeral Home bearing a fortune in stolen diamonds. Slumber greets him with such overbearing and phony hospitality that he might have made a successful politician. After delivering the diamonds, Slumber takes part in a double-cross and attempts to have Bond cremated. Agent 007 is saved only when Slumber realizes that the diamonds are fakes and they still need him alive to deliver the real ones. Amazingly enough, the producers used the name of a real funeral director for these scenes, as the Slumber Funeral Home actually existed.

007'S ALLIES

WILLARD WHYTE (Jimmy Dean)

The reclusive billionaire not too discreetly based on Howard Hughes. Whyte controls an enormous empire that includes hotels and casinos in Las Vegas and a construction site for building satel-lites and space craft in the Nevada desert. Whyte, who has not been seen in public for years, presents the ideal kidnap victim for Blofeld, who captures him and assumes the operation of his empire. Whyte, a shy, soft-spoken man from the American South, is the antithesis of a hard-nosed businessman. Yet, after James Bond rescues him, Whyte proves his courage by leading a helicopter attack on an oil rig from which Blofeld is masterminding his plans to destroy Washington DC. The choice of country singer Jimmy Dean for the part of a Howard Hughes-like character seemed ludicrous when announced. However, it proved to be one of the few truly inspired pieces of casting in the film, as Dean acquitted himself admirably in the role.

FELIX LEITER (Norman Burton)

This is the least likely incarnation of Bond's CIA colleague. Gone is the cool, slick hero played by Jack Lord and Rik Van Nutter. Instead, Norman Burton portrays Leiter as a somewhat bumbling, exasperated detective who is given to handing out bad one-liners. It's impossible to believe that this Leiter and Bond could have shared a close-knit friendship.

Below, left and right:

Trina Parks as Bambi and Donna Garrett as Thumper.

Lana Wood as Plenty
O'Toole.

requisite edginess apparent in the earlier films. This time, M must endure Bond showing off his superior knowledge of sherry to impress Sir Donald Munger. M does get in a few, not too subtle, insults, however, and reminds Bond that MI6 does function in his absence. This would be Connery and Lee's last screen appearance together and amply demonstates the unique chemistry between them.

Q (Desmond Llewelyn)
In this film the cranky gadgets genius enjoys the benefits of a field assignment by joining Bond in Las Vegas. Here, he saves the day by providing a makeshift imitation of Blofeld's voice simulator, thus allowing Bond to dupe his adversary by assuming Bert Saxby's identity. Later, Q demonstrates the one gadget which Desmond Llewelyn admits he wished actually worked: an electromagnetic RPM controller which causes all the slot machines to pay out each and every time.

MISS MONEYPENNY (Lois Maxwell)
Unfortunately, Moneypenny is relegated to a 'blink-and-you'll-miss-her' appearance. Disguised as a British customs official, she assists Bond in assuming the identity of smuggler Peter Franks. The film should have made more of the by-play between Sean Connery and Lois Maxwell, but the uninspired script falls short.

VEHICLES

MOONBUGGY Whilst fleeing from Willard Whyte's desert rocket site, Bond steals a moonbuggy that is being tested in a simulated lunar landscape. Designed by Ken Adam, it provides an entertaining, if rather slow-moving, chase sequence that is more comical than thrilling. Bond is truly a renaissance man when it comes to vehicles, as he is able to operate the moonbuggy with very few problems. (One doubts his training extended into 'Evasive Driving Techniques in Moon Machines'.) In the early 1990s, the moonbuggy was found, abandoned and neglected, by the James Bond Fan Club. It was completely rebuilt and is currently on display at Planet Hollywood in Las Vegas.

DIRT BIKES Made by Honda for the leisure market, these three-wheeled cycles, with large inflatable tyres, were designed for racing in sand dunes. The bikes – which were considered exotic at the time of the film's release – are used by

SIR DONALD MUNGER
(Laurence Naismith)
A respected expert in the field of diamonds, Munger informs Bond and M about his concerns that someone is stockpiling stolen diamonds and hoarding them for unknown purposes. He fears that the thieves will flood the market with the gems and thus greatly reduce their price around the world. Munger is played with dignity by Laurence Naismith, who seemed to have cornered the market in sophisticated English gentlemen roles in the 1970s. (He later appeared regularly in the Roger Moore television series *The Persuaders*.)

M (Bernard Lee)
It's great fun to witness Bernard Lee and Sean Connery together once more, albeit briefly. Despite Connery's four-year absence from the Bond films, the 007/M relationship picks up where it left off, with the pre-

Lois Maxwell is reunited with Sean Connery on location in Dover, England.

Willard Whyte's security guards as they pursue Bond in the moonbuggy.

BATHOSUB This mini-submarine is used by Blofeld in an attempt to escape from his doomed oil rig. However, Bond takes control of the crane which is lowering the bathosub into the water and uses it to smash through a control room, thus disabling the lethal laser satellite and giving Blofeld a rather bumpy ride. In reality, the sleek, silver bathosub was made of fibreglass and did not have any working features. The original, which is periodically displayed in public, is presently owned by The Ian Fleming Foundation, based in the USA.

TIFFANY'S MUSTANG MACH 1 As in *On Her Majesty's Secret Service*, the main chase sequence in *Diamonds Are Forever* required Bond to drive the heroine's car – in this case a 1971 Ford Mustang Mach 1, the ultimate muscle car of the decade. Whilst in Las Vegas, Bond is pursued through the neon-lit streets by the police in a spectacular stunt-laden chase which leaves numerous cars destroyed. The highlight is 007's escape through an alleyway only half the width of his car. Bond tilts the Mustang on to its side and drives it on two wheels through the impossibly narrow space. This sequence was filmed at two different locations. The entrance to the alleyway was constructed at Universal Studios; the exit was

Production designer Ken Adam's original sketch of Blofeld's oil-rig lair.

Bond's razor-edged finger clamp was used to devastating effect against one of Blofeld's bodyguards.

a real location in Las Vegas. Upon viewing the rushes, the producers realized that the car entered the alleyway on Tiffany's side, but emerged on Bond's side. This was cleverly rectified by filming an insert shot at Pinewood Studios in which Bond and Tiffany are seen shifting their respective positions. The Ford Motor Company, continuing their long-standing relationship with the 007 movies, supplied eight of these brand-new, sleek-looking sports cars. Today, only two of these are known to exist and they are in private collections.

GADGETS & WEAPONS

VOICE SIMULATOR Blofeld uses this device to imitate the voice of Willard Whyte and manages to convince the billionaire's business contacts that all is stable in the Whyte empire.

FINGER CLAMP Tucked inside 007's jacket, this spring-activated, razor-sharp clamp acts like a mini-bear trap when a SPECTRE guard attempts to remove Bond's pistol from his shoulder holster. The clamp snaps on the man's hand, almost severing his fingers.

FALSE FINGERPRINTS These are made of latex rubber and Q provides Bond with them so that he can successfully pose as Peter Franks. The invention comes in handy when Tiffany Case secretly tests Bond's fingerprints on a scanning machine which matches them to those of Franks. The false fingertips pass the test.

PITON GUN When Bond breaks into Willard Whyte's penthouse, he does so by using a piton pistol of the variety used by mountain climbers. This enables Bond to swing by rope to the roof and enter the penthouse. He is captured by Blofeld and relieved of his Walther PPK. However, Bond is able to access the piton pistol and fire a lethal bolt into Blofeld's head. He soon discovers that the man he has killed is merely one of Blofeld's doubles.

DIAMOND-ENCRUSTED SATELLITE Blofeld menaces the world with a diamond-encrusted satellite which is capable of using a deadly laser to pinpoint a target anywhere on earth. To demonstrate its power, the laser is used to destroy international military installations. These

Connery in Nevada, preparing to shoot the moonbuggy chase sequence.

sequences feature surprisingly ineffective special effects and the scenes of nuclear blasts appear to have been created with a child's science experiment kit, reducing the impact of Blofeld's threat.

BOMBE SURPRISE This is a time bomb hidden inside a lavish cake and served to Bond and Tiffany onboard a luxury cruise ship during the film's climax. The 'waiters' are actually Wint and Kidd. Fortunately, Bond recognizes Wint as an assassin. In the brief, but amusing, fight that follows, Bond engulfs Kidd in flames and tosses Wint overboard with the Bombe Surprise, which explodes seconds later.

MUSIC

John Barry provided another top-notch score for *Diamonds Are Forever*. As the film suffered from a weak script, the musical contribution became all the more important. Fortunately, Barry was up to the task and composed any number of memorable themes which add considerably to the mood and atmosphere of key sequences. Although *On Her Majesty's Secret Service* had relied on an instrumental title theme, the producers felt that with Connery back as Bond and Guy Hamilton as director, it would be appropriate to have Shirley Bassey sing the title song for *Diamonds Are Forever*. Although the song did not score as highly in the charts as Bassey's *Goldfinger* had done seven years previously, it is still a classic among Bond theme songs. As with *Thunderball*, however, some of John Barry's themes from the film did not make it on to the final soundtrack album, possibly due to time constraints and tight deadlines.

MARKETING & MERCHANDISING

'He's Back!' screamed the trailer for *Diamonds Are Forever* and, indeed, 'he' needed no introduction. Sean Connery's presence in the seventh Bond thriller was the primary selling point, although the print advertisements and posters were relatively modest about the fact that Connery had been absent for four years. A striking painting depicting Bond amidst many elements of the film was used internationally, although in Spain the scantily clad lovelies accompanying him had additional clothing added to soften the overt sexuality.

Although the film premiered in London at the Odeon Leicester Square in December 1971, an

Artist's concept for a teaser poster which was never produced.

extra gala presentation attended by Sean Connery took place in Edinburgh on 14 January 1972. A special brochure with a personal message from Connery announcing that all profits would benefit his Scottish International Educational Trust is a highly prized item amongst collectors today.

Surprisingly few merchandise tie-ins appeared apart from the soundtrack album and film edition paperback book. In Britain, Corgi Toys produced die-cast replicas of both the moonbuggy and the Ford Mustang Mach 1. A souvenir brochure was available in both Britain and Japan, but incredibly there was no merchandise produced for the US market.

THE BOX OFFICE

Diamonds Are Forever benefited from generally enthusiastic critical reviews and audience anticipation at seeing Sean Connery return as 007. The producers were quite nervous prior to the film's opening, as many industry insiders predicted the Bond phenomenon was over. Opening weekend grosses proved them wrong. *Diamonds Are Forever* posted the greatest seven-day gross in the history of the British cinema, and the biggest three-day opening ever in the USA. Ultimately, the film would post a very healthy worldwide gross of $116 million, proving that Bond's box-office appeal – like diamonds – was indeed forever. ■

LIVE AND LET DIE

(1973)

Director **GUY HAMILTON** Producers **ALBERT R BROCCOLI & HARRY SALTZMAN**
Screenplay **TOM MANKIEWICZ** Director of Photography **TED MOORE** Editors **BERT BATES,**
RAYMOND POULTON & JOHN SHIRLEY Supervising Art Director **SYD CAIN** Music **GEORGE MARTIN**

Release date: UK 5 July 1973, USA 27 June 1973. Running time: 116 minutes

B Y THE TIME PRE-PRODUCTION STARTED ON *LIVE*
And Let Die, it had become clear that no financial overture would
induce Sean Connery to play Bond yet another time. Therefore,
the producers had the unenviable task of finding a new 007. There
was concern on the part of some that inconsistency among the
actors would have a negative effect on audience enthusiasm. (This
would be the third actor to play Bond over a period of four years.)
Broccoli and Saltzman, whose relationship was becoming
increasingly strained due to differences on a number of matters,
agreed on one key decision: the new Bond would have to be an
established actor with significant credentials. The George Lazenby
affair had dampened their enthusiasm for casting an unknown. The
short list of candidates included Roger Moore and Timothy Dalton
(who was flattered but felt he was too young and too intimidated to
follow in Sean Connery's footsteps).

Ultimately, it was announced that Roger Moore would make
his debut as James Bond in *Live And Let Die*. On the basis of
credentials, his background was impressive. Moore had become an
icon among espionage fans for his long-running title role in *The
Saint*. More recently, he had gained an even wider audience starring
with Tony Curtis in the big-budget adventure series *The Persuaders*.
Unlike Connery, Moore was enthused about playing the role and
fully accepted the inevitable pitfalls: frenzied paparazzi, fanatical

Above: Bond meets some uninvited guests during his captivity at Kananga's crocodile farm.

Previous spread: Dr Kananga enjoying the fringe benefits of being a megalomaniac.

Opposite: Jane Seymour as the beautiful psychic Solitaire – whose powers of ESP are directly linked to her virginity.

Yet, *Live And Let Die* is a more satisfying film than its predecessor. Roger Moore successfully creates his own character of Bond – no easy task considering the impact Sean Connery had made in the role. Within minutes, we fully accept Moore as the new heir to the mantle and he would define the image of 007 for an entire generation. The rest of the film has its problems, but the idea of blending Bond into the world of voodoo and the occult is an effective one, even if prolonged action set-pieces seem more like padding than integral parts of the story. While *Live And Let Die* was not first-rate Bond, it certainly disproved the notion that 'Moore is less'.

THE ASSIGNMENT

James Bond is assigned to investigate the recent murders of MI6 agents in such diverse locations as New York, New Orleans and the Caribbean island of San Monique. Suspicion points to San Monique's *de facto* dictator, Dr Kananga, who is in New York to address the United Nations. Bond learns that Kananga has ties to a Harlem crime kingpin, Mr Big. While investigating their connection, Bond is captured and meets Kananga's 'kept woman', Solitaire, who has the power to foresee future events – providing she maintains her virginity. Bond escapes and follows Kananga to San Monique, where he turns his attention to finding and seducing Solitaire, who is a willing lover due to her desire to escape the oppressive Kananga. However, in making love with 007, Solitaire finds she has lost her power to predict the future. She and Bond discover that Kananga is growing massive fields of poppies for use in a scheme to gain a monopoly on the world's heroin market. The fields are protected by the imposing presence of Baron Samedi, who uses voodoo tactics to scare away the locals. Bond escapes with Solitaire to New Orleans, but they are captured by Mr Big, who reveals himself to be . . . Dr Kananga himself. Bond avoids death in a spectacular boat chase and returns to San Monique to pursue Kananga and rescue Solitaire. Here, 007 succeeds in destroying the heroin fields and kills Kananga in a hand-to-hand struggle.

007'S WOMEN

SOLITAIRE (Jane Seymour)
Like her mother before her, the beautiful and virginal Solitaire is treated like a personal possession by Dr Kananga, who uses her powers of extra-

fans and long shooting schedules. To maintain a sense of tradition, Guy Hamilton signed to direct his second consecutive Bond film.

Live And Let Die did not provide Moore with a powerful vehicle with which to make his debut as 007. He correctly chose not to imitate Connery but instead decided to establish his own unique interpretation of the role. However, Tom Mankiewicz's screenplay overindulges in Moore's personal preference for overt humour and continues to emphasize the comedy which was present in *Diamonds Are Forever*. Many of the situations ring false and the introduction of Sheriff Pepper represents the series' first embrace of a character who is so over the top that there isn't the slightest pretence that he is supposed to be taken seriously. The other unpardonable sin is the absence of Q from the film – the only time Desmond Llewelyn has been left out of the action since taking on the role.

sensory perception for evil purposes. Her unique ability to use tarot cards to predict the future makes her such an asset to the power-mad Kananga that he maintains the willpower to resist making love to her – an act which will deprive her of her mystical abilities. Solitaire, kept largely against her will by Kananga, is easily seduced by James Bond, who tricks her into thinking their affair is 'in the cards'. Although Bond, too, is using her for his own purposes, a genuine affection builds between the couple. Jane Seymour made her big screen debut with *Live And Let Die* and acquits herself admirably, although her talents are somewhat diluted by the script which makes Solitaire appear to be little more than a glorified Lois Lane. She is the typical helpless female who excels only in getting captured and making the hero risk life and limb to rescue her.

MISS CARUSO (Madeline Smith)
This voluptuous Italian agent risks her career to enjoy a fling with 007. While her superiors search worldwide for her, Miss Caruso is enjoying a pre-sumably extended stay in 007's flat, giving the audience only the second opportunity to view Bond's bachelor pad (the first was in *Dr. No*). Madeline Smith has the distinction of being the first Bond girl of the Roger Moore era.

007'S VILLAINS

DR KANANGA/MR BIG (Yaphet Kotto)
On the exterior Dr Kananga is a diplomat from the poor Caribbean island of San Monique who fights valiantly to improve the lot of his people. In reality he is the island's unchallenged dictator who rules through fear and oppression. His scheme is to cultivate enormous crops of poppies, turn them into heroin and capture a virtual monopoly on the international drug trade. Kananga has bases of operation in New York and New Orleans, disguised as the Fillet of Soul restaurants which are ostensibly run by local crime kingpin Mr Big. Only a handful of people realize that he and Kananga are one and the same.

Kananga is played with convincing menace by Yaphet Kotto, who fires off the customary witti-cisms and threats of a Bond villain with suitable panache. Kananga's demise is largely ineffective, however. He bites into a pressurized bullet and lit-erally blows up. The sequence is symptomatic of much of the script in that it dilutes an otherwise interesting character by going for a quick laugh.

Above: The voodoo threat of Baron Samedi claims a real victim: double agent Rosie Carver.

Right: Tee Hee willingly feeds Old Albert, the crocodile who relieved him of his arm some years before. (The name was a joking dig at Albert R. Broccoli.)

Far right: David Hedison as Felix Leiter, the only actor to date to play the role twice.

ROSIE CARVER (Gloria Hendry)

This is a completely unconvincing character who is played with charm by the fetching Gloria Hendry. Although their relationship allows Bond his first inter-racial affair, the role of Rosie is poorly written and her ineptness is used to exaggerated comedic effect. She plays a hopeless CIA agent in league with Kananga, but it defies belief that Kananga would think Bond would be deceived by someone so immature. Hendry looks terrific in a bikini but it is a pity the script does not allow her to play a character of any depth. Her ultimate demise is neither shocking nor very effective for either the audience or Bond.

BARON SAMEDI (Geoffrey Holder)

An enigmatic, fascinating character, Baron Samedi adds immeasurably to the supernatural overtones of the film. In a wonderfully appropriate bit of casting, noted choreographer Geoffrey Holder makes a visually stunning Samedi, bedecked in outlandish outfits and frightful make-up. It is understandable that the population of San Monique fears this mythical figure. Happily, the script allows some ambiguity concerning

Samedi's mortality. Bond clearly kills him by tossing him into a casket filled with poisonous snakes. However, in a truly inspired finale, the mocking Samedi appears on the front of the train carrying Bond and Solitaire. Is he there literally or just symbolically? Samedi remains one of the more memorable of the Bond villains and Geoffrey Holder is wonderful in the role.

TEE HEE (Julius W Harris)

Tee Hee is an imposing henchman of Dr Kananga who bears some unique physical characteristics: he is a virtual giant and has a steel arm, the result of having lost his real one to a crocodile some years before. Naturally, being a Bond villain, this is not just *any* steel arm. This one features pincer hooks capable of twisting the barrel of a gun. Tee Hee is used effectively in the film and the performance of Julius W Harris is consistently amusing. In the best sequence, Tee Hee brings Bond to a crocodile farm then good-naturedly leaves him stranded on a small island with an army of the hungry creatures closing in on him. Tee Hee appears in the film's sting-in-the-tail climax – a well-directed fight sequence aboard a train, from which he is unceremoniously tossed by 007.

WHISPER (Earl Jolly Brown)

Whisper is the obese, seemingly slow-witted, henchman to Kananga. The origin of his unusual

nickname is hardly a mystery, as he talks with a raspy, barely audible voice. Although he is a competent killer, Whisper's haplessness seems to spare his life when Bond locks him into a large canister during the fight at Kananga's underground lair. Whether he escaped or is still in there is a subject of debate.

007'S ALLIES

FELIX LEITER (David Hedison)
Following the unsatisfactory casting of Norman Burton in *Diamonds Are Forever*, the character of Felix Leiter gets a new lease of life through the performance of David Hedison. Hedison, a friend of Roger Moore's since their days as struggling actors, plays the role with understated charm. Frustratingly, this script – like most of the others – does not provide Leiter with much to do, but Hedison and Moore enjoy some genuine chemistry. Hedison is the only actor to play the role twice, reappearing as Leiter in *Licence To Kill* in 1989. Curiously, it is in the novel *Live And Let Die* that Leiter is mutilated by a shark but that sequence would not appear onscreen until Hedison's appearance in *Licence To Kill*.

SHERIFF J W PEPPER (Clifton James)
You know the boat chase in this film is too long when James – an actor who appears solely in that scene – receives prominent billing in the credits.

To classify Sheriff Pepper as an ally of Bond may be stretching things. The uneducated, prejudiced lawman is constantly frustrated in his attempts to capture 007 during the chaotic chase. The inclusion of Pepper in a Bond film made the purists' jaws drop, as he is to subtlety what Kananga is to compassion. Having established that Pepper is synonymous with the weaker aspects of the Roger Moore films – that is, humour at any cost – it has to be admitted grudgingly that Clifton James's performance does evoke laughter. He's a terrific character actor and when he shouts warnings about 'a swamp full of Black Russians', it's difficult not to relish the moment. The character was so popular with the masses that he reappeared in the next Bond film. Pepper also seems to be the clear inspiration for the Southern sheriff played by Jackie Gleason in the *Smokey and the Bandit* films, a genre for which this type of character is far more appropriate.

Above: Geoffrey Holder as the evil Baron Samedi, whose flute doubles as a two-way radio.

TOP SECRET CAST & CREW DOSSIERS

✳ The name of Dr Kananga is derived from **Ross Kananga**, the real-life owner of the crocodile farm where Bond finds himself menaced. The sequence did not originally appear in the script. However, when Syd Cain and Guy Hamilton stumbled upon the location in Jamaica, they were so impressed by the 'Trespassers Will Be Eaten' sign that they suggested a scene in which Bond must battle with the alligators. Ross Kananga performed the incredibly dangerous stunt, in which he doubles as Bond, running across the backs of the crocodiles. He had to do numerous takes and almost fell victim to the beasts. For his efforts, the producers rewarded him by naming the film's villain after him.

Clifton James (right) on the set with Sheriff Pepper's 'car boat' in Louisiana.

QUARREL JR (Roy Stewart)

It's a nice touch introducing the son of Quarrel, Bond's brave but ill-fated ally from *Dr. No*. Unfortunately, the script fails to mention the connection between Bond and his father. The younger Quarrel, like his father, works for the CIA and poses as a deep-sea fisherman, though junior is far more sophisticated.

M (Bernard Lee)

For reasons known only to screenwriter Tom Mankiewicz, M ludicrously decides to drop in on Bond in the middle of the night to inform him of his assignment. The situation provides an opportunity for some low-level humour when Bond plays a cat-and-mouse game to prevent M from seeing the scantily clad Miss Caruso. M does have one of the film's best lines, however, after Bond uses a preposterously noisy and ornate machine to make a cappuccino for his boss. After being presented with the drink, M stares in disbelief at the machine and asks rhetorically, 'Is that all it does?'

MISS MONEYPENNY
(Lois Maxwell)

Moneypenny saves the day again when she conspires to help Miss Caruso hide in Bond's closet, thus avoiding detection by M. This type of behaviour is more befitting teenagers trying to keep a tryst from their parents than sophisticated MI6 agents. Sadly, the film provides no other secondary action between Bond and Moneypenny – truly unfortunate, since Roger Moore and Lois Maxwell are real-life friends.

VEHICLES

GLASTRON SPEEDBOATS The extended speedboat chase was filmed in Lousiana's bayou country. Here, stunt arranger Jerry Comeaux spent over two weeks orchestrating the dramatic sequence. One of the major stunts included a scene in which Bond's boat leaves the water and soars high above a strip of land (and Sheriff Pepper's police car) before landing back in the water. This 120-foot leap was achieved by Comeaux (with the aid of a ramp) and completed in just two takes. Over four dozen Glastron boats were used, all powered by Evinrude jet propulsion motors. (The stunts would not have been possible with conventional propeller motors.) Other stunts resulted in occasional mishaps. For the scene in which a boat skids through a wedding reception, three Glastrons were destroyed. By the time filming was complete, over a dozen boats had been wrecked. Today, the boat chase in *Live And Let Die* – though overlong – still impresses with its originality.

AROUND THE WORLD WITH 007

Location shooting took place in **New Orleans** and the surrounding bayou country. For the fictional island of San Monique, the film-makers went back to **Jamaica** where *Dr. No* was filmed. They made the most of the **New York City** locations, playing up Bond's fish-out-of-water presence in Harlem. Interiors and sequences requiring sets were done at **Pinewood Studios**, where art director Syd Cain built Kananga's impressive underground lair.

LONDON BUS In another unique chase scene, Bond commandeers a double-decker bus while Kananga's henchmen pursue him on Harley Davidson motorcycles. Using daring manoeuvres, Bond dispenses with the speeding bikes by skidding in a circle on the road's wet surface, causing his pursuers to ditch their cycles in order to avoid the oncoming bus. With two police cars still chasing him, Bond speeds through a low overpass, causing the entire top section of the bus to be sheared off and fall on to his pursuers. For this scene, Maurice Patchett, a driving instructor for bus drivers in London, gave Roger Moore a 'crash course' in the fundamentals of handling the double-decker. To achieve the stunt, production designer Syd Cain placed the top deck of the bus on rollers. Filmed in Montego Bay, these scenes, which last only minutes on film, took four days of intense work to achieve.

GADGETS & WEAPONS

HANG GLIDER Bond uses the hang glider to infiltrate Kananga's headquarters by flying unnoticed at night. It floated at fifty feet above the ground and was kept in place by a wire and guided by a crane. Roger Moore did his own stuntwork without the aid of a harness or safety strap which would have been visible onscreen.

FELIX LIGHTER In one scene, Bond is in CIA agent Strutter's car and is able to communicate with Felix Leiter via a small transmitter concealed in the vehicle's cigarette lighter – hence Bond's unpardonable pun, 'A genuine Felix lighter!'

ROLEX WATCH This unique timepiece contains a magnetic field capable of deflecting a bullet at long range. The watch also has a small buzz saw built into the face which enables Bond to free himself while tied up in Kananga's lair, though this latter function is never explained to the audience in advance (thus violating a strict Bondian rule). More appropriate is his use of the watch's magnet to unzip the dress of Miss Caruso, a feat he attributes to 'sheer magnetism'.

Roger Moore took a 'crash' course in driving a London bus for an extended chase sequence.

HAIRBRUSH TRANSMITTER Agent 007's hairbrush conceals a small transmitter which he uses to communicate with Quarrel Jr by Morse code. The device also features a 'bug detector' which allows Bond to scan his hotel room for listening devices.

COMPRESSED-AIR BULLET With an impact like a small grenade, this bullet is activated by withdrawing a pin. It then shoots out enough compressed air to inflate its victim, causing him to explode. Although it is designed to battle sharks, Bond uses the unique invention to hasten Kananga's demise.

KANANGA'S SCARECROWS Used to guard Kananga's secret poppy fields, the scarecrows keep away the locals, who fear they are possessed by evil spirits. In reality, they conceal closed-circuit television cameras in their eyes and guns in their mouths. Rosie Carver becomes one of the victims of these sentinels of death.

DART-SHOOTING CAR MIRROR The right-side mirror of Whisper's 'pimp mobile' features a hidden device which shoots a poison-tipped dart into the neck of the agent driving James Bond into Manhattan, thus leaving Bond frantically steering his car from the back seat.

Above: Bond utilizes a hairbrush with a built-in communicator to signal Quarrel Jr.

Right: Bond arrives in New York with a bang after avoiding an assassination attempt by Whisper.

MUSIC

Musically *Live And Let Die* is significant among the Bond films because it represents the first time John Barry did not contribute the score. Beatles producer George Martin rose to the task, providing a number of atmospheric tracks. However, Martin's use of the music is often erratic. During the prolonged boat chase sequence, for example, major portions of the scene are left unscored. When Martin does finally use music for the climax of the chase, the excitement level picks up considerably.

Paul McCartney and Wings provided the film with a terrifically exciting title song, and it quickly rose on the international charts to become a major hit. (It also earned an Oscar nomination for best song, but lost to 'The Way We Were'.)

MARKETING & MERCHANDISING

To ensure the public were aware that Roger Moore was now the James Bond of the hour, a public relations blitz accompanied the film. Unlike Sean Connery, Roger Moore enthusiastically made the talk show round internationally, gamely telling anecdotes and winning over audiences with his unique, self-deprecating sense of humour. Major promotional tie-ins were done with Glastron boats and Evinrude motors (both producing posters that are now highly collectable). In Britain, Schick featured a Bond advertising campaign to emphasize 007's razor of choice. Both Jane Seymour and Gloria Hendry featured prominently in a *Playboy* spread devoted to the film. For the poster campaign, Moore was depicted in a typical Bond pose à la Connery, with his gun crossed over his chest. The artwork on the poster heavily emphasized the occult theme of the movie and the tarot cards which feature so prominently in the story. The cards, which were designed by young Scotsman Fergus Hall specifically for the film, were impressive enough to be marketed in 007 packaging as a consumer game.

Other merchandise included a British poster of Roger Moore in action produced by Scandecor, 3-D Viewmaster sets, a 'James Bond Super Action Set' from Lone Star Toys of England comprising a gun, walkie-talkie, grenade and other 'necessities' for young spies, *Roger Moore's James Bond Diary*, a highly readable paperback account of the star's day-by-day experiences filming *Live And Let Die* (though the British edition is inexplicably sans

Early prototype of the film poster.

Moore's fascinating introduction found in the US version), and the standard souvenir brochure sold in UK theatres.

THE BOX OFFICE

Any doubts about public acceptance of Roger Moore as James Bond were quickly eradicated when international box-office grosses exceeded those for *Diamonds Are Forever* at $161 million. Broccoli and Saltzman could breathe a sigh of relief. After years of very public controversies with Lazenby and Connery, they now had an actor who not only relished the role of 007, but who had been clearly accepted by the public – if not the critics, who predictably compared Moore unfavourably with his predecessor. Moore was nonplussed and, to his credit, continued to play his own unique version of the character. ■

TOP SECRET CAST & CREW DOSSIERS

❋ **Derek Meddings**, a master of miniature model building, created the poppy fields which are destroyed at the end of the film. Because of his unique talents, Meddings became a regular in the Bond stock company, and would go on to win an Oscar for *Superman*.

THE MAN WITH THE GOLDEN GUN

(1974)

Director **GUY HAMILTON** Producers **ALBERT R BROCCOLI & HARRY SALTZMAN**
Screenplay **RICHARD MAIBAUM & TOM MANKIEWICZ** Directors of Photography **TED MOORE &
OSWALD MORRIS** Editor **RAY POULTON** Production Designer **PETER MURTON** Music **JOHN BARRY**

Release date: UK and USA 19 December 1974. Running time: 125 minutes

THE WEAKEST OF THE BOND FILMS TO DATE, *THE MAN With The Golden Gun* represents the series at an artistic nadir. Perhaps because the relationship between Broccoli and Saltzman had reached breaking point (this would be their last film as partners), almost every aspect of the film seems uninspired. The emphasis on overt humour reaches its peak here, with the movie often resembling a slapstick comedy. The screenplay is also tepid and filled with inconsistencies and absurd situations. All of the characters are ill-tempered and there is little affection displayed even among the regulars. The heroine, Mary Goodnight, is an immature high school-type girl who strains all credibility as a seasoned MI6 agent, and Bond's constant irritation with being in her presence is fully understandable. No Bond film is without merit, however, and *Golden Gun* ironically features one of the best villains of the series: Scaramanga, who is played with such skill and charm by Christopher Lee that we almost end up cheering him on!

THE ASSIGNMENT

The world energy crisis results in the superpowers vying to possess the Solex Agitator, a device which can convert radiation from the sun into electricity. James Bond is assigned to recover the device, but has a slight distraction: there are indications that he has been

Above: Between takes on the set of Scaramanga's laboratory at Pinewood Studios.

Previous spread: Christopher Lee perfectly cast as Francisco Scaramanga, the world's highest paid assassin.

TOP SECRET: CAST & CREW DOSSIERS

❋ **Roger Moore** and **Christopher Lee** filmed an extended beach duel in which Bond fires his pistol into a Thermos bomb, causing it to explode. The scene was cut from the final print but appears in the teaser trailers.

❋ **Christopher Lee** is a distant cousin of **Ian Fleming**. When *Dr. No* began production, Fleming asked Lee to play the title role. Lee declined the offer, much to his regret. Thus, he welcomed the chance eventually to play a Bond villain in *Golden Gun*.

marked for death by notorious assassin Francisco Scaramanga, known as 'The Man With The Golden Gun'. However, both men are being used as pawns by Scaramanga's mistress Andrea Anders who hopes that Bond will kill her lover, thus freeing her from virtual captivity. Bond is assigned to work with beautiful but bumbling MI6 agent Mary Goodnight to recover the Agitator, which has fallen into Scaramanga's possession. He has a face-to-face confrontation with Scaramanga on his private island and learns that the charismatic assassin intends to sell the Agitator to the highest-bidding nation, thus guaranteeing a virtual monopoly on the sun's power. Scaramanga, who respects Bond as a rival, arranges an elaborate duel inside his deadly funhouse. Bond manages to best him, but barely, and has to resort to his wits to outgun his rival. Agent 007 ultimately recovers the Agitator and embarks on a long-delayed romantic journey with Mary.

007'S WOMEN

MARY GOODNIGHT
(Britt Ekland)
This beautiful MI6 agent, stationed in Hong Kong, is assigned to work with

Bond to recover the Solex Agitator. Mary, who was a daring and competent ally in Fleming's novel, is portrayed as someone so inept she makes Inspector Clouseau seem like Sherlock Holmes. The running joke in the film is that Mary's romantic encounters with 007 are never consummated due to various interruptions. At one point, she suffers the indignity of being shoved in Bond's closet while he seduces Andrea Anders in the same room. (Bond must have a thing about women in his closet. Witness Ms Caruso in *Live And Let Die*.) Britt Ekland performs gamely, but no actress could bring dignity to this character.

ANDREA ANDERS (Maud Adams)
Although technically a supporting character, Andrea should have been the leading heroine in the film instead of a sacrificial lamb. In contrast to Mary Goodnight, she is an intriguing and realistic presence in an otherwise outlandish film. The haunted mistress of Scaramanga, Andrea is willing to risk her life to escape his clutches. Before every assassination, Scaramanga makes love to her in the belief that it will ensure his mission succeeds. Alas, Bond does not treat her much better. He beds her then insists that before he will rescue her she must retrieve the Solex Agitator – an act which costs her her life when she is shot by Scaramanga for her betrayal. Maud Adams gives a strong performance as the tragic Andrea, bringing a sense of conviction to the role. Adams has the distinction of being the only actress to date to play major characters in two Bond films. (She played the title role in 1983's *Octopussy*.)

007'S VILLAINS

FRANCISCO SCARAMANGA
(Christopher Lee)
A classic Bond villain, Scaramanga considers himself the dark side of James Bond's character and finds similarities between their two personas, a notion 007 naturally rejects. The son of a Cuban circus ringmaster and a British snake charmer, Scaramanga spent his early years under the big top perfecting his expertise in marksmanship. By the time he was a teenager, he had already gained a reputation as a feared gunman. He was recruited by the KGB, but later went freelance, commanding $1 million per 'hit'. He became known as 'The Man With The Golden Gun' because of his infamous trademark weapon: a golden pistol. He prides himself on needing only one bullet to do the job.

Left: Bond follows Andrea Anders from Macau to Hong Kong aboard *The Flying Sandpiper* hydrofoil.

Below: Between takes, Christopher Lee films a British commercial endorsing milk. Roger Moore and Sean Connery had appeared in previous promotions.

Scaramanga, though apolitical, does favours for the Red Chinese and consequently is able to establish a massive base of operations on a small island in Chinese territorial waters. Here he and his loyal manservant, Nick Nack, live virtually in seclusion in the midst of a lavish lifestyle. (Scaramanga is rather a skinflint when it comes to employees. Disappointingly, he has only one nondescript technician running his entire operation, which makes for a rather weak finale.) Scaramanga has ensured that there are no existing photographs of him, but he can be identified by a peculiar physical characteristic: a third nipple. He meets his death in an elaborate one-to-one duel with James Bond inside his extravagant funhouse. Christopher Lee is an inspired casting choice in an otherwise uninspired film. He is sexy, witty and charming and the scenes in which he and Bond verbally duel are highlights. The same cannot be said for the physical duel, which is a rather limp and predictable affair. (The moment we see that Scaramanga has a wax replica of Bond in his museum, we just know 007 will ultimately end up switching places with it to outwit his adversary.)

NICK NACK (Herve Villechaize)
An intriguing and unique villain, the midget Nick Nack is a very suitable henchman for Scaramanga, and the two make bizarre partners in crime. Nick Nack is Scaramanga's 'cook, chef and chief bottle washer', performing everything from preparing gourmet meals to carrying out assassinations. Wonderfully played by Herve Villechaize, his

humiliated by his pint-sized adversary (whose fate is left ambiguous).

Herve Villechaize played a similar character a few years later in the television series *Fantasy Island*, co-starring with Ricardo Montalban who suspiciously resembled a rather benign version of Scaramanga. Tragically, Villechaize would commit suicide in 1993.

HAI FAT (Richard Loo)

This corrupt Hong Kong industrialist employs Scaramanga to kill Gibson, the inventor of the Solex Agitator, and steal the device for his own purposes. He is not fooled when 007 masquerades as Scaramanga. He has Bond captured and brought to his kung fu school where 007 narrowly escapes death. In one of the film's best sequences, Scaramanga politely accepts a tongue-lashing from Fat, all the while and unnoticed assembling his golden gun which he uses to murder him. He then assumes control of Fat's business empire.

CHULA (Chan Yiu Lam)

The top student at Hai Fat's kung fu school, Chula is the adversary Bond is forced to fight to the death. The sequence, which has the two men squaring off in front of other students as though in a tournament, is quite entertaining – until Chula and his cronies are ludicrously defeated by a pair of teenage girls. He then pursues Bond on a yawn-inducing boat chase through Bangkok's canals.

Above: Herve Villechaize as Nick Nack, Scaramanga's murderous right-hand man.

Below: This Guinness promotional poster is now considered to be a valuable collectable.

character is kept in restraint most of the time and is refreshingly not used for most of the overt humour found in the film. Nick Nack acts as a sort of gruesome version of the servant Kato in *The Pink Panther* films in that he tries to keep his boss in peak condition by subjecting him to random attacks – in this case employing actual would-be assassins to match their skills against Scaramanga. Although Nick Nack is an interesting character, his appearance at the end of the film in a battle with Bond is more embarrassing than thrilling, as it's difficult to watch the great 007

007'S ALLIES

LIEUTENANT HIP (Soon-Taik Oh)

The Hong Kong police officer assigned to work with Bond to recover the Solex Agitator, Hip is not the most interesting of allies, nor the brightest. When he pretends to arrest Bond following the assassination of Gibson, he inexplicably fails to tell 007 that he is actually bringing him to a meeting with M, thus causing Bond to have to initiate an escape. Later, after he and Bond flee Hai Fat's henchmen, Hip speeds away in his car leaving Bond behind in the dust to fend for himself. Hip later suffers the indignity of disguising himself as a peanut vendor at a boxing stadium. Although he succeeds in recovering the Agitator, Hip makes the mistake of entrusting it to Mary Goodnight.

SHERIFF J W PEPPER (Clifton James)

Fans who could barely tolerate this character in *Live And Let Die* were even less enamoured with

his indefensible return in this film. Here, we are asked to believe that the sheriff is 'coincidentally' on holiday with his wife in Bangkok at precisely the same time that Bond is wreaking havoc on his foes. Absurdity piles upon absurdity as Pepper mugs, slobbers, shouts and otherwise undermines the dignity of the film in scenes that are actually painful for Bond purists to watch. First he is tossed into a canal by an elephant, then he becomes Bond's reluctant ally in a wild car chase in pursuit of Scaramanga. Clifton James's performance this time is so over the top it makes his previous appearance look like a scene from *Hamlet*. Although the producers erred drastically in reviving this character, they at least recognized the mistake and allowed Pepper to retire from future missions.

M (Bernard Lee)

Bond's boss is particularly ill-tempered this time and he does not hesitate to insult and berate his top agent for any number of transgressions. He has the honour of delivering the one genuinely funny line in the film. When Bond asks who would pay a million dollars to have Scaramanga assassinate him, M replies, 'Jealous husbands. Outraged chefs. Humiliated tailors. The list is endless!'

Q (Desmond Llewelyn)

After his unforgivable absence from the previous film, Q returns, although he has little to do in this mission. He does provide Bond with a highly unusual gadget – a phoney nipple which 007 uses to impersonate Scaramanga. (The request leaves the usually unflappable Q a bit flustered and embarrassed.)

MISS MONEYPENNY (Lois Maxwell)

Moneypenny's appearance is a brief one, as she reflects with Bond on the killing of agent 002 and how it might be tied in with the Scaramanga affair. Apart from that, the usual good-natured banter is virtually absent with Moneypenny storming off into M's office in a temper when Bond refuses to follow up on her advances.

VEHICLES

AMC HORNET HATCHBACK If the
1970s could be termed 'the decade that style

Above: Filming Scaramanga's flying car at Pinewood Studios.

Right: Japanese advertising material emphasizing how the incredible Golden Gun is assembled.

forgot' in terms of fashion (seeing 007 in a leisure suit is traumatic), the same could be said of most of the cars of the period. This is evidenced by the film's promotion of an AMC Hornet hatchback, an incredibly boring vehicle. Bond steals the car from a Bangkok showroom where Sheriff Pepper is demanding a test ride. (Why Pepper would be purchasing a car in Thailand is just another absurdity left unexplained.) Bond and the sheriff indulge in a mundane car chase in pursuit of Scaramanga. The highlight occurs when Bond attempts to make a 360-degree jump over a half-fallen bridge to get to the other side of a canal. Stunt specialist Jay Milligan had successfully overseen a performance of the seemingly impossible stunt and convinced Broccoli and Saltzman to replicate it in *Golden Gun*. He used a computer at Cornell University to calculate the mathematical ratios, the first time this technology was used for such purposes. Milligan devised a special car with a central steering column and lightweight interior. Specially built ramps were disguised as the half-sunken bridge and eight cameras were positioned to capture the amazing feat. The stunt was so dangerous that ambulances, cranes and frogmen stood by to rescue driver 'Bumps' Willard. To the relief of all, Willard did the leap in one take and Cubby Broccoli celebrated with champagne all round. Months of hard work went into a scene which lasts only fifteen seconds onscreen. Incredibly, the entire impact is lost due to the presence of Sheriff Pepper and the addition of a cartoonish sound effect that was added in post-production.

AROUND THE WORLD WITH 007

Golden Gun featured a number of exotic locations, including **Macau**, **Hong Kong** and **Thailand**. Extensive use was made of sites in **Bangkok** and on Thailand's exotic island of **Phuket**, where Scaramanga's hideaway is located.

SCARAMANGA'S FLYING AMC MATADOR One of the more unusual vehicles to appear in a Bond film, the AMC Matador appears to be an ordinary car owned by Scaramanga – until he escapes from Bond by flicking a switch and converting the vehicle into an aeroplane, complete with wings and jet motor. Special-effects wizard John Stears built the flying attachments to full scale and filmed the transformation sequence at a local airfield in England and at Pinewood Studios. The car seen flying was a highly detailed model with a wingspan of twelve feet. It is virtually impossible to distinguish the miniature from the full-size car – a testament to the highly talented technicians.

SCARAMANGA'S JUNK This is the arch villain's personal mode of transport from his island base to exotic ports of call. Bond and Mary Goodnight commandeer the junk to escape Scaramanga's exploding island. However, Nick Nack has stowed away and attempts to assassinate Bond in the film's rather ludicrous conclusion. (Equally absurd is the fact that M reaches Bond on the junk's phone. Surely the world's most secretive killer would have invested in an unlisted phone number.)

GADGETS & WEAPONS

THE GOLDEN GUN Scaramanga's deadly, custom-made, 4.2 calibre gold-plated pistol is

an ingenious invention. Assembled from seemingly innocent component parts, it is a classic weapon. The pistol is made up of a cigarette case (the handle), lighter (the bullet chamber), fountain pen (the barrel) and cuff link (the trigger). The weapon fires one gold bullet made by an infamous Portuguese gunsmith named Lazar, who operates out of Macau. Scaramanga conceals the bullet in his belt buckle. Thus, the entire golden gun can be disassembled into everyday fashion accessories.

SOLEX AGITATOR The key to the Golden Gun mission is this innocuous-looking device which is about the size of a cigarette case. However, it possesses the power to harness solar power and turn it into an instrument of mass destruction. Scaramanga and Bond play a cat-and-mouse game for possession of the Agitator following the assassination of its inventor, Gibson.

Cubby Broccoli greets Guy Hamilton, Britt Ekland and Roger Moore on the set in Phuket, Thailand.

MUSIC

John Barry returned for his eighth Bond score, contributing an oriental flavour to the now familiar 007 theme overtures, as he did with *You Only Live Twice*. Unfortunately, this score falls short of that previous film. Barry's incidental compositions are adequate but the title song (sung by Lulu) is instantly forgettable and hampered by absurd lyrics. ('If you want to get rid of someone, the Man with the Golden Gun will get it done. He'll shoot anyone with his golden guuuunnnn ...') It's doubtful that anyone left the cinema humming any of the themes from the film.

MARKETING & MERCHANDISING

Golden Gun featured one of the more anaemic advertising campaigns of the series. Even the poster art seemed like a rehashed version of the campaign for *Live And Let Die*, although a rarely seen poster depicting Scaramanga and previous villains is today considered to be a valuable collectors' item. A teaser poster showing the disassembled golden gun was far more impressive in its impact than the main advertising campaign.

As usual, there were numerous product tie-ins. In the UK they included Fabergé toiletries (which Roger Moore had ties with at the time), Dupont carpets, Nikon cameras and Colibri cigarette lighters – the company assisted in the design of the Golden Gun. In the USA, the American Motor Company promoted their vehicles' involvement with the movie.

On the merchandising front, licensed products were few. In addition to the standard paperback and soundtrack album, British fans could buy a souvenir poster magazine and Lone Star Toys re-issued their generic 007 pistol (now in gold) with a caption indicating the product was inspired by the new film. In recent years, a gold-plated replica of Scaramanga's gun was produced (complete with engraved '007' bullet) and marketed to serious collectors for $700.

THE BOX OFFICE

While international box-office grosses for *Golden Gun* ($98 million) would have been considered huge by most standards, they reflected a precipitous drop compared with those of previous Bond films. In the USA the film grossed a disappointing $21 million – a forty per cent drop on *Live And Let Die*. Neither critics nor fans were impressed with or enthused by the film, and those reactions – combined with the forthcoming break-up of Broccoli and Saltzman – left many wondering if Agent 007 had finally met his most lethal enemy – audience apathy. ∎

TOP SECRET CAST & CREW DOSSIERS

✳ In 1997, **Christopher Lee** returned to Phuket to revisit the location of Scaramanga's hideaway. In 1974, the island had been so isolated that the production company feared attacks by local pirates. When Lee and his wife arrived this time, they were startled to find that Phuket had become the centre of a booming tourism business, with hundreds of souvenir shops. Despite trying to keep a low profile, Lee was immediately recognized by one fan who said, 'Well, I suppose *you* feel at home here!'

THE SPY WHO LOVED ME

(1977)

Director **LEWIS GILBERT** Producer **ALBERT R BROCCOLI** Screenplay **CHRISTOPHER WOOD &
RICHARD MAIBAUM** Director of Photography **CLAUDE RENOIR** Editor **JOHN GLEN**
Production Designer **KEN ADAM** Music **MARVIN HAMLISCH**
Release date: UK 7 July 1977, USA 3 August 1977. Running time: 125 minutes

F OLLOWING THE LUKEWARM RECEPTION ACCORDED
The Man With The Golden Gun, Cubby Broccoli knew the stakes
were high for this tenth James Bond thriller, and he had much to
prove to the fans, to United Artists and ultimately to himself.
Conventional wisdom said that the 007 franchise was on life-
support. Broccoli made an all-out gamble to prove that theory
wrong. Freed of the distraction of his rocky relationship with Harry
Saltzman, Cubby re-energized himself and was determined to do the
same with the series. He wisely took his time in bringing *The Spy
Who Loved Me* to the screen. Initial screenplays involved any
number of diverse scenarios contributed by a host of well-known
writers. The original intention was to revive SPECTRE but those
plans were shelved due to a court injunction obtained by producer
Kevin McClory, who was attempting to stage a remake of *Thunderball*
with a script written by Sean Connery and Len Deighton.

Ultimately, the final script was approved, although for all the
effort it bore a startling resemblance to *You Only Live Twice*. Cubby
was warned by production designer Ken Adam that no sound stage
in the world was big enough to contain the massive sequences envisioned. 'Then build it,' was Cubby's simple command. Thus, Adam
created the famed '007 Stage' at Pinewood Studios, the largest sound
stage in the world. Cubby's go-for-broke gamble received full
backing from United Artists, which willingly raised the budget to
a then whopping $13.5 million. The results show on the screen.

Above: The *Liparus* was big enough to devour three nuclear submarines.

Below: Richard Kiel as Jaws, with Milton Reid as Sandor.

With *The Spy Who Loved Me* premiering a full two-and-a-half years after *The Man With The Golden Gun*, audiences were eager to experience Mr Bond once more. Broccoli gave them the biggest Bond epic yet produced, an eye-popping extravaganza that combined all the traditional elements which made the series so popular.

As a film *The Spy Who Loved Me* is a success on almost every level. The humour is more controlled and mature and there are sequences featuring genuine suspense, something long absent from the franchise. The film also features a marvellous cast and the type of larger-than-life production values reminiscent of the earlier Bond movies. *The Spy Who Loved Me* features at least two memorable components destined to rank among the most enduring images from the series: the introduction of the villainous Jaws and the gadget-equipped Lotus Esprit, which rivalled the classic Aston Martin DB5 in terms of its ingenious design. Audiences responded enthusiastically and the film fulfilled its boast that 'This summer of '77 belongs to James Bond, 007'.

THE ASSIGNMENT

Allied and Soviet nuclear submarines are mysteriously disappearing and both M and his KGB counterpart General Gogol suspect a third party is responsible. They assign James Bond and top Soviet spy Major Anya Amasova to work together to investigate the situation. The two form an uneasy alliance, but gain mutual respect as they hop the globe from Egypt to Sardinia tracing clues.

Bond and Anya suspect reclusive billionaire shipping magnate Karl Stromberg is behind the crisis. The two agents discover that he has been using his gigantic cargo ship, the *Liparus*, to capture the submarines and imprison their crews. He plans to use the subs to launch nuclear missiles in the hope of destroying civilization and ruling over an undersea kingdom from his amphibious power base, Atlantis. In a fierce battle with Stromberg's forces, Bond and the freed crews from the submarines narrowly avert a nuclear holocaust. Bond kills Stromberg and escapes the exploding Atlantis with Anya.

007's WOMEN

ANYA AMASOVA (Barbara Bach)

The impact made by Barbara Bach's stunning visual presence as Anya makes the audience overlook her rather shaky Russian accent. Despite having the traditional trappings of the buxom Bond woman, Anya is indeed a new breed of heroine for the series. She is 007's equal in terms of intellect, courage and self-sufficiency. Known as Agent 'Triple X' in the KGB, she is regarded as one of the bureau's top field operatives. She is in love with fellow agent Sergei Barsov and is shattered by his death. Ever the professional, she carries on with her mission until she learns that 007 was the one who killed Barsov in the course of an assignment. She vows revenge, but ultimately is won over by Bond. Given all her attributes, it's no wonder Bond is virtually a one-woman man during the course of the entire mission. Barbara Bach remains one of the most beautiful women to grace a Bond film.

007's VILLAINS

KARL STROMBERG (Curt Jurgens)

This billionaire shipping magnate has a unique base of operations: Atlantis, a gigantic city in the sea capable of supporting life above or below the surface. Stromberg is obsessed with bringing civilization to the depths of the ocean but for megalomaniacal purposes: he dreams of establishing himself as dictator of the new world order. Like any good Bond villain, Stromberg is witty and ever respectful of 007's talents as an adversary. Played in a low-key fashion by noted German actor Curt Jurgens, Stromberg is rather dull compared to previous villains. Although Jurgens is effective and often amusing, his character basically sits around Atlantis pushing buttons and issuing ultimatums. His demise – he is shot by Bond – is also a bit anticlimactic.

JAWS (Richard Kiel)

Jaws is an innovative and memorable addition to the Bond Rogues' Gallery. He is a dim-witted but intensely determined assassin who doesn't let a few hundred setbacks dissuade him. Hired by Stromberg as a henchman, the seemingly mute giant uses his razor-sharp steel teeth to kill anyone who stands in his way. The towering terror almost succeeds in finishing off 007, but Bond inevitably uses his wits to counter Jaws' brute strength. The original ending of the film had Jaws dying in an inferno. However, Cubby Broccoli suspected the character had enormous appeal and shot an alternative ending in which he survives, thus allowing the character to reappear in the next Bond epic *Moonraker*. Jaws is never a terrifying presence in the film because he is used increasingly for comic effect. Yet he is so engagingly played by Richard Kiel, an actor with genuine screen presence, that the audience welcomes his frequent appearances.

Above: Barbara Bach as Anya Amasova, the KGB's Agent 'Triple X'.

Previous spread: In Sardinia, Q greets Bond with the new Lotus Esprit – and a warning to return it intact!

Bond and Anya with the murderous genius Stromberg.

NAOMI (Caroline Munro)

This stunningly beautiful assistant pilot to Stromberg initially brings Bond (posing as a marine biologist) to Atlantis to greet her boss. Naomi's sultry presence and perfect figure (barely covered in a bikini) certainly impress 007, though they do not stop him from terminating her during a life-and-death chase. Caroline Munro, a veteran of several Hammer horror films, continues to charm fans who queue for her autograph at collectors' shows internationally.

SANDOR (Milton Reid)

This hulking, bald-headed henchman of Stromberg is assigned to work with Jaws. Stromberg orders Sandor to 'obey' Jaws – not an easy task, bearing in mind the steel-toothed giant is not a man known for his oratory skills. Sandor kills the beautiful Felicca before she can provide information to Bond about the submarine tracking system. In one of the better fight sequences from a Moore film, an uncharacteristically harsh 007 makes Sandor divulge information then lets him plummet to his death from a rooftop. Actor Milton Reid played one of Dr No's henchmen fifteen years previously.

TOP SECRET CAST & CREW DOSSIERS

✳ **Ian Fleming** was never happy with his novel *The Spy Who Loved Me*. In the bizarre book, written from the heroine's viewpoint, 007 does not even appear until late in the story and much of the action takes place in a motel room. Therefore, when Fleming sold the film rights to the 007 books to Broccoli and Saltzman, it was with the specification that *TSWLM* was to be reinvented for the big screen and only the title could be used.

FEKKESH & MAX KALBA

(Nadim Sawalha, Vernon Dobtcheff)

These two are the key players in the search for the sub tracking system. Fekkesh is murdered by Jaws in an eerie and atmospheric sequence set during a light show for tourists at the pyramids. A notebook on his body leads Bond to Max Kalba, the owner of an Egyptian nightclub who instigates a bidding war between Bond and Anya for microfilm of the sub tracking system. However, he too is murdered by Jaws (who is posing rather conspicuously as a telephone repairman).

007'S ALLIES

GENERAL GOGOL (Walter Gotell)

With this film comes the first of what would become semi-regular appearances by the KGB chief. Depending upon the script, Gogol is either a friendly enemy or a strong ally. The producers, seeming to sense an eventual warming in East–West political relations, presented Gogol as a Communist with compassion. In this film, Bond is shocked to arrive at MI6's Egyptian HQ (ingeniously hidden inside a pyramid) only to find General Gogol there to greet him. Gogol has formed an unusual alliance with M to locate the missing nuclear subs. Walter Gotell, who would go on to play Gogol for the next decade, made his first appearance in a Bond film as the villainous Morzeny in *From Russia With Love*. The tall, imposing actor has great screen presence and would become a valuable member of the 007 stock company.

M (Bernard Lee)

After his ill-tempered appearance in *The Man With The Golden Gun*, a more traditional M appears in this film. In fact, he even gives Bond a rare 'well done' for besting Anya in his knowledge of facts about the Stromberg link to the missing subs. M is also on excellent terms with General Gogol, who refers to him by his first name, Miles (the only time his Christian name is mentioned in the course of the series).

Q (Desmond Llewelyn)

The Spy Who Loved Me provides Q with some wonderful scenes, including a glimpse into his highly creative Egyptian workshop located in a pyramid. Here he and his technicians demonstrate a number of amusing (if somewhat impractical) gadgets. At one point Q observes a tea set on a razor-brimmed tray which is used to decapitate a dummy sitting at a dining-table. 'I want that ready for Akbar's tea party,' he instructs nonchalantly, gaining a large guffaw from the audience. Q is also instrumental in providing valuable insights into the submarine

Above: Former model Caroline Munro in her brief but memorable role as Naomi.

Left: The amphibious Lotus Esprit en route to Atlantis.

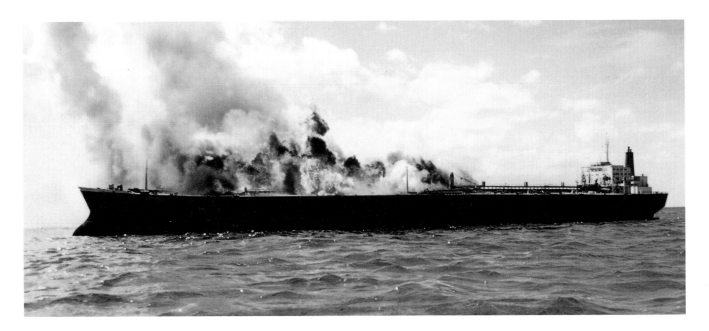

Stromberg's supertanker the *Liparus* under siege by Bond and his allies.

tracking system and he personally drives the Lotus Esprit to deliver it to Bond in Sardinia.

MISS MONEYPENNY (Lois Maxwell)
The expansion of the roles of M and Q seems to have been at the expense of poor Moneypenny. In this mission, none of the flirtatious secondary action with Bond is evident and Moneypenny, though on a field assignment to Egypt, is basically reduced to showing Bond into M's office.

FREDERICK GRAY (Geoffrey Keen)
In the first of several appearances, Geoffrey Keen is the picture of dignity as the minister of defence. Gray is involved with high-level strategy sessions involving the submarine crisis. Curiously, Bond is introduced to him as though they have never met before, but minutes later he feels comfortable enough to refer to the minister as 'Freddie' (this informality would not reappear in the series). The stodgy Gray gets an eyeful at the film's conclusion when he, Gogol, M and Q witness Bond and Anya making love in Stromberg's escape pod.

CAPTAIN CARTER
(Shane Rimmer)
The captain of the *USS Wayne* nuclear submarine, Carter and his men play a prominent role in assisting Bond in thwarting Stromberg's plans for an atomic holocaust. Carter is a heroic figure who personally leads his men into the spectacular battle in

the hull of the *Liparus*. The role was played by Shane Rimmer, who previously had minor roles in *You Only Live Twice* and *Diamonds Are Forever*.

VEHICLES

LOTUS ESPRIT Nicknamed 'Wet Nellie' as a tribute to Bond's autogyro 'Little Nellie' (from *You Only Live Twice*), the introduction of the seemingly indestructible Lotus was a major highlight of the series. To this day it almost ranks with Bond's Aston Martin DB5 as a truly classic vehicle. The inclusion of a new 'Bondmobile' added a much-needed boost to the series after Bond's lacklustre transportation in *The Man With The Golden Gun*. The highly armed Lotus is amphibious and capable of travelling under water at a relatively fast speed. At the flick of a switch, the wheel arches turn into fins, propellers extend from the back of the car and Bond can navigate the Lotus with the help of a small periscope on the roof. Weapons include front-mounted underwater rockets, an underwater smoke screen, a limpet mine dispenser and radar-guided surface-to-air missiles. On land, the car is equally impressive. Cannons hidden behind the back number plate can be used to spray cement on pursuing vehicles.

Six different cars were used to achieve the land to sea transformation, with one full-sized car and a three-foot model capable of submersible actions. Filmed in the Bahamas by Derek Meddings and his team, the full-scale Lotus was built by Perry Oceanographics from a body shell supplied by Lotus of England. Today, one of these six vehicles is owned by The Ian Fleming Foundation and

AROUND THE WORLD WITH 007
The film-makers had truly to globetrot to exotic locations around the world. Major sequences were filmed in **Egypt**, **Sardinia**, **Scotland** and the **Bahamas**. Interiors were shot in England on the '007 Stage' at Pinewood Studios. It's been said that audiences knew the old Bond formula still worked when 007 skied off a cliff in the famous pre-credits sequence, causing fans to erupt in applause. The stunt – one of the most notable in film history – was performed by Rick Sylvester and was shot by multiple cameras on location at **Asgard** in the remote Auquittuq National Park on Baffin Island in Canada.

makes appearances at various Bond-related events around the world.

THE *LIPARUS*

The second largest super-tanker in the world is the pride of Stromberg's shipping fleet. However, it has been designed to include several unorthodox options: its bow opens to reveal an interior which acts as a full-scale harbour, complete with submarine ports and loading docks. There is also an armoured control room, hovercar and a heavily armed crew that serves as Stromberg's personal army. The tanker's width can easily accommodate the three full-sized nuclear submarines which are literally swallowed by the *Liparus* as part of Stromberg's scheme for nuclear destruction. It is from this ship that he launches the submarines as 'instruments of Armageddon' to destroy New York and Moscow. The climactic battle is one of the most elaborate action sequences in any Bond film. It was filmed on the enormous '007 Stage' at Pinewood Studios and the magnificent set rightly earned production designer Ken Adam an Oscar nomination.

WETBIKE

Designed by Nelson Tyler, this bike (which is now a common recreation vehicle found on beaches all round the world) had not been commercially released at the time of the film's premiere. Hence, it had considerable impact on audiences when they witnessed it could be assembled from parts carried in a large tote bag. Bond uses the wetbike (which resembles an exercise bike on skis) to ride to Atlantis in a desperate attempt to rescue Anya.

ROCKET-FIRING MOTORCYCLE

In Sardinia, Bond's Lotus is pursued by a motorcycle driven by a henchman of Stromberg. The cycle features a sidecar which turns out to be a rocket-powered pod packed with high explosives. Bond narrowly escapes the mobile bomb by manoeuvring the Lotus between two lorries, one of which bears the brunt of the explosive. The cycle fares even worse, plunging over the side of a cliff.

STROMBERG'S HELICOPTER

Piloted by the stunning Naomi, Stromberg's Jet Ranger helicopter is fitted out with powerful machine guns which are used extensively in a dramatic chase with Bond's Lotus. Eventually the helicopter forces the Lotus into the ocean. The unsuspecting Naomi smirks in victory, not knowing Bond is activating a surface-to-air missile from his amphibious vehicle which will destroy her chopper and send it plunging into the sea.

JAWS' VAN

Masquerading as a telephone repairman, Jaws systematically rips apart his Sherpa van which Bond and Anya are trying to use as an escape vehicle. They eventually succeed in a highly amusing sequence in which Jaws reduces the van to little more than a wreck. One unanswered question: if Jaws is supposed to be an Egyptian repairman, why is the sign on the van in English?

TOP SECRET CAST & CREW DOSSIERS

❋ **Robert Brown**, who portrays Admiral Hargreaves, would later go on to play M.

❋ **Richard Kiel** reported that Jaws' steel teeth were so painful that he could only wear them for five minutes at a time.

The model of Atlantis is towed out to sea in the Bahamas.

HOVERCAR/SPEEDBOAT Used to transport equipment and personnel around the interior of the *Liparus*, the car, which hovers on a metallic surface, is also Stromberg's escape vehicle. It is jettisoned through a large 'porthole' in the ship, whereupon it discards its outer shell revealing it to be a speedboat. (The model used for this scene belongs to the James Bond Collectors' Club and is on display at Planet Hollywood in London.)

MINI-SUBMARINE This missile-firing, two-man mini-submarine is deployed by Stromberg to destroy Bond's Lotus Esprit in a brief but entertaining underwater battle. Agent 007 uses limpet mines to send the sub to the bottom of the ocean.

STROMBERG'S ESCAPE POD Designed by Stromberg for a fast escape from Atlantis, the pod is used by Bond and Anya to flee from the sinking city in the sea. Small and spherical, it is equipped with all the luxuries a megalomaniac would never leave home without: luxury bed, stereo, champagne – and of course, curtains. Bond should really have drawn the curtains because he is so engrossed in making love to Anya that he does not realize the pod has been scooped up by a Royal Navy vessel whose crew – along with several dignitaries – are observing the action.

The original storyboard depicting Bond's battle with Jaws.

GADGETS & WEAPONS

SEIKO WATCH The watch contains a ticker-tape message device that alerts Bond to call HQ. Unfortunately, the urgent message causes him to interrupt bedding a beautiful woman on a bearskin rug.

ANYA'S CIGARETTE Smoking is dangerous to your health, but even Bond cannot predict the dual use of Anya's cigarette. It contains a sleep-inducing substance which she blows into Bond's face, causing him to nod off immediately.

SKI-POLE RIFLE Whilst escaping from Russian agents in the film's thrilling pre-credits sequence, Bond uses this device to kill Anya's lover Sergei Barsov. The grip of the ski pole acts as a trigger which unleashes a powerful mini rocket.

MICROFILM VIEWER Bond converts a cigarette case and lighter into an instant microfilm viewer as he travels with Anya on a barge on the Nile. This allows him quickly to analyse the microfilm plans for the sub tracking system.

MUSIC

For the second time in the series, John Barry did not provide the score. This time, Oscar-winning composer Marvin Hamlisch accepted the assignment, providing a classic theme song 'Nobody Does It Better'. Sung by Carly Simon, the tune became an instant pop hit. It also earned an Oscar nomination as best song, along with another nomination for Hamlisch's score. Alas, he lost in the latter category to John Williams' magnificent score for *Star Wars* and unjustly lost in the former category to 'You Light Up My Life' from the film of the same name. Hamlisch's score, while certainly effective, has a somewhat dated feel to it today. Like other Bond composers he is also occasionally guilty of leaving parts of major action and suspense sequences unscored. Nevertheless, Hamlisch proved to be a valuable asset to the film, although his campy, honky-tonk rendition of 'Nobody Does It Better' at the film's climax is all wrong.

MARKETING & MERCHANDISING

With *The Spy Who Loved Me*, Broccoli sensed he had a winner and launched a massive marketing

Production designer Ken Adam with Cubby Broccoli during the construction of the massive '007 Stage' at Pinewood Studios. A brochure was produced to promote the stage.

campaign. Artist Bob Peak produced an unusual, somewhat avant-garde poster design that played down the 007 character and emphasized the epic feel of the film. In Britain, the Open University on the BBC broadcast a lengthy documentary on every aspect of the film's creation. The cast and crew travelled the world publicizing the film in every media outlet imaginable and Roger Moore filmed special unique introductions for the US television advertisements.

On the merchandising front, a wide array of products was released. After a six-year absence, Corgi Toys of England renewed their long-standing association with the Bond franchise by producing the most comprehensive selection of die-cast toys ever tied-in with a specific 007 film. With their Aston Martin DB5 having been acclaimed as the biggest-selling toy car of all time, Corgi realized that Bond's latest vehicle – the amphibious Lotus Esprit – also had significant sales potential. Released in June 1977, the James Bond Lotus Esprit became the single biggest-selling item in Corgi's range since 1973. During the first six months, some 660,000 cars were sold. By the time it was withdrawn in 1981, this figure totalled over 1.5 million units. (Such was the durability of its popularity that Corgi reissued the 007 Lotus Esprit as a twenty-first anniversary commemorative limited edition.) To accompany the Lotus, a die-cast model of Stromberg's Jet Ranger helicopter was produced. Both the Lotus and helicopter were manufactured to a smaller scale, commonly known as Corgi Juniors. These two toys – along with a Mercedes car (complete with cement on its windscreen), a speedboat on a trailer and Jaws' telephone van – were packaged as part of 'The Spy Who Loved Me Gift Set'.

In Australia, bubble bath was packed in a Lotus-shaped bottle. In Japan, a highly detailed model of the car was available. A battery-powered version of the Lotus which could operate in water was available in the USA. Other collectables included a US souvenir brochure and a series of children's puzzles in Canada.

THE BOX OFFICE

Any doubt that Bond was back in vogue with the public was quickly dispelled by the box-office results of *The Spy Who Loved Me*. It grossed a towering $185 million internationally, including $47 million from the US market (more than twice the US gross of *The Man With The Golden Gun*). For the film's release, United Artists reverted to a policy of showing the film in a limited number of selected cinemas in the USA instead of opening countrywide. The strategy worked and *The Spy Who Loved Me* was regarded as a major hit – despite the record-breaking grosses being accumulated by *Star Wars*, which had opened just weeks before. Critics were also kind to the film, apparently grateful that Broccoli had returned to the formula of old. ∎

MOONRAKER

(1979)

Director **LEWIS GILBERT** Producer **ALBERT R BROCCOLI** Screenplay **CHRISTOPHER WOOD**
Director of Photography **JEAN TOURNIER** Editor **JOHN GLEN** Production Designer **KEN ADAM**
Music **JOHN BARRY**
Release date: UK 26 June 1979, USA 29 June 1979. Running time: 126 minutes

EVIDENCE THAT BIGGER IS NOT NECESSARILY BETTER is exemplified by *Moonraker*, a $30 million James Bond epic which cost more than twice as much as *The Spy Who Loved Me*. Although *For Your Eyes Only* was supposed to be the eleventh 007 film, the success of *Star Wars* encouraged Cubby Broccoli to send James Bond out of this world – literally. As Ian Fleming's original novel was now too dated to translate to the screen, screenwriter Christopher Wood retained only the essence of the characters and the premise of a megalomaniac using the space programme for his own scheme. Wood erred dramatically in reverting to the anything-for-a-laugh philosophy of *The Man With The Golden Gun*. The resulting emphasis on slapstick negates many otherwise thrilling sequences.

However, it must be said that *Moonraker* fulfilled Cubby's promise to put every penny up on the screen. Because of prohibitive British tax laws, the film-makers shot the massive production at two major studios in France – Studio de Boulogne in Epinay and Eclair in Paris. Here, production designer Ken Adam constructed the largest sets ever seen in the French film industry. The crew worked 222,000 man hours to ensure the sets were ready in time for principal photography. Bond still retained his British 'home' as the extensive special-effects shots were done at Pinewood Studios. The film is filled with exotic locations, beautiful people, space-age technology and enough special effects to merit the Oscar nomination which visual-effects supervisor Derek Meddings ultimately received. There's also a good film hidden between the outrageous sight gags. A little careful editing would have improved the film

Above: Roger Moore with Lois Chiles as Holly Goodhead.

Previous spread: James Bond averts destruction of the human race at the climax of *Moonraker*.

THE ASSIGNMENT

On the trail of the Moonraker space shuttle, which has mysteriously vanished, James Bond flies to California to question Hugo Drax, the billionaire builder of the machine. Bond seduces Corinne Dufour, one of Drax's employees, and learns that Drax has hijacked the Moonraker as part of a top-secret scheme. Several attempts are made on Bond's life and Corinne is ultimately murdered. Bond follows the trail to Venice where he discovers Drax's laboratory is developing a mysterious deadly gas for reasons unknown. Working with CIA agent Holly Goodhead, Bond travels to Rio de Janeiro where he is menaced by the hulking Jaws, now a henchman for Drax. Bond and Holly ultimately discover Drax's secret headquarters in the Brazilian jungle. Here, they learn that he intends to use the deadly gas to destroy life on earth and preside over a master race on his secret, opulent space station. Bond and Holly join the US Marines in a massive battle on the space station, during which Drax is killed and his plans for domination of the universe are thwarted.

007'S WOMEN

DR HOLLY GOODHEAD (Lois Chiles)
This lady is a courageous CIA agent who infiltrates Drax Industries in California and becomes an employee in the space programme. Holly is a genuine scientist, as well as a field agent, in addition to being a fully trained astronaut. As is the custom, she takes an instant dislike to James Bond and engages in a game of one-upmanship to prove her superiority. Equally predictable is the inevitability that she will be seduced by his charm (although, refreshingly, it is she who initially treats 007 as a one-night stand).

The role of Holly is intelligently written and Lois Chiles is most satisfactory in the part. However, the character is rather bland and remains one of the least memorable of Bond's onscreen lovers.

CORINNE DUFOUR (Corinne Clery)
Played with understated charm by French actress Corinne Clery, Corinne is personal assistant/pilot to Drax at his California estate. She gives James Bond a detailed tour of Drax Industries and later is even more generous on a personal level. Agent 007 seduces the beautiful girl and persuades her to allow him to photograph secret papers from Drax's safe. For her betrayal, she pays a terrible

enormously. A perfect example is the amazing pre-credits sequence in which Bond and a villain skydive while they battle for a single parachute. The superbly edited and filmed scene is marred only by the inexplicable appearance of Jaws in a highly comic turn.

Moonraker tries to be all things to all fans, and ends up falling short in almost every department. The first half-hour is quite intriguing but the film quickly becomes a hit-and-miss affair in which the parts are more impressive than the whole. Despite the aforementioned criticisms, it should be noted that *Moonraker* was both a critical and financial success. The public seemed to enjoy it tremendously, but Bond purists were dissatisfied and made their protests clear to Cubby Broccoli. Ultimately, even the film-makers agreed they had gone overboard on comedy and excess. Despite the success of the film, Cubby promised to bring Bond back to earth in the next film, *For Your Eyes Only*.

price – Drax unleashes his Dobermans on her and she is torn to shreds in a truly harrowing and suspenseful sequence.

MANUELA (Emily Bolton)

Manuela is the field agent attached to Station VH in Rio and assigned to work with Bond in locating and investigating Drax's warehouse. She makes it clear that she definitely prefers to mix business and pleasure and becomes romantic with Bond immediately upon his arrival in Rio. Later, as they investigate the warehouse, the couple are menaced by Jaws, who is in costume as part of a Mardi Gras parade. While the sight of a giant with steel teeth heading your way would undoubtedly startle anyone, Manuela – obviously more skilled in the boudoir than in fieldwork – barely makes a token attempt at resistance and has to be rescued by 007.

007's VILLAINS

HUGO DRAX (Michael Lonsdale)

An internationally respected billionaire whose Drax Industries constructs space shuttles for the US government, Drax, a highly cultured, soft-spoken man, has a dry sense of humour and an eye for beautiful women. He indulges in every imaginable luxury and owns a palatial château in California (transported brick by brick from France) and significant businesses in Venice and Brazil. It is in the jungles of Brazil that he has built a gigantic hidden headquarters from which he is capable of launching his private Moonraker shuttles to his secret space station. Like the villain of Fleming's novel, Drax is held in high esteem throughout the world. However, unlike the grotesque-looking character in the book, actor Michael Lonsdale is the picture of dignity. His performance, criticized by many as being too low-key, is actually very entertaining. Lonsdale delivers his droll one-liners in a manner that continuously upstages Roger Moore, though Moore does get an appropriate laugh when he mortally wounds Drax and pushes him from the space station saying, 'Take a giant leap for mankind.'

JAWS (Richard Kiel)

The return of Jaws in *Moonraker* was a subject of controversy with fans. Everyone seemed to agree that he was a unique villain for *The Spy Who Loved Me*, but there were fears that an encore performance would result in a Sheriff Pepper-style embarrassment. The fears were partially justified.

Jaws, who was fairly cartoonish in the previous film, is now the centre of slapstick comedy sequences. On the positive side, however, there is at least an attempt to give the character some interesting personality traits and his transformation from villain to ally of 007 is intriguing. Richard Kiel embellishes Jaws with a degree of pathos and makes a previously one-dimensional character quite interesting.

CHANG (Toshiro Suga)

In introducing this servant/henchman of Drax, the intention was obviously to bring back memories of Oddjob. Chang is a silent, menacing figure

Above: Drax takes a giant leap for mankind after being shot by Bond's wrist dart gun.

Below: Executive producer Michael G Wilson plays a cameo role as a NASA technician. Wilson has also made Hitchcock-like appearances in *Goldfinger* and every film since *The Spy Who Loved Me.*

Above: Richard Kiel didn't complain about re-takes of this sequence – the cable he is biting was made of liquorice.

Right: The murderous Chang about to unleash vicious Dobermans on the helpless Corinne.

who is more than eager to carry out Drax's command to 'Look after Mr Bond. See that some harm comes to him.' Chang makes a failed attempt to kill Bond by manipulating a centrifuge to breakneck speeds. It's the best sequence in the film because there is genuine suspense and Bond looks terrified by the ordeal. Later, Chang corners Bond in a Venetian glass factory where the two engage in a magnificently staged fight sequence with the predictable shattering of virtually every object. However, like so many other scenes in the film, the impact is reduced because it ends on a comedic note. One wonders how inconspicuous the oriental assassin dressed in Kendo regalia really was among the population of Venice.

007'S ALLIES

M (Bernard Lee)

Bond's boss is a little less crusty during this mission – despite the fact that 007 damages a priceless painting in his office by firing a dart into it while experimenting with Q's wrist gun device. When Bond stages a raid on Drax's Venetian headquarters which backfires, M gives his top agent the benefit of the doubt and suggests he takes a leave of absence to pursue the case privately. Later, M greets Bond in the Brazilian HQ of MI6, where they discuss strategy regarding Drax's activities. Sadly, this was Bernard Lee's last performance as M. He died before production began on the next Bond film. Fans and co-workers will long remember the dignity he brought to the role and his contributions to the eleven films in which he appeared cannot be overestimated.

Q (Desmond Llewelyn)

Q meets Bond at the MI6 Brazilian HQ, which is disguised as an old monastery. Here, amidst robe-clad agents with Friar Tuck haircuts, he demonstrates a variety of weapons, including exploding bolas. Q is also instrumental in identifying the source of a rare orchid which Drax is using as the basis for a deadly gas which will kill human beings but leave other forms of life unaffected.

MISS MONEYPENNY (Lois Maxwell)

Here is another disappointingly brief appearance for this valued member of the MI6 staff. Although Moneypenny gets a field assignment to Brazil, she has little to do there. The charmingly flirtatious bantering between Bond and Moneypenny is all but eliminated during the Roger Moore era.

FREDERICK GRAY (Geoffrey Keen)
When Bond stages a misguided raid on Drax's secret laboratory in Venice, he insists that Gray and M don gas masks to prevent them from inhaling the deadly substance they expect to find. The trio are humiliated to find the location contains nothing more than Drax's office. The *faux pas* causes a red-faced Gray to apologize humbly to Drax and to insist that Bond be taken off the case.

DOLLY (Blanche Ravalec)
Along with Sheriff Pepper, Dolly is the most inappropriate character ever to appear in a Bond film. The pint-sized, bespectacled, pig-tailed Aryan girl possesses super strength – and an ample bosom. In one of the most embarrassing sequences in the entire series, Jaws falls madly in love with her and the duo become inseparable for the rest of the film. Richard Kiel reports that the original intention was to pair Jaws up with a woman of Amazon proportions. When the film-makers protested that Jaws could never be involved with Dolly because of their considerable size difference, Kiel won the day by reminding them that his real-life wife was the same height.

GENERAL GOGOL (Walter Gotell)
Seen only fleetingly in this affair, Gogol agrees to delay military action against Drax's secret space station, which he suspects may have been placed there by the US government, in order to give the US Marines time to establish its origin. Amusingly, Gogol is seen in his Moscow bedroom clad in red silk pyjamas in the company of a scantily clad beauty who is waiting for him under the covers.

007's VEHICLES

THE 'BONDOLA' This Venetian gondola is fitted out with a hidden steering column and propeller-driven motor. The boat also converts to a hovercraft, thus enabling it to travel on land. Bond uses this absurd invention during a prolonged and highly improbable boat chase through the canals (some of which is taken almost directly from a similar scene in *The Man With The Golden Gun*). The idea of turning a gondola into a speedboat is acceptable enough, but when Bond crosses St Mark's Square in it, all credibility is lost as we see sight gags such as pigeons doing double takes and waiters spilling drinks on customers.

GLASTRON BOAT/HANG GLIDER While cruising on a Brazilian river in his sleek, highly armed craft, Bond is attacked by Jaws and a fleet of motorboats. In a spectacular chase sequence, he employs hidden mines and torpedoes to demolish his pursuers. However, with the gigantic Iguacu Falls looming ahead, Bond deploys a hang glider built into the boat's roof, thus allowing him to soar to safety and eventually land near Drax's secret

Bond's high-powered speedboat concealed an array of defensive weapons – and a hang-glider.

Above: Q demonstrates the wrist-activated dart gun which ultimately saves 007's life.

Right: A Moonraker space shuttle model was placed on display for the London premiere.

him to transport his master race of henchmen and women to his space station, where they will begin a new civilization. Ironically, one of Drax's own shuttles leads to his downfall when Bond and Holly use it to infiltrate the space station. Cubby Broccoli took great pains to assure fans that he had received NASA's co-operation to ensure that all aspects of the shuttle were true to life.

GADGETS & WEAPONS

CIGARETTE-CASE X-RAY MACHINE
The lid of the cigarette case doubles as an X-ray screen which discloses the internal workings and combination of Drax's safe, gaining Bond access to top-secret plans.

MINI CAMERA This small compact camera is similar in size to a cigarette lighter. The lens is positioned in the middle of the '0' on the engraved '007'. (Surely Bond could be a bit more subtle.) Bond uses the camera to photograph the contents of Drax's safe.

DETONATOR WATCH Bond's wrist watch (another Seiko) contains a small amount of explosive and detonator cable accessed by removing the rear plate. Agent 007 uses this gadget to escape being fried under the rocket bay of the Moonraker shuttle.

jungle HQ. Again, a terrific action sequence is marred by comedy, as we get a close-up of an exasperated Jaws about to topple over the falls.

SPACE SHUTTLE The Moonraker space shuttles are built by Drax for the US space programme. However, his own private fleet allows

HOLLY'S HANDBAG Holly's standard CIA issue weaponry includes: a dart-firing diary, a flame-throwing atomizer, a radio receiver and aerial, and a hypodermic syringe concealed in the barrel of a fountain pen.

WRIST DART GUN This dart gun is similar in design to a watch and is activated by nerve impulses from the wrist muscles. Agent 007 is supplied with five blue-tipped armour-piercing darts and five red-tipped cyanide darts which are capable of killing in thirty seconds. 'Very novel, Q, we must get them in the stores for Christmas,' is Bond's nonchalant opinion of his latest gizmo. It is this device that save's Bond's life on the centrifuge and that he uses to kill Drax.

LASER GUNS First seen being demonstrated by technicians in Q's lab, these deadly hand-held laser guns are more appropriate weaponry for *Star Wars*, not the world of 007. During the film's climactic battle, the platoon of US Marine astronauts carries these deadly weapons, which are capable literally of melting an opponent.

MUSIC

Although *Moonraker* is one of the weaker 007 efforts, the same cannot be said about the score. John Barry provided some lovely atmospheric themes that perfectly reflect the film's outer-space setting. The main title song, sung by Bond veteran Shirley Bassey, is a haunting melody. The song is reprised over the title credits in a faster tempo more reflective of the disco era in which the film was produced. Both versions are equally effective. Barry also makes liberal use of the stirring '007' theme during the boat chase in Brazil. It's a nice touch and provides at least a minor link from this space-age comedic Bond film to its early predecessors.

MARKETING & MERCHANDISING

Moonraker saw the largest merchandise and publicity campaign for any Bond film since 1965's *Thunderball*. The advertising campaign began in the USA with two different teaser posters, one a

Above: The square-jawed Roger Moore action figure.

Below: Lone Star's 007 Space Gun toy.

magnificent painting of Bond blasting off into outer space, the other depicting 007 with a bevy of Drax's beauties. The main poster art was somewhat disappointing, reflecting comic-book-style art showing a montage of characters from the film. In the USA, a ten-minute behind-the-scenes featurette entitled *James Bond in Rio* was shown on television. The Museum of Modern Art in New York City held a Bond celebration which was open to the public. Cubby Broccoli, Ken Adam and director Lewis Gilbert presided over question-and-answer sessions with fans.

In terms of merchandise, a huge range of collectables was manufactured. Corgi released both regular- and junior-sized versions of the Moonraker shuttle and Drax's helicopter. Lone Star Toys of England had a cap-firing replica of a laser gun. Mego of the USA produced twelve-inch dolls of Bond, Drax, Holly and Jaws. Other collectables included shuttle model kits from Airfix and Revell, a children's annual in Britain, US and UK souvenir brochures, bubble bath in a 007-shaped bottle, a sleeping bag and Hallowe'en costumes.

THE BOX OFFICE

Although hard-core Bond fans were turned off by the lack of reverence for the more serious side of Agent 007, critics were impressed with *Moonraker*, describing it as a fun summer extravaganza. Perhaps they just didn't remember how little this offering reflected the traditional Bond film. In any event, there could be no debating the success of *Moonraker*. The film grossed a huge $62 million in the USA and a worldwide total of $203 million, making it the highest-grossing entry in the series until *GoldenEye* in 1995. ■

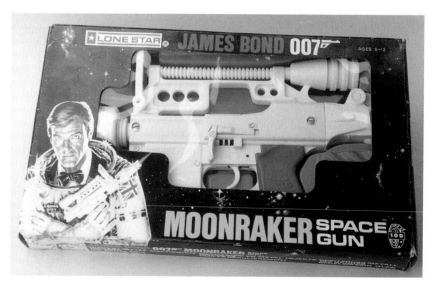

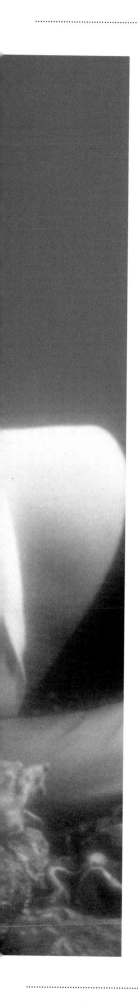

FOR YOUR EYES ONLY

(1981)

Director **JOHN GLEN** Producer **ALBERT R BROCCOLI** Screenplay **RICHARD MAIBAUM &**
MICHAEL G WILSON Director of Photography **ALAN HUME** Editor **JOHN GROVER**
Production Designer **PETER LAMONT** Music **BILL CONTI**
Release date: UK 24 June 1981, USA 26 June 1981. Running time: 127 minutes

STUNG BY CRITICISM THAT *MOONRAKER* HAD STRAYED too far from the 007 formula, Cubby Broccoli made good on his promise to make *For Your Eyes Only* a more realistic thriller. He succeeded quite admirably, although the first half of the film is a decidedly mixed bag. The pre-credits sequence is extremely well done, but its impact is largely negated by an over-the-top villain and some very exaggerated jokes. The extended chase sequences in cars and by skis are technically proficient, but so overlong that they appear to be used as padding. The film takes off with the introduction of the villainous Kristatos and his rival Columbo – two fascinating characters played superbly by Julian Glover and Topol. The pair re-energize the film and ensure that the story becomes far more involving. The film also boasts the directing debut of long-time Bond editor John Glen, who acquits himself admirably with his first of five 007 films.

For Your Eyes Only features one of Roger Moore's best performances as Bond. He downplays the tongue-in-cheek jokes and actually appears to be taking the proceedings seriously. He has a strong leading lady in Carole Bouquet. Despite their dramatic age difference, their relationship is a believable one. The film sacrifices the standard climactic battle for a small-scale, but far more dramatic, assault by Bond and his allies on Kristatos' mountain hide-out. There is genuine suspense, and the sequence in which Bond falls precipitously from the mountain peak while trying to

Above: Bond pays his respects to his late wife Tracy in the pre-credits sequence.

Previous spread: The keel-hauling sequence, which originally appeared in the novel *Live And Let Die*.

THE ASSIGNMENT

The British trawler *St George's*, in reality a spy ship, sinks in Albanian territorial waters. The vessel was equipped with ATAC, a top-secret device which is used to transmit orders to Polaris submarines. If the ATAC falls into the wrong hands, it can be used to programme the subs to attack their own nation and allies. The sinking results in a scramble between the British and Soviets to retrieve the ATAC from the ocean floor. Unable to launch official recovery efforts in Albanian waters, both nations initiate covert activities. James Bond is assigned to locate the wreck and bring back the ATAC. His mission is complicated by Melina Havelock, a young woman out to avenge the murder of her parents – two marine archaeologists who were secretly assisting MI6 in the search for the *St George's*. In Greece, Bond and Melina succeed in recovering the ATAC but are captured by a local shipping magnate, Kristatos, who plans to sell the device to the Soviets. With the aid of Kristatos' old rival, Columbo – a charming smuggler with massive resources – the couple infiltrate their enemy's compound in the Greek mountains. Kristatos dies at the hands of Columbo, and Bond chooses to destroy the valued ATAC rather than let it fall into the hands of the KGB.

007'S WOMEN

MELINA HAVELOCK (Carole Bouquet) Half-British, half-Greek, Melina is the beautiful daughter of two marine archaeologists who are murdered when they attempt to help MI6 find the wreck of the *St George's* and the missing ATAC. Vowing revenge, she embarks on a wide-ranging pursuit of Kristatos, the man who ordered her parents' death. When she crosses paths with 007, she impresses Bond as a strong-willed, courageous woman who is not hesitant about using her proficiency with a crossbow to eliminate her enemies and she plays a vital role in the destruction of Kristatos. French actress Carole Bouquet plays Melina with genuine conviction, making her character a haunted woman with a mission of vengeance. She and Bond don't even share a romantic moment until the last sequence of the film – an unusual situation for 007, but a scenario that makes the plot much more convincing.

BIBI DAHL (Lynn-Holly Johnson)
This spoiled, rebellious teenage ice-skater is

outmanoeuvre a would-be assassin is riveting. Another outstanding action scene is the one in which Kristatos keelhauls Bond and Melina through shark-infested waters. (The sequence is from the novel *Live And Let Die*.) Critics and audiences were initially startled by the lack of the huge sets and massive battles which had become a staple of the series. However, in retrospect, the film-makers made a wise choice. After sending 007 into outer space, there was nowhere else to go but back to earth. In *For Your Eyes Only* Bond is once again a man who relies primarily on his wits and ingenuity instead of merely pushing buttons or operating gadgets.

sponsored by Kristatos as an Olympic hopeful. Although Bibi lives in luxury and travels the world, she desires the life of a normal teenager instead of rigorous training routines. She is instantly smitten by Bond, whom she sees as her ticket to escaping her confined life with Kristatos. Starved of affection, she attempts to seduce Bond – but for once 007's resistance is strong enough to decline politely. When she learns of Kristatos' connection to the Soviets she rebels and incurs his wrath. Bibi is a character wholly out of place in a Bond film and she is largely superfluous to the plot. Agent 007 should not be interacting with pouting teenagers and the scene in which Bibi attempts to seduce Bond is awkward and unconvincing.

COUNTESS LISL (Cassandra Harris)

The countess is the expensive mistress of Columbo and a regular at the casino in which he is a silent partner. Lisl, who poses as an Austrian countess, is in fact an everyday girl from Liverpool. Bond encounters her when Columbo has her seduce him in order to learn more about his identity and mission. Agent 007 spends a passionate evening with her, but she is murdered by Locque during an exciting chase sequence on a beach. Lisl is played with infectious charm by Cassandra Harris, the wife of Pierce Brosnan. It

was always her dream to see Pierce play the role of 007, but she tragically died before he was chosen for *GoldenEye*.

Above: Melina Havelock, out to avenge her parents' murder.

Left: Lynn-Holly Johnson as the naïve Olympic hopeful Bibi Dahl.

007'S VILLAINS

ARIS KRISTATOS (Julian Glover)

Decorated with the King's Medal for his resistance against the Nazis, Kristatos is regarded as a well-respected shipping magnate. Bond discovers that, despite his reputation as an ally to MI6, he is playing a double-cross. Kristatos attributes crimes committed by himself – such as heroin smuggling – to his arch rival, Columbo, in the hope that 007

The late Cassandra Harris with husband Pierce Brosnan at the film's premiere in London.

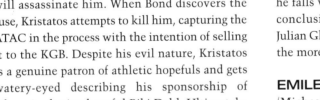

Michael Gothard as Kristatos' henchman Locque.

will assassinate him. When Bond discovers the ruse, Kristatos attempts to kill him, capturing the ATAC in the process with the intention of selling it to the KGB. Despite his evil nature, Kristatos is a genuine patron of athletic hopefuls and gets watery-eyed describing his sponsorship of Olympic skating hopeful Bibi Dahl. Ultimately, he falls victim to Columbo in the film's riveting conclusion. Kristatos is wonderfully played by Julian Glover, who succeeds in making him one of the more cultured villains Bond has faced.

EMILE LEOPOLD LOCQUE
(Michael Gothard)
A well-known figure in the Brussels underworld, Locque escapes from prison by strangling his psychiatrist. He later becomes a hit man for Kristatos, personally murdering Countess Lisl and Ferrara. In an extremely exciting and well-directed chase, Bond pursues Locque's car on foot and causes it to dangle precariously over a cliff. In a move uncharacteristically harsh for Roger Moore's 007, he ruthlessly kicks the vehicle over the edge, sending Locque to his death. It's a terrific sequence, although it would have been even more satisfying if Locque had been a more developed character.

ERIC KRIEGLER (John Wyman)
This handsome but ruthless KGB agent moonlights as an East German skiing champion with an eye on the Olympics. Kriegler makes an unsuccessful attempt to murder Bond in a prolonged, but not particularly enthralling, chase sequence. He later arranges for the KGB to buy the ATAC from Kristatos. During the dramatic attack by

Bond and his allies on Kristatos' hide-out, Kriegler is killed in a brutal fight with 007.

HECTOR GONZALES (Stefan Kalipha)

This Cuban hit man is employed by Kristatos to murder the Havelocks before they can retrieve the ATAC. When 007 is captured spying on Gonzales at his Spanish estate, he orders that Bond be killed. Bond is spared when Melina Havelock uses her crossbow to kill Gonzales as he dives into his swimming pool.

GENERAL GOGOL (Walter Gotell)

This time round, Gogol is an enemy of MI6 in a desperate race to retrieve the ATAC. He personally arrives at Kristatos' mountaintop hide-out to buy the device. Alas, his trip is in vain. When Kristatos is killed, Bond opts to destroy the ATAC rather than hand it over to Gogol. The general seems unconcerned about the situation, perhaps because he knows his charming mistress Rublevich awaits him back in Moscow.

VILLAIN IN WHEELCHAIR (John Hollis)

In the pre-credits sequence, a bald villain confined to a wheelchair menaces Bond by using remote control to commandeer the helicopter which carries 007. The sequence, shot at Becton Gasworks in England, features imaginative stunt-work but is marred by a bad guy who delivers his lines unconvincingly. Bond's disposal of him by scooping up his wheelchair with the helicopter and dropping him into a smokestack is also a bit much to take, especially when the panic-stricken villain starts pleading with Bond and offering to buy him a delicatessen in stainless steel. (The relevance of this line has long perplexed Bond fans who continue to debate its meaning.)

007'S ALLIES

MILOS COLUMBO (Topol)

A charismatic smuggler of gold and diamonds, Columbo runs a large organization in Corfu where he engages in constant rivalry with Kristatos. He convinces a sceptical 007 that he is his ally and that Kristatos has been framing him for any number of crimes which he has personally committed. Columbo is one of the strongest supporting characters ever to appear in a Bond film and he has larger-than-life characteristics which bring back memories of Kerim Bey in *From Russia With Love*. He is wonderfully played by Topol, who is so engaging in the role that he

Kristatos attempts to escape with the ATAC.

steals every scene in which he appears. Indeed, the film itself becomes far more compelling with his introduction and the plot device about his rivalry with Kristatos is very intriguing.

JACOBA BRINK (Jill Bennett)

Brink is a stern-faced former ice-skating champion from behind the Iron Curtain. Of late, she has been employed by Kristatos to act as trainer for Bibi Dahl. Brink shares Bibi's disdain for Kristatos, but reminds her that he has the wealth to ensure she becomes a leading candidate for the Olympics. Brink works Bibi constantly despite the younger girl's protests. However, she also shows

TOP SECRET CAST & CREW DOSSIERS

❋ Cubby Broccoli's son **Tony** served as one of the second assistant directors on this film and *Octopussy*.

❋ Beautiful **Robbin Young** won a competition sponsored by *Playboy* to appear in a James Bond film. Her prize was a small role as the girl in the flower shop in Cortina.

Topol as Columbo, Bond's most charismatic ally since Kerim Bey.

Q (Desmond Llewelyn)

As usual, there is a humorous glimpse into Q's workshop, complete with such gadgetry as a spiked umbrella which snaps closed on the user's neck when exposed to moisture and a spring-loaded plaster cast for an arm. Q later makes a welcome reappearance in Greece disguised as a priest in a local village – complete with phoney beard. When Bond enters the confessional and says, 'Forgive me, father, for I have sinned,' Q replies 'That's putting it mildly, 007.'

FREDERICK GRAY (Geoffrey Keen)

Typically grumpy, Gray is on hand in Tanner's office to assign Bond to retrieve the ATAC. As is customary, he shows up at the film's climax only to be humiliated once again by Bond. Geoffrey Keen would have been very appropriate to assume the role of M, though Robert Brown would eventually get the part.

MISS MONEYPENNY (Lois Maxwell)

At last Moneypenny and Bond share a few flirtatious moments – a rarity in the Roger Moore era. Also shown is Moneypenny's hi-tech make-up case, which is concealed in a filing cabinet and springs up when the drawer is opened.

FERRARA (John Moreno)

This Italian MI6 agent is assigned to work with Bond in Cortina. Ferrara introduces Bond to Kristatos and is murdered by Locque shortly afterwards. The character is a weak and unconvincing one and is seemingly squeezed into the story merely to act as a sacrificial lamb.

VEHICLES

LOTUS ESPRIT Following the car's triumphant debut in *The Spy Who Loved Me*, James Bond is seen once more behind the wheel of not one, but two, Lotus Esprits. When one of Gonzales' thugs attempts to break into the vehicle he disregards the 'Burglar Protected' sticker on the window. When the villain (played by stunt man Bob Simmons) smashes the window, the car blows up, blasting the gunman into oblivion. (Presumably, the average Lotus has a more humane security system.) Later, in Q's workshop, we see a metallic bronze Lotus. Bond quips, 'Oh, I see you've managed to get the Lotus back together again.' This Lotus, a 1980 turbo capable of 0–150mph in fifteen seconds, had a new engine developed from the 2 litre 907 and 910 2.2 litre turbo. This latest

compassion in an almost romantic way, although Bibi seems oblivious to that behaviour. When Brink discovers that Kristatos is a KGB agent, she attempts to escape with Bibi, in the process assisting Bond and his allies.

TANNER (James Villiers)

Tanner is M's chief of staff who fills in for his boss when M is on leave. (In reality, his absence is due to the death of Bernard Lee, which occurred shortly before production began. As a sign of respect, the film-makers did not recast the role for this film.) Tanner, a character in the novels, is stiff and humourless enough to make M seem like a stand-up comedian. He would not reappear again until *GoldenEye*, when he is introduced as a completely different character.

model, with interior design by Guigiaro of Italy, is seen in only two brief sequences when Bond goes to Cortina. Unlike its predecessor, this Lotus does not feature any gadgetry.

CITRÖEN 2 CV Probably the most unlikely car ever to appear in a 007 chase, the Citröen 2 CV, driven by Melina and Bond, is pursued by henchmen of the assassin Gonzales. Even Bond reacted in shock when he saw he would have to rely on the little French car to negotiate mountain roads at high speed. Supervised by Remy Julienne, one of the world's top car stunt experts, the chase scene required the boxy Citröen to roll over, speed backwards and fly across the roof of another car. The car chase sequence is ingeniously planned but lacks suspense.

YAMAHA MOTORCYCLE In Cortina, Bond is pursued down the ski slopes by Kriegler's men who ride Yamaha motorcycles which have been souped up to feature machine guns (activated by the handle grips) and spiked tyres which give

them traction in the snow. The sequence features some amazing stuntwork and the motorcycles pursue Bond by crashing through fences, restaurants and finally down a bobsled run. However, like the Citröen 2 CV chase, it becomes wearying after several minutes.

Above: The Citroen 2 CV was an honoured guest at the London premiere.

Below: Melina faces assassination.

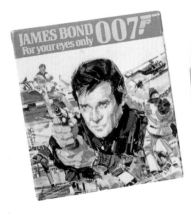

Above: The 007 Zeon wristwatch: the perfect gift for the Bond fan who likes to have time on his hands.

Below: Roger Moore takes a break during filming.

THE _NEPTUNE_ This is a small submarine used by Bond and Melina to search for the ATAC in the wreck of the _St George's_. In a tense sequence it is almost sunk when an armed one-man sub attacks them. The _Neptune_ was created for the film by production designer Peter Lamont.

It measures twenty-three feet long and eight feet wide. Two Neptunes were actually built, one fully functional and the other made from fibreglass and used in the scene in which the vessel is lifted from the water. The latter sub now resides in a theme park on the Isle of Wight in England, while the operational model is owned by The Ian Fleming Foundation.

GADGETS & WEAPONS

RADIO/WATCH This was the third successive film in which a Seiko watch was featured although each had different functions. In _For Your Eyes Only_, the watch has a radio/transmitter which Bond leaves on a parrot perch while he skinny-dips with Melina. Q and Frederick Gray think they have Bond speaking to the prime minister, when in fact it is the parrot. The scene is a bit out of place in a Bond movie, but it's difficult not to laugh at Janet Brown and John Wells' hilarious impersonation of Margaret and Denis Thatcher.

ATAC The Automated Targeting Attack Communicator is a device that emits a low-frequency coded transmission to order British Polaris submarines where and when to launch their missiles. The ATAC is hidden aboard the British spy trawler _St George's_ and goes to the bottom of the sea when the vessel strikes a mine. Bond's assignment is Operation Undertow: to locate and secure the ATAC before it falls into Soviet hands.

3-D VISUAL INDENTAGRAPH Bond and Q use this inventive device to identify Emile Locque. The user simply inputs physical characteristics then manipulates sketches of the individual until it resembles the person targeted. The data is then put into a database comprising files from the top police agencies in the world. If successful, an immediate response identifies the person and provides all known data on his or her background.

MUSIC

Bill Conti provided an outstanding theme song for the film. Sung by Sheena Easton, it became a major hit on radio stations throughout the world. His incidental music is less impressive, however. Although he captures the flavour of the various nations in which the film was shot, some of the music seems more loud than inspired. When the

On the set, left to right: Roger Moore, Barbara, Cubby and Dana Broccoli and director John Glen.

title song was nominated for an Oscar, it was performed by Sheena Easton in a huge production number featuring elaborate stunts and sets (not to mention the presence of Richard Kiel and Harold Sakata). Unfortunately, the award was lost to the theme from *Arthur*, although Conti's song is the one which will endure with the public.

MARKETING & MERCHANDISING

'Nobody Comes Close to James Bond, 007' read the provocative cinema poster for the film. In the UK Bond is depicted through the back of a pair of woman's legs, surrounded by a montage of scenes from the film. In the USA, however, the advertisements were far more controversial because a genuine photograph was used and showed the derrière of the female model. Although she was clad in a bikini, the poster designer opted to turn the swimsuit round to make it skimpier. The result was a striking advertising campaign which set off a media frenzy.

Virtually every model claimed to be the possessor of the gorgeous legs and several conservative newspapers objected to the advertisements as being too sexual. (One even painted black boxer shorts over the bikini.) All of this helped ensure a good box office, of course.

There were a number of licensed merchandising items of note. Corgi released large and small versions of the Citroën 2 CV. Crescent manufactured a die-cast cap gun. In the UK a souvenir brochure featured highlights from the film. Other items included a film poster magazine, a Marvel comic adaptation, a children's annual in Britain, a series of toy guns from Coibel, four promotional posters sold in stores, a Japanese resin figure model of 007 and a line of watches from Zeon. The chrome wristwatch had the film's logo and played the Bond theme, and Prince Charles was presented with a gold-plated version at the premiere.

THE BOX OFFICE

Any concerns that audiences would not respond to a Bond film that was not hi-tech were quickly dissipated by initial box-office returns. Although US grosses totalled $52 million ($11 million less than *Moonraker*), international totals of $195 million ensured that *For Your Eyes Only* was classified as a major hit. ■

AROUND THE WORLD WITH 007

Exotic locations abound in *FYEO* with extensive sequences filmed on the Greek island of **Corfu** and in the resort town of **Cortina d'Ampezzo** in northern Italy. In the small Greek town of **Kalambaka** in the Meteora mountains, the film-makers ran into an unexpected problem. Monks at a neighbouring monastery protested at the presence of the crew by hanging signs designed to ruin the camera angles. The incident received international attention, although the film-makers insisted they were not in any way disturbing the natural beauty of the area. Roger Moore quipped, 'I don't see what the fuss is all about . . . they seem to forget that I was once a "Saint" myself.' The moving sequence in which Bond pays a visit to the grave of his late wife Tracy (a wonderful touch) was shot at **Stoke Poges** church near **Pinewood Studios**, where the interiors were filmed. Certain underwater scenes were filmed by Al Giddings in the **Bahamas**.

OCTOPUSSY

(1983)

Director **JOHN GLEN** Producer **ALBERT R BROCCOLI** Screenplay **GEORGE MACDONALD FRASER, RICHARD MAIBAUM & MICHAEL G WILSON** Director of Photography **ALAN HUME** Supervising Editor **JOHN GROVER** Production Designer **PETER LAMONT** Music **JOHN BARRY**

Release date: UK 6 June 1983, USA 10 June 1983. Running time: 131 minutes

*O*CTOPUSSY IS ONE OF THE BEST FILMS OF THE ROGER Moore era. It boasts a very complex and interesting screenplay filled with exotic characters. Although the plot centres on a megalomaniac, this time the political overtones make his threat of a nuclear crisis quite plausible and the co-operation between East and West to stop him signifies the end of the Cold War. The film not only features one of Roger Moore's most effective performances as 007, but also presents an impressive and talented cast. The producers wisely keep silly humour to a minimum, although a bit of it does manage to creep in. (Bond gives a Tarzan yell while swinging on a vine, for example.) Ironically, the sequence which could have been mishandled quite easily – Bond trying to disarm a nuclear bomb at a circus while dressed as a clown – is played seriously and generates a good deal of tension.

The breathtaking visuals of India make a unique background for a Bond film, and the local sites are creatively used to their utmost potential. (Alan Hume's cinematography ignores the poverty and makes the nation look like a paradise.) The film also benefits from some well-directed action sequences and a pre-credits scene that ranks among the best of the series. Aided by a wonderful John Barry score, *Octopussy* comes close to hitting an all-time high for Roger Moore's 007.

THE ASSIGNMENT

Renegade Soviet General Orlov is infuriated by the warming of relations with the West. When his suggestion to attack NATO forces in Europe is rejected, he decides to enact the plan with a group of loyalists. He forms a partnership with Kamal Khan, an

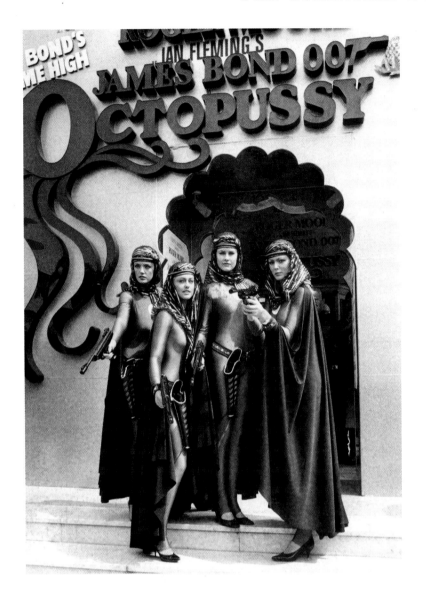

Above: Pre-production publicity at the Carlton Hotel in Cannes.

Previous spread: Maud Adams as Octopussy holds the Fabergé egg – a key element in the script.

aristocratic smuggler of gems who operates out of India. Orlov agrees to steal valued jewels from the Kremlin and sell them to Khan. The entire scenario is part of an elaborate plot in which Orlov will detonate a nuclear bomb on a US military base in West Germany. He predicts the USA will be blamed and be forced to withdraw their forces, thus leaving Western Europe open to Soviet attack. Khan has a business relationship with fellow smuggler Octopussy, the beautiful owner of an exotic travelling circus. When James Bond is assigned to the case he forms an alliance with Octopussy, who eventually discovers that her circus has unwittingly carried the nuclear bomb to the US Army base. Bond manages to deactivate the device with a second to spare, then attempts to rescue Octopussy who has been captured by Khan. In a hand-to-hand battle with Gobinda atop Khan's aeroplane, Bond eventually saves Octopussy and sends Khan to a flaming death.

007's WOMEN

OCTOPUSSY (Maud Adams)

The beautiful owner of a travelling circus based in India, Octopussy is as exotic as her name. Having revived the ancient Octopus cult, she lives in splendour in a palace guarded by an all-female army of gymnasts. She uses her circus as a cover for her partnership with Kamal Khan in the international gem-smuggling business. The daughter of disgraced British agent Dexter Smythe, Octopussy is grateful to James Bond for allowing her father to commit suicide rather than face the scandal of a high-profile court martial on charges of theft and murder. She and 007 become lovers and when she is captured by the traitorous Khan Bond must race against time to rescue her.

Maud Adams is one of the most accomplished actresses to appear in a Bond film. She exudes considerable chemistry with Roger Moore and ensures her status as one of the most memorable of Bond's ladies. As a side note, Adams is the only actress to date to have major roles in two Bond movies (she had previously appeared as Andrea Anders in *The Man With The Golden Gun*).

MAGDA (Kristina Wayborn)

This beautiful blonde serves as right-hand woman to Octopussy. Magda is assigned to seduce 007 in order to recover a stolen Fabergé egg. During the course of their encounter in bed, Magda utters one of the film's best lines by raising a champagne glass and informing 007 suggestively that 'I need refilling'. She also proudly displays the Octopus tattoo (referred to as 'my little Octopussy') which identifies her as part of Octopussy's cult. Magda represents the earlier type of Bond girl: buxom, leggy and oozing sexuality. She is extremely well played by Kristina Wayborn, who also gets the opportunity to show her athletic prowess when Magda uses her fighting skills to help Bond in the assault against Kamal Khan.

007's VILLAINS

KAMAL KHAN (Louis Jordan)

In typical Bond villain fashion, Khan is an aristocratic snob who still has the good manners to wine and dine 007 in elegance while making plans to assassinate him. Jordan is a good choice for the role and he brings his considerable acting skills to bear, making Khan one of the more interesting bad guys of recent years. A corrupt Afghan prince, Khan lives lavishly in India. He eventually double-crosses Octopussy and marks her for death when he teams up with General Orlov to use her circus as the catalyst for a nuclear disaster. When he is defeated, Khan tries to escape by plane, using Octopussy as a hostage – a strategy that backfires when he meets a spectacular death. Jordan has a number of memorable sequences, the best being his silent smouldering as Bond forces him to bid an outrageous price for a Fabergé egg at a Sotheby's auction. There is also a terrific scene in which Bond bests him at gambling, causing Khan to warn him to 'spend the money quickly, Mr Bond'.

GOBINDA (Kabir Bedi)

Gobinda is the tall, silent, handsome Indian henchman of Kamal Khan. He is virtually always at his employer's side and is more than willing to carry out murder and mayhem. Gobinda tries to assassinate Bond in a chaotic chase through an Indian marketplace. Later, in a very effective scene, he attempts to kill Bond in a battle on top of a speeding train. In the edge-of-the-seat finale,

Gobinda and Khan discover that Bond is hanging on to the roof of their plane. 'Go out and get him,' orders Khan. For once, even the stoney-faced Gobinda looks incredulous at the prospect of climbing atop an airborne plane. In the brief struggle with 007, he falls to his death. The role is effectively played by Indian star Kabir Bedi who has considerable screen presence.

GENERAL ORLOV (Steven Berkoff)

In an era of increasing détente, Orlov finds himself out of step with the more pragmatic bureaucrats in the Kremlin who are looking to improve relations with the West. Orlov is a hot-tempered, power-crazed relic of the rapidly diminishing hard-line Communist order. He comes within one second of realizing his dream of a nuclear holocaust in Western Europe. Ironically, he meets his demise when he is shot by Soviet troops loyal to

Above: Faces of evil – Kamal Khan and Gobinda plot the death of James Bond.

Left: Steven Berkoff as the power-crazed General Orlov.

Bond and Vijay observe one of Q's least impressive achievements!

the Kremlin. Orlov is played by noted stage and screen actor Steven Berkoff, but his performance – quite good throughout the remainder of the film – has a shaky start with his over-the-top speech before the Kremlin leaders. Here, Berkoff's impact is far less effective than the quiet rage exuded by Walter Gotell's General Gogol.

MISCHKA & GRISCHKA
(David and Tony Meyer)
Played by real-life identical twins, the handsome but murderous circus knife throwers are in the employ of Kamal Khan. They are excellent villains, largely because they are presented without exaggerated character traits. The two murder 009 at the beginning of the story, then attempt to do the same to Bond. However, 007 manages to kill both brothers in separate confrontations.

007'S ALLIES

VIJAY (Vijay Amritraj)
Indian tennis professional Vijay Amritraj makes his big screen debut as Bond's likable ally in India. Vijay's cover is – appropriately enough – a tennis professional working at a resort owned by Kamal Khan. He also poses as a snake charmer who contacts 007 by playing the 'James Bond Theme' on his flute – a nice gag. Although gentle and humorous, Vijay distinguishes himself as a fearless field agent. He becomes the film's sacrificial lamb when he dies an agonizing death at the hands of Gobinda and the thugs in his employ. The death of Vijay touches Bond deeply and allows for some of the most poignant moments of the film.

M (Robert Brown)
Bond finally gets a new superior in this film. The role of M had been left unfilled in *For Your Eyes Only* out of respect for the late Bernard Lee. M, played by Robert Brown – an old friend and acting colleague of Roger Moore – gives Bond the prerequisite lecture about the importance of his mission (Operation Trove). He later joins 007 in West Berlin to plan strategy. Brown is a fine actor who looks perfect for the role of Bond's crusty superior but the image of Bernard Lee is indelible. Not helping Brown is the fact that the character is noticeably softened, which seems to diminish the air of authority so prominent in Lee's performances.

Q (Desmond Llewelyn)
This is one of Q's biggest roles to date and one of his most amusing. He is shown demonstrating outlandish devices in his Indian laboratory, then gives Bond several important gadgets, including a homing device built into a Fabergé egg. Q later gives Bond a lift to the scene of the battle at Octopussy's palace via a hot-air balloon. He gets some unwanted attention from Octopussy's girls after he saves their lives. He shrugs off their kisses claiming there is no time for frivolity, but does leave the door open saying, 'Later, perhaps.'

GENERAL GOGOL (Walter Gotell)
A proponent of increased détente, Gogol bravely admonishes General Orlov for his militaristic threats against the West. It is Gogol who later pursues the renegade Orlov and exposes him as a thief who has stolen precious gems from the Kremlin. Gogol has the satisfaction of being the last man Orlov sees after he has been shot by

The Big Three – General Gogol, M and Frederick Gray.

Soviet troops loyal to the government. The character of Gogol is either an enemy or an ally of 007, depending upon circumstances. Fortunately, Walter Gotell is skilled enough to carry off both scenarios successfully.

FREDERICK GRAY (Geoffrey Keen)

The minister of defence is in a relatively cheerful mood during this caper and even returns a precious jewel to General Gogol after the mission has been successfully completed. For once, Gray is spared the indignity of inadvertently interrupting one of Bond's romantic liaisons at the film's conclusion.

JIM FANNING (Douglas Wilmer)

This art expert is employed by MI6 to attend the Sotheby's auction of a rare Fabergé egg. It is Fanning's job to identify the buyer and seller of the precious gem. Unfortunately, he opts to take along 007 who decides to call the bluff of Kamal Khan by bidding against him – an action which almost causes Fanning to have a nervous breakdown. The Sotheby's sequence is quite good, establishing a unique atmosphere and providing genuine tension. Roger Moore is at his best here,

gently tweaking Fanning by upping his bids to astronomical levels.

BIANCA (Tina Hudson)

This sexy Hispanic MI6 agent assists Bond in his initially ill-fated attempt to sabotage a radar system in a Caribbean nation. When 007 is captured, Bianca flirts with his guards and distracts them long enough for Bond to escape.

MISS MONEYPENNY & PENELOPE SMALLBONE

(Lois Maxwell, Michaela Clavell)
M's office has an abundance of charm as Moneypenny introduces Bond to her lovely younger assistant Miss Smallbone – a sequence that provides some good laughs as Bond pretends he is not distracted by the new girl's beauty. The role of Miss Smallbone was obviously meant to be a possible replacement for Moneypenny, but the character never appeared again. She was played by the daughter of author James Clavell. Incidentally, Lois Maxwell recalls making a Freudian

Hats off to Moneypenny! Three 007 actors have indulged in the traditional tossing of their *chapeaux* on to her hat rack: George Lazenby, Sean Connery and Roger Moore. Changing styles have precluded Timothy Dalton and Pierce Brosnan from participating in the ritual. Lois Maxwell reports that it often took dozens of takes to hit the target.

dressed as a clown – frantically tries to escape from a circus with the Fabergé egg that is the key to the plot. He is stalked through an East German forest by Mischka and Grischka in a tense and haunting sequence which is very effectively directed. The scene comes to an eerie conclusion when the mortally wounded 009 crashes through the doors of the British Embassy into the middle of a grand party, letting the egg roll on to the floor in front of the startled guests.

VEHICLES

ACROSTAR MINI JET This fabulous one-man jet was designed, built and flown by stunt pilot 'Corkey' Fornof. The Acrostar Mini Jet (also known as the Bede Jet) is capable of flying at over 300mph. Its power is supplied by a single jet engine, a micro-turbo TRS-18 and it is the world's smallest jet plane. The one concession to artistic licence in the film is the plane's retractable wings – needed to enable Bond to hide the Acrostar behind a phoney horse's rear end in a trailer. In the spectacularly exciting pre-credits sequence (one of the best of the series), Bond uses the jet to escape his enemies. However, it looks like curtains when he can't shake off a heat-seeking missile. He daringly races through an airline hangar as the villains try to close the door and trap him. The Acrostar makes it through by inches but the

slip during filming by introducing her assistant as 'Penelope Smallbush'. As the cast and crew laughed hysterically, Roger Moore said, 'Oh, we know where *your* mind has been, Miss Moneypenny.'

AGENT 009 (Andy Bradford)
One of the most suspenseful and sinister sequences in the film occurs when Agent 009 –

missile doesn't. Thus, the bad guys are destroyed in the resulting explosion. The sequence was achieved by using full-scale replicas, the real jet and miniatures – each of which is indistinguishable from the other (a testimony to the professionalism of the technicians and special-effects department). Two of the replicas are on display at Planet Hollywood restaurants in Las Vegas and Dublin.

TUK-TUK 'COMPANY TAXI' The standard Tuk-Tuk taxi is a small, three-wheeled vehicle which resembles a motorized rickshaw and is used in India's metropolitan areas. Vijay's Tuk-Tuk 'company taxi' allows him to demonstrate his evasive driving skills in a wild and amusing chase through city streets with Gobinda and his men in hot pursuit. Vijay makes the taxi ride on its two rear wheels and actually gets it to fly through the air to the amazement of the locals.

Q'S HOT-AIR BALLOON Q transports 007 to the Monsoon Palace to rescue Octopussy in the midst of a large-scale battle. The balloon, proudly decorated with the Union flag, is equipped with a closed-circuit television and a video camera which allow Q to monitor the action below. The notion of Bond and Q depending on this mode of transport is ludicrous, of course, but it is nonetheless amusing. For the sequence, both a full-size and a model hot-air balloon were used.

CROCODILE SUBMARINE
To gain access to Octopussy's island palace undetected, Bond uses a one-man submarine in the form of a crocodile – surely ranking this as the gadget least likely to be used again. Access to the submarine was gained through the crocodile's mouth.

GADGETS & WEAPONS

DEMOLITION CASE This small briefcase conceals bombs underneath its false bottom. Bond uses it in his attempt to destroy the Caribbean air base at the beginning of the film.

YO-YO BUZZ SAW This is a razor-sharp circular saw which runs up and down a wire, in similar fashion to a child's yo-yo. The weapon is employed by one of the thugs Gobinda hires to assassinate Bond and Octopussy and features prominently in a well-staged fight sequence. Tragically, Vijay falls victim to the saw and is subjected to a torturous death (although in the tradition of the Bond films, good taste prevails and

Desmond Llewelyn and the *Octopussy* girls with the Acrostar Mini Jet at Pinewood Studios.

The toy replica of the deadly spin saw.

we are spared the gory details). Despite the weapon's horrific nature, a toy company produced a children's version in Britain.

SEIKO WRISTWATCH When Bond wears a watch, you can bet it does more than merely tell the time. Probably the most creative of all 007's timepieces, this one contains a liquid crystal television monitor behind its face which, when connected to Q's video camera, allows Bond to survey various locations live. At the beginning of the film Bond also wears a different watch which houses a radio directional finder.

An original prop from the film – the fictitious programme for Octopussy's circus.

MONT BLANC FOUNTAIN PEN This eighteen-carat gold Mont Blanc pen contains a receiver to enable 007 to track the bug in the Fabergé egg. The barrel also holds a portion of acid capable of dissolving metal. Bond uses this to escape from his imprisonment in Khan's palace by burning through metal bars on the window. The pen also contains an earpiece which works in conjunction with the bug in the Fabergé egg, allowing 007 to listen in on conversations between Orlov and Khan.

MUSIC

John Barry's score for *Octopussy* is one of his most haunting, and his title song, 'All Time High' – sung by Rita Coolidge with lyrics by Tim Rice – quickly became a standard. Barry also provides a number of impressive incidental themes which stress romance over action, finding new and exciting ways to arrange and incorporate the 'James Bond Theme' into the score. Barry's soundtrack was the first Bond soundtrack to be released on CD. Unavailable for many years, an original copy could command up to $200 on the collectors' circuit. Due to popular demand, it was reissued as a de luxe edition in 1997, complete with extensive production notes, mini poster and the trailer on CD-ROM.

MARKETING & MERCHANDISING

Octopussy marked a notable anniversary of the Bond films and was celebrated by an internationally syndicated one-hour television special titled *James Bond: The First 21 Years*. It featured many amusing tributes from well-known celebrities ranging from President Reagan to Frank Sinatra. A more obscure, but very informative, one-hour special was *Bonds Are Forever*, featuring extensive interviews with the cast and crew of *Octopussy* as well as alumni from the series.

Cubby Broccoli ensured the film received a first-class publicity campaign. This time, Bond's biggest competition was . . . James Bond. The original 007, Sean Connery, was returning in the *Thunderball* remake *Never Say Never Again* and the press made much ado about who would win the 'Battle of the Bonds'. Roger Moore and Connery, real-life friends, played down the competition but the seemingly suicidal plan to release the films simultaneously fell apart when production problems delayed the premiere of *Never Say Never Again* for months.

The advertising campaign made clever use of the *The Spy Who Loved Me* theme song 'Nobody Does It Better' by creating a striking poster of Octopussy with eight arms wrapped around 007. The tag line read 'Nobody Does Him Better'. A teaser poster featured thirteen James Bonds to indicate the number of films made to date.

Most of the *Octopussy* merchandising was centred in the UK. Among the must-haves for fans were a hardback annual, a Zeon watch which played the Bond theme, the infamous yo-yo buzz saw toy, badges, stickers, key rings, a Corgi Junior gift pack consisting of the Acro Star Mini Jet, and a horse trailer. On the promotional front, in the UK Smith's Crisps produced fifteen million packets with promotionals for the film, including a competition. Nabisco Shredded Wheat created a series of collectors' stickers and fans in the USA and UK could buy souvenir brochures in cinemas. Starlog also produced a full-length magazine devoted to *Octopussy*. Japanese schoolchildren could carry their writing implements to school in the *Octopussy* pencil case.

THE BOX OFFICE

With the much-heralded 'Battle of the Bonds' a non-event due to the delay of *Never Say Never Again*, there was still considerable interest in which film would be the biggest grosser. *Octopussy* was the clear winner, chalking up worldwide box-office grosses of $184 million. Although international grosses were down marginally from *For Your Eyes Only*, the film reawakened interest in the franchise in the USA, where it grossed a significant increase over *For Your Eyes Only* at $68 million. *Never Say Never Again* was also a sizable hit, posting the largest autumn opening weekend gross in US history. However, *Octopussy* had opened in the summer, a much stronger time for a major film to premiere. ■

AROUND THE WORLD WITH 007

Octopussy was shot largely on location in **Udaipur**, India. Other key sequences were filmed in **Berlin** and **London**. UK locations included the **Nene Valley Railway** near Peterborough and the **RAF Northholt** base, which was transformed into a banana republic for the film's amazing pre-credits sequence. Footage of the Acrostar Mini Jet in flight was largely shot in the USA. Interiors were filmed at **Pinewood Studios**, as was the scene in which Bond drives the Acrostar to a petrol station and says 'Fill 'er up'. (This was the site where the Fort Knox set for *Goldfinger* had been built almost twenty years previously.)

Roger Moore is a bit shaken and stirred on the set in India.

A VIEW TO
A KILL

(1985)

Director **JOHN GLEN** Producers **ALBERT R BROCCOLI & MICHAEL G WILSON**
Screenplay **RICHARD MAIBAUM & MICHAEL G WILSON** Director of Photography **ALAN HUME**
Editor **PETER DAVIES** Production Designer **PETER LAMONT** Music **JOHN BARRY**
Release date: UK 12 June 1985, USA 22 May 1985. Running time: 131 minutes

P RIOR TO PRODUCTION ON *A VIEW TO A KILL*, IT SEEMED
that Roger Moore would make good his oft-stated intention to retire
from the series. However, Moore strapped on the shoulder holster for his
seventh appearance as 007. In retrospect, this time it was a mistake in
judgment. *A View To A Kill* presents an unworthy swan song for Moore's
James Bond. For the first time since *The Man With The Golden Gun*, a
Bond film seems tired and uninspired. This is apparent in the screenplay,
which borrows liberally from *Goldfinger*, and is a great shame because
For Your Eyes Only and *Octopussy* had presented a re-energized Bond
and strong storylines. There is also an inexplicable return to the kind
of overt humour and sight gags that alienated audiences in *Moonraker*.
(For example, the film's otherwise credible pre-credits sequence is undermined by the inclusion of 'California Girls' on the soundtrack as Bond
snow-surfs away from his pursuers.)

A *View To A Kill* is certainly up to Bondian standards in terms of
scope and production values, with impressive cinematography, sets and
score. There are also several wonderful performances, Christopher
Walken, Grace Jones and Patrick Macnee among them. Unfortunately,
some of the other casting choices, such as Tanya Roberts and Willoughby
Gray, are not so successful. This time the large-scale action scenes are
often superfluous. There is a wild fire-engine chase through the streets
of San Francisco that is spectacularly staged but played totally for laughs.
Stunt man B J Worth's amazing leap from the top of the Eiffel Tower is
ruined by a ludicrous car chase sequence in which Bond endangers more

innocent people's lives than Zorin's scheme does.
More successful is the scene in which 007 is forced
into a deadly steeplechase race on Zorin's estate
and the film's climax, with the action carrying
over from a mine disaster to a terrific sequence in
which Bond battles Zorin hand-to-hand atop the
Golden Gate Bridge.

Although *A View To A Kill* is not one of his
more glowing cinematic missions as James Bond,
the film closed the book on the Roger Moore era.
Over the course of twelve years and seven films,
Moore had achieved what many people had
thought would be impossible: replacing Sean
Connery in the role and embellishing Bond with his
own unique and equally successful interpretation.

THE ASSIGNMENT

Millionaire industrialist Max Zorin is suspected by
MI6 of selling top-secret information about
microchips to Soviet intelligence. James Bond is
assigned to investigate and infiltrates Zorin's
estate posing as a prospective buyer of the racehorses which Zorin breeds. His
identity is eventually revealed and he
narrowly escapes an attempt on his
life by Zorin and his exotic mistress
May Day. Bond makes an alliance
with Stacey Sutton, a young woman
whom Zorin is trying to force to sell
her shares in her late father's oil
company. When she refuses, she is
also marked for death. Bond and
Stacey learn that Zorin intends to
corner the microchip market by
destroying Silicon Valley, California,
where most of the world's microchips are made.
Bond – with the unlikely assistance of May Day –
manages to thwart Zorin and send him to his death
from the top of the Golden Gate Bridge.

007'S WOMEN

STACEY SUTTON (Tanya Roberts)
One-time heiress to the Sutton Oil Company
fortune, Stacey has fallen on hard times and is
working as a geologist for the California department of oil and mines when she teams up with
James Bond. The majority of her company has been
swindled by Max Zorin as part of his scheme to
gain control of the world microchip market, and
when she refuses to sell him her remaining shares
her life is placed in danger. She becomes involved
in helping 007 prevent Zorin from carrying out his
destructive scheme. The character of Stacey is the
least inspired and convincing of any Bond girl. She
does little but dangle precariously in lift shafts and
from cliffs and bridges while screaming 'Help me,
James!' On the few occasions Tanya Roberts – who
admittedly is a very sexy screen presence – is supposed to relate technical information, her delivery
elicits more laughs than credibility.

POLA IVANOVA (Fiona Fullerton)
Attractive KGB agent Pola Ivanova is not above
sharing a little détente with 007 between the
sheets. She encounters him when they make
simultaneous attempts to infiltrate Zorin's oil
refinery. When their missions go awry, she and
Bond end up in a hot-tub where they reminisce
about their previous erotic encounters over the
years. Pola absconds with what she thinks is

Bond's cassette of Zorin's conversations – only to discover that 007 has switched it for a tape of classical music. The role of Pola is played with great charm and skill by Fiona Fullerton, who would have made a wonderful leading lady in a Bond film.

007'S VILLAINS

MAX ZORIN (Christopher Walken)

This twisted genius owes his intellect to the perverted experiments of Dr Carl Mortner. Zorin was born to a prisoner in a Nazi concentration camp. Mortner had injected his mother with steroids in order to create an artificial form of superior intelligence. The experiment succeeded on that level, but a side effect was Zorin's psychotic penchant for murder. Zorin became a KGB agent and the Soviets used his intellect and charisma to their advantage, ensuring he became an internationally successful businessman with corporations in the West. Zorin would then export top-secret technology to his Soviet bosses. Ultimately, however, he resigned from the KGB to initiate Project Main Strike, his daring plan to gain a monopoly on the world microchip market by destroying Silicon Valley.

One of the strengths of *A View To A Kill* is the casting of Oscar winner Christopher Walken as Zorin. Walken, who has made a career of playing odd characters, is very good in the role and wisely chooses to underplay the part of the merciless, but undeniably charming, villain. His best scene is the

realization that he is about to plummet to his death from atop the Golden Gate Bridge. Walken allows Zorin a brief smile and giggle as though appreciating the fact that the joke is on him.

MAY DAY (Grace Jones)

An exotic, Amazon-like martial arts trainer and girlfriend to Max Zorin, May Day is a humourless,

Above: Tanya Roberts was cast as Stacey after Cubby Broccoli had been impressed with her appearance in *The Beastmaster*.

Left: May Day, Scarpine and Zorin examine evidence of an intruder at the pumping rig.

Patrick Macnee's onscreen chemistry with Roger Moore was a highlight of the film.

but highly sexual, woman who relishes dressing in outlandish clothing. She possesses extraordinary strength and is more than efficient in the art of murder. (She personally assassinates three of Bond's colleagues.) When she is left to die by Zorin in the film's climactic mine cave-in, she sacrifices her life to prevent a bomb from causing a cataclysmic series of earthquakes. May Day is one of the most original and interesting characters to appear during the Roger Moore era. Jones steals most of the scenes in which she appears – including a very funny one in which she beds Bond but ensures it is she who is on top.

DR CARL MORTNER (Willoughby Gray)
The doctor's real name is Hans Glaub. He is a former Nazi physician with a penchant for immoral medical experiments on concentration camp inmates. Mortner theorizes that superior intelligence can be created artificially by injecting pregnant women with steroids. The by-product of this illicit practice is Max Zorin, for whom Mortner is a father figure. Mortner is the only person for whom Zorin shows any sign of affection and the two twisted geniuses mutually plan Project Main Strike. He is killed in his misguided attempt to avenge Zorin's death. The character of Mortner is a stereotypical mad doctor – complete

with monocle – and is none too convincingly portrayed by Willoughby Gray.

SCARPINE (Patrick Bauchau)
Scarbine is head of Zorin's security team and his chief henchman. Bond is introduced to him in the sequence in which he infiltrates Zorin's spectacular French estate while posing as a horse buyer. Scarpine also enthusiastically assists his boss in the wholesale murder of the miners in the film's climax. He ultimately perishes when Zorin's airship goes up in flames. Patrick Bauchau has little to do in the role, as Scarpine is largely a one-dimensional character with no particularly interesting character traits.

W G HOWE (Daniel Benzali)
Ostensibly the director of the state of California's division of oil and mines, Howe is actually a paid yes-man to Max Zorin. He helps to cover up Zorin's illegal activities on his oil pumping station off the San Francisco coast and ensures that Stacey Sutton is fired when she starts to unravel compromising information. Alas, Howe's loyalty to Zorin only results in tragedy when the billionaire shoots him in cold blood and attempts to frame the murder on Bond and Stacey. The scene in which Howe is murdered is rather chilling and one of the better moments in the film.

BOB CONLEY (Manning Redwood)
Conley is the corrupt supervisor of Zorin's mining operations as well as his oil pumping rig in San Francisco Bay. He willingly aids and abets his boss by taking steps to ensure that the Hayward Fault in California is flooded with seawater in an attempt to cause a catastrophic earthquake. He also helps plant the bomb in the Main Strike Mine. However, when he learns of Zorin's plans to murder his workers, he objects and is shot to death by Scarpine.

007'S ALLIES

SIR GODFREY TIBBETT
(Patrick Macnee)
This upper-crust MI6 agent has a vast knowledge of horses. He is assigned to pose as Bond's manservant when the duo visit Zorin's French estate. Supposedly, Bond and Tibbett are there to examine racehorses for sale. In reality, they discover that Zorin is using steroids to give his horses an extra 'rush' which ensures they will win each race. Tibbett is a wonderful character and he is played

with great charm by Patrick Macnee. He and Roger Moore enjoy a genuine chemistry onscreen and the scenes in which Bond takes delight in berating his 'servant' are particularly enjoyable. Unfortunately, Tibbett is assassinated – rather implausibly – in a car wash by May Day. This is a pity because Macnee's presence would have been an asset to future 007 films.

CHUCK LEE (David Yip)

A CIA agent who poses as a fish salesman on San Francisco's Fisherman's Wharf, Lee informs Bond of strange goings-on at Zorin's oil pumping facility and is strangled shortly afterwards by May Day. The character exists only to act as a sacrificial lamb and Lee is even denied the dignity of having Bond express any regret about his death.

Q (Desmond Llewelyn)

Q informs M, Bond and Frederick Gray that the KGB now has access to a top-secret microchip which is immune from damage should a nuclear blast occur in the atmosphere. This casts suspicion on Zorin, whose company has manufactured the chip.

M (Robert Brown)

M gives Bond his full support to investigate Zorin's activities but chastises his top agent when the French police charge MI6 six million francs for the damage Bond causes in his reckless car chase of a parachutist through the streets of Paris. (A sequence in which Bond is arrested by Parisian police was filmed but not included in the final print.)

MISS MONEYPENNY (Lois Maxwell)

This is Lois Maxwell's farewell appearance as Moneypenny and she leaves the series in style by taking part in a field assignment. She – along with M and Q – dress elegantly to meet 007 at a racecourse to observe the suspicious winning streak of Zorin's horses. Moneypenny, however, is less interested in the mission than in the bets she has placed.

When Cubby Broccoli informed Lois that this would be her last Bond film, following Roger Moore's retirement from the role, Lois suggested that she be allowed to play M henceforth. The idea was rejected on the grounds that the public would not accept a female in the role. Within the next ten years, however, such prejudices had changed significantly enough for Judi Dench to be accepted enthusiastically as Bond's boss. Bond will always

have a Moneypenny in his life, but Lois Maxwell certainly set the standard for all who follow her.

FREDERICK GRAY (Geoffrey Keen)

Gray balks at the suggestion that a respected industrialist like Max Zorin could be in league with the KGB, yet reluctantly agrees to have M launch an investigation. As usual, Gray's instincts are all wrong.

GENERAL GOGOL (Walter Gotell)

Gogol is sympathetic to 007's cause in this mission because Zorin has dared to resign from the KGB. This leads Gogol to initiate an ill-fated mission to blow up Zorin's oil rig. He appears at the end of the film and informs M that the KGB has granted Bond the Order of Lenin for stopping Zorin. When M says he would think that the Kremlin would have wanted Zorin to destroy Silicon Valley, Gogol gets a good laugh by reminding him that Soviet technology is completely dependent upon what can be stolen from American technology.

VEHICLES

BOND'S ROLLS-ROYCE Sir Godfrey

Tibbett (masquerading as 007's chauffeur) is strangled by May Day in the vintage 1962 Rolls-Royce he and Bond are using. Later, Bond is knocked unconscious and left in the car, which May Day pushes into a lake. In a cleverly written sequence, Bond stays alive under water by breathing the air from one of the tyres.

Renault, who provided the taxi for the Parisian chase sequence, promoted their 1985 11 Turbo in conjunction with the film's release.

The 007 toy that never was! Matchbox's prototype of the *View To A Kill* vehicle set which was never released.

RENAULT TAXI After May Day's spectacular parachute jump from the Eiffel Tower, Bond commandeers a taxi to pursue her in a high-speed chase through the streets of Paris. Although far too comical and far-fetched to be suspenseful (the slapstick scenes of the harried taxi driver running after Bond are very silly), the sequence is amazing from a technical point of view – particularly when Bond's car continues to drive after it has been sheared in half.

ZORIN'S AIRSHIPS This time, not only is Bond's adversary full of hot air but so are his modes of transport. His gigantic helium-filled airship, contains a full conference centre complete with scale model of Silicon Valley and a junior version which can be hidden inside a construction caravan and inflated at the touch of a button. The larger vehicle contains a handy device for unwanted passengers: a stairway that converts to a slide, thus ensuring the victim makes a very hasty and fatal exit (in this case a man who refuses to be part of Zorin's briefing for Project Main Strike). Although the scene is virtually a remake of the scenario with Mr Solo in *Goldfinger*, it does provide a very entertaining moment. Later, Zorin forces Stacey aboard the smaller airship and sets in motion the well-staged fight to the death between himself and 007 atop the Golden Gate Bridge – a scene which climaxes with the airship exploding and plunging into San Francisco Bay.

ICEBERG SUBMARINE In the pre-credits sequence, Bond escapes Siberia in this novel submarine disguised as an iceberg. The unique vessel is complete with luxury facilities, state of the art technology and an automatic pilot which ensures Bond's voyage with the beautiful agent Kimberly Jones is smooth sailing.

GADGETS & WEAPONS

CAMERA RING Bond uses this rather gaudy ring which has a hidden camera in it to take photographs of Carl Mortner and other guests at Zorin's estate.

SHAVER BUG DETECTOR To avoid a close shave later, Bond uses a Philips shaver with a built-in bug detector to weed out listening devices in his room at Zorin's French château.

POLARIZING SUNGLASSES These ordinary-looking sunglasses greatly reduce glare and give Bond the ability to spy through a window. He uses them to observe Zorin paying Stacey in a business transaction – a suspicious development which he immediately investigates.

MINI COPIER Bond uses this notebook-sized device to scan Zorin's chequebook in order to get an impression of the cheque he wrote to Stacey. It reveals a mysterious $5 million payoff to the young woman and makes Bond determined to investigate their relationship.

JOCKEY'S WHIP The secret to the winning streak of Zorin's racehorses is the fact that he has implanted steroids in the thoroughbreds. The steroids are released when the jockey uses a device in his whip to activate them, thus giving the horse the boost required to win the race.

ZORIN'S COMPUTER Zorin uses this device to establish Bond's real identity. The computer is located behind his desk and supposedly contains a database of hereditary information about the horses he has for sale. In reality, a hidden video camera photographs Bond and instantly relays the image on to the computer. Zorin is then able to identify Bond as a British agent.

'SNOOPER' One of the more preposterous gadgets from Q Branch, this dog-like robot scampers about rather conspicuously. 'Snooper' features a retractable neck and its eyes contain video cameras which allow Q to monitor various locations – including Stacey's bathroom, where he discovers she is in the shower with Bond. (Why Q – who is frantically searching for the couple – employs the cumbersome device instead of merely ringing the doorbell is never explained.)

MUSIC

Although *A View To A Kill* was by all accounts one of the weaker Bond films, it did boast a very strong score from John Barry. The title song written (with Barry) and performed by Duran Duran was one of the most exciting and became an international smash hit – both in record shops and on MTV, where the very first 007 music video made its debut.

MARKETING & MERCHANDISING

Roger Moore's last Bond film received the usual massive media promotion. In the USA, three cinema posters were created, two of them advance teasers. The first – and least impressive – depicted Bond hanging from the Eiffel Tower with May Day parachuting behind him. More successful were the second teaser featuring Bond and May Day back to back and the one-sheet poster depicting Bond and

Stacey on the Golden Gate Bridge.

Most of the merchandising was done in the UK and mainland Europe. Smith's Crisps made a series of action posters which were given to consumers. Lone Star Toys of England manufactured the *A View To A Kill* gun and holster set and Hestair Hope provided two jigsaw puzzles. Philips launched major promotions for their devices used in the film and Matchbox created toy versions of the Parisian taxi and Bond's Rolls-Royce. A 007 alarm clock by Zeon was released and Starlog published a souvenir magazine. In Holland a set of trading cards and accompanying photograph album were available. The film had its US premiere in San Francisco – a courteous nod to the city's extraordinary co-operation in letting the production company stage the elaborate chase scenes.

Shortly before filming, the '007 Stage' at Pinewood Studios burned down. The production team rebuilt it in record time. At the dedication ceremony, the new building was renamed 'The Albert R Broccoli 007 Stage'.

THE BOX OFFICE

Although worldwide box-office grosses were still sizable at $152 million, *A View To A Kill* grossed about $30 million less than *Octopussy*. Critics and fans criticized the emphasis on comedy and the tired feel of the film. Producers Cubby Broccoli and Michael G Wilson realized that the franchise needed to be reinvigorated and they set about the unenviable task of finding a replacement for Roger Moore. His popularity and box-office clout over the last twelve years had proved to be considerable – despite the popular consensus that *Octopussy* should have been his last cinematic mission as 007). ∎

AROUND THE WORLD WITH 007

A View To A Kill features some stunning locations. The pre-credits sequence was filmed in **Iceland** (doubling for Siberia) and there are some very atmospheric scenes shot in **Paris** and at **Château Chantilly**, the breathtaking mansion in the French countryside which represented Zorin's estate. Other sequences were filmed in and around **London**, with interiors completed at **Pinewood Studios**.

THE LIVING DAYLIGHTS

(1987)

Director **JOHN GLEN** Producers **ALBERT R BROCCOLI & MICHAEL G WILSON**
Screenplay **RICHARD MAIBAUM & MICHAEL G WILSON** Director of Photography **ALEC MILLS**
Production Designer **PETER LAMONT** Editors **JOHN GROVER & PETER DAVIES**
Music **JOHN BARRY**

Release date: UK 29 June 1987, USA 31 July 1987. Running time: 130 minutes

THE SEARCH FOR A NEW ACTOR TO PLAY 007 FOLLOWING Roger Moore's retirement from the series with *A View To A Kill* caused a predictable media frenzy. Rumoured candidates ranged from the plausible (Sam Neill) to the unlikely (Christopher Reeve stated he had been approached) to the virtually impossible (an unknown Australian model named Finley Light). Ultimately, it appeared just about certain that Pierce Brosnan would be the next James Bond in *The Living Daylights* and Cubby Broccoli had all but officially anointed him as the new 007. Clearly, he was a popular choice with the public, who felt Brosnan's experience playing a detective on the recently cancelled television series *Remington Steele* gave him the necessary background for the role. However, when NBC sought to reactivate the series, Brosnan was forced to endure the heartbreak of losing the role. (Ironically, the new *Remington Steele* was cancelled shortly thereafter.)

Broccoli approached Timothy Dalton, whom he had long considered a strong candidate for the role of Bond. When Dalton enthusiastically accepted, the publicity juggernaut was put into motion to ensure every Bond fan on earth knew that he had inherited Roger Moore's mantle. The casting of Dalton was a strategically sound one. His intense acting style ensured that the Bond films would return to the genre of serious thrillers. Indeed, *The Living Daylights* is refreshingly devoid of embarrassing sight gags and over-the-top humour. Dalton took the Bond role seriously and

Above: Maryam d'Abo as Kara Milovy with her prized Stradivarius cello named 'The Lady Rose'. The cello helps Bond to locate the villainous Koskov.

Previous spread: The new Bond sported a casual, contemporary look compared to his more traditional predecessors.

THE ASSIGNMENT

James Bond is assigned to Bratislava, Czechoslovakia, to arrange for the defection of top Soviet General Koskov. Their daring escape succeeds and Koskov informs MI6 that the KGB General Pushkin has initiated a programme of assassinations against British agents. To forestall any further casualties, Bond is assigned to terminate Pushkin. In the process, however, 007 discovers that the operation is merely a ploy by Koskov to have MI6 kill Pushkin, who was about to arrest him for stealing government funds. Bond learns that Koskov is actually in league with international arms dealer Brad Whitaker and that the pair have initiated an ambitious scheme to use Soviet money for an arms deal to finance the purchase of opium, which they will then sell at enormous profits. Bond forms an alliance with Pushkin and enlists Koskov's jilted girlfriend Kara Milovy to help track him down. The trail leads to a Soviet military base in Afghanistan. Here, Bond is able to convince the leader of the resistance, Kamran Shah, to launch an attack on the base and help foil Koskov's scheme. Bond tracks Koskov to Whitaker's estate in Tangier. In a brief but furious gun fight, Bond manages to kill the ruthless arms dealer and Pushkin arrests Koskov – who has a grim fate awaiting him.

007'S WOMEN

KARA MILOVY (Maryam d'Abo)

A beautiful and talented Czech cellist, Kara is the naïve girlfriend of Koskov, who persuades her to pose as a KGB sniper in order to authenticate his 'defection' to the British. Bond convinces her that she is being made the victim in Koskov's deadly double-cross. The betrayed Kara sides with Bond to thwart Koskov and distinguishes herself in action by bravely joining the Afghan resistance in a fierce battle against Soviet troops. Later, she manages to keep a cargo plane aloft while Bond fights the killer Necros. For her efforts, she is granted asylum in the West, where her talents as a cellist ensure she becomes an immediate sensation. Kara is one of the more interesting and believable of Bond's women. She is innocent but brave and fiercely self-sufficient. The role is played with considerable skill by the lovely Maryam d'Abo, who proved to be a very appropriate leading lady for Timothy Dalton's more serious interpretation of 007.

immersed himself in reading Fleming's novels to ensure he gave 007 a dangerous edge. Indeed, if Dalton had one drawback it was his uncomfortable way of delivering the one-liners that are obligatory for any actor playing Bond. Mercifully, the script keeps these to a minimum.

By all accounts, *Daylights* succeeded on both an artistic and financial level. The movie is an engrossing thriller with a diverse and interesting cast, exotic locations and an excellent score by John Barry. Highlights include a terrific pre-credits sequence and an even more impressive fight between Bond and a would-be assassin aboard a cargo plane – one of the most impressive stunt sequences to appear in any of the films. Weaknesses included smaller-than-life villains and a lack of romance for Bond, who is monogamous this time (with one brief exception). The Dalton era had begun, although no one realized at the time that his considerable contribution to the series would be limited to only two films.

007'S VILLAINS

GENERAL GEORGI KOSKOV
(Jeroen Krabbe)

This high-ranking Soviet general pretends to defect to the West in order to spread disinformation. Koskov is a charming but ruthless rogue who seeks to play off the British and Soviets against each other as part of his and Whitaker's scheme to use KGB arms funds secretly to finance the purchase of a large opium shipment. Dutch actor Jeroen Krabbe's performance is played too broadly to make it believable that this man could have risen to the rank of general in the Soviet Army. His overly patronizing gestures and exaggerated expressions of friendship would not dupe anyone. Krabbe is a very competent actor, but he makes a lightweight Bond villain.

BRAD WHITAKER (Joe Don Baker)

This egotistical US arms dealer models himself on history's most notorious dictators. In between orchestrating international arms deals, Whitaker enjoys re-creating battles with his vast dioramas and toy soldiers. His Tangier mansion contains an array of life-like wax figures of Hitler, Napoleon

and other megalomaniacs – each of which bears the face of Whitaker. His fanaticism about military history ironically causes his demise when he is crushed under a statue of Wellington. Whitaker is not very interesting by Bond villain standards, and although Joe Don Baker is amusing he is somewhat miscast in the role. He plays Whitaker as an oaf from the American South and we never believe for a moment that Bond will have any trouble besting him. More successful was Baker's eventual casting as Jack Wade in *GoldenEye*.

NECROS (Andreas Wisniewski)

Necros is the most intriguing of the film's trio of main villains. He is a silent, humourless, but extremely handsome assassin who tends to use a Walkman as a strangulation device. The role is well played by Andreas Wisniewski, who provides the film with a much-needed sense of menace. Necros' clever infiltration of an MI6 safe house is an excellent sequence as he masterminds the

Above: Jeroen Krabbe as General Georgi Koskov; he is about to feign defection in Bratislava.

Left: Posing as a milkman, Necros infiltrates MI6's safe house – with deadly results.

Above: Art Malik portrays Kamran Shah, the courageous and powerful leader of a group of Afghan freedom fighters.

Right: Caroline Bliss makes her debut as the amorous and ever-faithful Miss Moneypenny, replacing Lois Maxwell who had appeared in the role since *Dr. No.*

thwart Koskov and the Soviet forces by leading his men in a cavalry raid on an air base. This sequence – the most effective large-scale action piece in a Bond film in many a year – is extremely well staged. The character of Shah is very well written and convincingly played by Art Malik.

SAUNDERS (Thomas Wheatley)

The film's obligatory sacrificial lamb, Saunders is Bond's contact in Bratislava in the mission to help Koskov defect. The two men don't like each other and when Bond hesitates to assassinate Kara (who is posing as a KGB sniper), Saunders files a formal complaint with M accusing 007 of dereliction of duty. Later, however, he develops a grudging respect for Bond and agrees to help him cut through red tape to get Kara out of the country. He is later assassinated by Necros at an amusement park in Austria in a highly effective sequence. Thomas Wheatley is very good as Bond's colleague and antagonist, and Saunders' death has an impact on the audience.

Q (Desmond Llewelyn)

Q gets the film's best line when he introduces Bond to his latest gadget, a portable stereo with a built-in bazooka: 'Something we're making for the Americans,' he explains. 'It's called a ghetto-blaster.' Q also helps arrange to transport Koskov to the West via a special device that catapults him through an oil pipeline.

'kidnapping' of Koskov from the British. In reality, Necros is a partner of Koskov and Whitaker, although it is he who is assigned the job of performing actual assassinations. The fight between Bond and Necros aboard an airborne cargo plane is a superbly filmed sequence and is filled with cliff-hanging suspense.

007'S ALLIES

GENERAL LEONID PUSHKIN

(John Rhys-Davies)

Pushkin is the KGB chief who has replaced General Gogol. He is being framed by Koskov as the leader of an assassination campaign against MI6 agents. Bond is assigned to terminate him but believes Pushkin's story that he is being used as Koskov's dupe. Bond and Pushkin concoct a plan wherein 007 'assassinates' the KGB chief in the hope that it will make Koskov show his hand. The role of Pushkin is a strong one and Rhys-Davies plays the part with infectious wit and humour.

KAMRAN SHAH (Art Malik)

Shah is the Oxford-educated leader of the Afghan resistance movement, the Mujahedeen. When Bond frees him from a Soviet jail (and certain death), the rebel repays the favour and helps 007

The Aston Martin Volante makes light work of Bond's pursuers.

M (Robert Brown)

M is seen on a field assignment in his plane above the Rock of Gibraltar. Here, he sends the 00s on a training mission by having them parachute over the rock and try to take over a military installation below. M later dismisses Bond's suspicions that his assignment to kill Pushkin is part of a double-cross by Koskov. Although this sequence should be tense (as in the Bond/M confrontations in *Goldfinger* and *On Her Majesty's Secret Service*), Robert Brown is far too avuncular in the role to give much bite to M.

MISS MONEYPENNY (Caroline Bliss)

The task of following on from Lois Maxwell in the character of Moneypenny after her fourteen performances is not an enviable one. Caroline Bliss fails to register a significant impact as the love-starved secretary but this is because the script does not provide much of the flirtatious banter that is traditional between Moneypenny and Bond. Dalton's Bond doesn't even seem aware of her affections and his relationship with Moneypenny is not in the least suggestive.

FREDERICK GRAY (Geoffrey Keen)

Gray helps to interrogate Koskov, then later goes into his predictable panic mode when he must inform the prime minister that the KGB has captured their prize defector.

FELIX LEITER (John Terry)

The unexpected pleasure of having Leiter on hand once more (he had not been seen in a Bond film since *Live And Let Die*) is undermined by the fact that he has almost nothing to do other than greet Bond on a yacht and communicate with him briefly by radio. There is no attempt to build any sentiment between the men and Leiter's character may just as well have been a stranger to 007. The part is played this time by John Terry, who has virtually no chemistry with Dalton.

GOGOL (Walter Gotell)

Now a member of the Soviet foreign office, Gogol has bequeathed his former assignment as head of the KGB to General Pushkin. He makes a welcome, but all too brief, appearance. This is due to the fact that it was originally envisioned that the Pushkin role would be that of Gogol. However, when Walter Gotell suffered an illness, Cubby Broccoli could not get him insured for a substantial role in the film. According to Gotell, Cubby even offered to pay a rather extravagant sum for insurance out of his own pocket but still could not get coverage. Thus, the Pushkin character was created. Gotell was given a small role at the finale of the film in which he has a cordial meeting with Kara and arranges to get her a visa to visit the Soviet Union at will. This was the last appearance for the character and Gotell, who graced the Bond films with his considerable screen presence for many years.

VEHICLES

1986 ASTON MARTIN VOLANTE

Linking new Bond Timothy Dalton to tradition, the producers arranged for him to have his own unique Aston Martin to use in the film. Like its

Location filming was centred largely in **Morocco**, for the sequences set in Tangiers as well as Afghanistan. The pre-credits sequence combined footage shot in **Gibraltar** and the **USA** (for part of the aerial jump). There was also extensive work done in **Austria**. Other scenes were shot in and around **London**, with interiors done at **Pinewood Studios**.

illustrious predecessor, the DB5, this latest model was customized with an array of hi-tech gadgetry. Bond and Kara escape from Bratislava in the vehicle and manage to elude Soviet pursuers. During the chase, 007 deploys each of his car's hidden gadgets. These include a laser beam, installed in the front hubcap, which is used to saw a police car from its axle; retractable skis and spiked tyres to assist the car on ice; a police band radio; bullet-proof windows; front-mounted rockets hidden behind the fog lights; and a rocket booster to give the car extraordinary power. As in the DB5, the armaments are hidden in the arm rest, with the missile's visual display target projected on to the windscreen. Like the Lotus in *For Your Eyes Only*, the Volante has a self-destruct mechanism which Bond uses to prevent the car from falling into enemy hands. In the film, the car is seen in two guises: as a hardtop and as a convertible. In reality, two different vehicles were used: the Volante (hardtop) and a Vantage (convertible). The transformation was explained by a sequence in which Q's assistants are shown 'winterizing' the car (that is, fitting a hardtop section over it). Today, the Vantage – complete with gadgetry – still appears at car shows and conventions. The vehicle is a worthy successor to the DB5 and the action sequences featuring it are exciting and imaginatively staged.

Playboy magazine has a long association with 007. Maryam d'Abo graced this issue with a stunning pictorial.

GADGETS & WEAPONS

WALTHER SNIPER'S RIFLE Bond uses this outsized weapon to prevent a KGB sniper from assassinating Koskov as he attempts to defect. The cumbersome gun features an infrared scope which pinpoints precisely the target area on the victim. (In this case, Bond recognizes the sniper – Kara – as a novice and shoots the rifle from her hand instead of killing her.) The gun takes either soft-tipped or steel-tipped bullets (Bond prefers the latter).

WHITAKER'S ASSAULT RIFLE Brad Whitaker is armed with an automatic assault weapon as he hunts Bond in their climactic confrontation. The rifle takes a clip containing up to eighty rounds of ammunition which are disbursed in seconds with devastating effect. Whitaker has also added a bullet-proof face shield which successfully deflects Bond's shots.

PHILIPS KEYRING FINDER Activated by 007 whistling the first notes of 'Rule Britannia', the magnetic fob emits a stun gas capable of disorienting an opponent for up to thirty seconds, providing he is within a five-foot range. It also contains a highly concentrated plastic explosive which is detonated by Bond giving a wolf whistle. (The latter proves to be the undoing of Whitaker.) The fob also contains a series of keys capable of opening ninety per cent of the world's locks.

EXPLOSIVE MILK BOTTLES Necros' victims don't have a chance to cry over this spilled milk – each bottle contains high explosives. Necros uses these to deadly effect when he impersonates a milkman to gain access to the MI6 safe house to 'kidnap' Koskov.

PUSHKIN'S WATCH When Bond gets the drop on Pushkin and his mistress in a Tangier hotel suite, the KGB chief presses a silent alarm which notifies his bodyguard that he is in danger. Bond relies on a normal male weakness to distract the guard by forcing Pushkin's mistress to stand naked in the doorway. The momentary diversion works and Bond is able to get the upper hand.

MUSIC

The Living Daylights finds John Barry at his best, contributing a highly atmospheric and memorable score. He teamed with the Norwegian rock band a-ha to write the title theme. One of the liveliest of the series, the song reached number five in the British charts. Another rock band, The Pretenders, contributed the song which is heard over the end credits, 'If There Was a Man', as well as an incidental track heard fleetingly in the film, 'Where Has Every Body Gone?'. Both were satisfactory efforts but neither made an impact on the international charts.

MARKETING & MERCHANDISING

No expense was spared to remind the world that Timothy Dalton was the new Bond. Massive advertising campaigns began long before the film was released. Trade advertisements depicted the front number plate of an Aston Martin bearing the news that a new Bond film was coming. A teaser poster featured an extreme close-up of Dalton looking very intense. Indeed, the entire campaign was designed to inform fans that the dangerous element of 007 was back. A teaser trailer featured this aspect repeatedly (even if it was rather anti-climactic by showing most of the highlights of the terrific pre-credits sequence). The British quad poster featured a superb painting of Bond inside a gun barrel surrounded by a collage of scenes and characters from the film. For reasons unknown, the US one-sheet poster was far less effective, with the main emphasis on a girl in a see-through nightgown. (Fans also complained that Dalton's head appeared too big for his body.) A one-hour television special, *Happy Anniversary, 007*, was ostensibly to celebrate the twenty-fifth anniversary of the series. In reality, the show – hosted by Roger Moore – was designed to promote the new Bond. (It was later released with additional footage on home video.)

Promotional tie-ins were plentiful. In the UK, Unigate offered free tickets to the film on their orange juice, Trio chocolates featured stickers in each packet, Philips heavily promoted their products in conjunction with the film, and Bollinger launched an aggressive advertising campaign featuring a special promotional poster, as did Carlsberg beer. Products included a line of one-inch hand-painted figurines of Bond and characters from the film, and series, from Little Lead Soldiers (the same company provided the military dioramas for the film). LLS also produced leather address books, golf accessories, driver's licence holders and other products. Two books

were released to considerable fanfare: *The James Bond Movie Book*, a brief look at the making of the individual films and *The James Bond Movie Poster Book*, which offered reproductions of the US one-sheet posters suitable for framing. In Germany, the ASS Company created a beautifully packaged board game and in Australia an entire series of toy guns and accessories was created. The rarest item connected with the film, however, is a promotional replica of the Philips keyring finder. Today, it can sell for over £200.

THE BOX OFFICE

Box-office grosses for *The Living Daylights* were far superior to those of *A View To A Kill* with a worldwide total of more than $191 million. The results cheered Eon Productions because it proved there was still an enthusiastic audience for Bond and that their efforts to revitalize the franchise had succeeded. Many house records were broken throughout the world. Critics were more anaemic, however. Most gave the film respectable, if unenthusiastic, reviews. Dalton's acting skills were uniformly cited as excellent but some critics complained that he lacked the sexual aggressiveness of Connery and the wit of Moore. They missed the point. Dalton was not attempting to emulate any of his predecessors and was determined to create his own unique interpretation of the role. Judging by the box-office returns, he succeeded admirably. ■

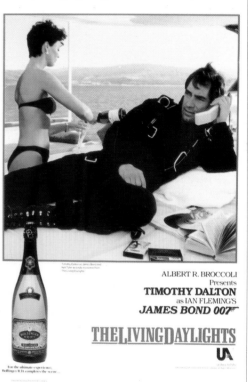

BOLLINGER
The Champagne of James Bond 007

ALBERT R. BROCCOLI
Presents
TIMOTHY DALTON
as IAN FLEMING'S
JAMES BOND 007
THE LIVING DAYLIGHTS
UA

Since *A View To A Kill*, Bollinger has promoted itself as 'The Champagne of James Bond', as illustrated in this poster.

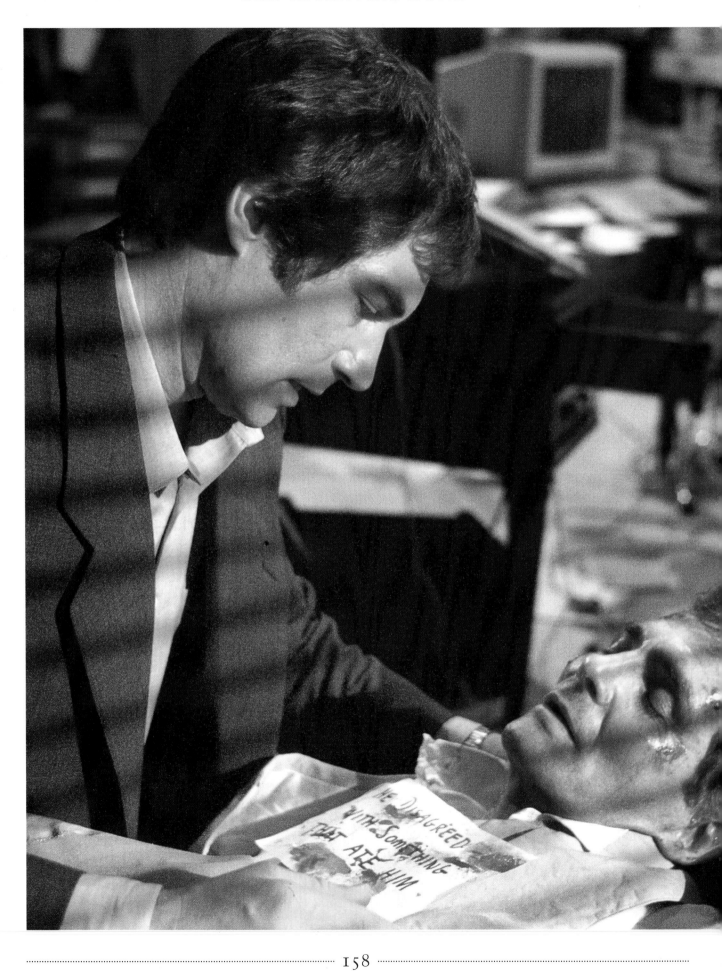

LICENCE TO KILL

(1989)

Director **JOHN GLEN** Producers **ALBERT R BROCCOLI & MICHAEL G WILSON**
Screenplay **RICHARD MAIBAUM & MICHAEL G WILSON** Director of Photography **ALEC MILLS**
Production Designer **PETER LAMONT** Editor **JOHN GROVER** Music **MICHAEL KAMEN**
Release date: UK 13 June 1989, USA 14 July 1989. Running time: 133 minutes

Timothy Dalton's second – and ultimately last – appearance as James Bond would prove to be one of the most controversial films of the series. Determined to make 007 a more realistic, down-to-earth hero, screenwriters Richard Maibaum and Michael G Wilson created a storyline sending Bond on a mission of personal vengeance. Virtually everyone agreed that this was a superior thriller but for many fans it simply wasn't 'Bondian' enough. The locations were certainly exotic but gone were the extravagant sets and the villain was, for many, an all-too-believable drug baron instead of a power-crazed megalomaniac. Despite criticism that 007 was straying too far from his cinematic roots, for many other fans *Licence To Kill* is one of the best Bond films of recent years and harkened back to the 'it could actually happen' style of *From Russia With Love* and *On Her Majesty's Secret Service.*

The film boasts an engrossing and tightly scripted screenplay, an exceptional cast and several excellent action set-pieces. In one, Bond wreaks havoc on a boat, and in the space of seconds dives overboard, fights with frogmen and ends up atop a seaplane in a battle to the death with its pilot. It's a superbly staged sequence – only in a Bond movie could such a scenario seem plausible. The film's climactic tanker lorry chase is clearly the other high point. Associate producer Barbara Broccoli won great respect overseeing production of this ambitious and excitingly staged set-piece.

Above and previous spread: Bond makes a horrific discovery at the home of Felix and Della Leiter.

petition at the box office backed by a weak advertising campaign. The result was a very anaemic performance at the US box office (although international grosses were more impressive). Ultimately, Danjaq became embroiled in legal issues with MGM/UA. No one could have realized it at the time, but the legalities would preclude another Bond film from opening for a period of six years. By then, Timothy Dalton had decided to leave the role he respected so much in order to work on different projects. His tenure as Bond was brief but impressive. It can be said that the Dalton era truly restored James Bond to a serious action figure and his contribution to the series cannot be overstated.

THE ASSIGNMENT

On the day of his wedding in Key West, Florida, Felix Leiter is informed that an opportunity exists to capture Franz Sanchez, a notorious international drug baron. Leiter and his best man James Bond stage a spectacular airborne arrest of Sanchez. However, their triumph is short-lived. Sanchez escapes and extracts a terrible revenge: Felix is mutilated and his new bride is murdered. When Bond ignores M's warning not to embark on a personal vendetta to avenge the Leiters, he becomes a rogue agent acting on his own. With the aid of Pam Bouvier, a daring pilot who has flown missions for the CIA, and Q who uses a leave of absence to assist his colleague, 007 gains Sanchez's confidence at his home base of Isthmus City in South America. Bond is invited to a gigantic facility where Sanchez has developed the ability to dissolve heroin in gasoline and reclaim it after it has been transported in tanker lorries. Agent 007 pursues Sanchez in a spectacular chase which culminates in the drug baron being burned alive. His enemy thwarted, Bond rejoins MI6 as an active agent – taking time out for a well-deserved romantic fling with Pam.

007'S WOMEN

PAM BOUVIER (Carey Lowell)
One of the most intriguing of Bond's ladies, Pam Bouvier is a tough-as-nails, courageous freelance pilot who works periodically for the CIA. She has a chameleon-like ability to change from a hardened field operative to a sultry beauty – a talent she uses to her advantage. She becomes a reluctant ally of James Bond in his quest to locate Sanchez and gets ample opportunity to

Licence To Kill is notable on several other levels. For one, it represents the last appearances in the series of Robert Brown's M and Caroline Bliss's Moneypenny. It would also be John Glen's final Bond film. No one has directed as many 007 films and the former editor emerged as a talented film-maker in his years with the series. Additionally, this was screenwriter Richard Maibaum's last Bond script (he died shortly after the film was released). *Licence To Kill* would also be the last Bond film in which Cubby Broccoli acted in his traditional role as producer.

Sadly, the film's legacy was not a happy one. At the time MGM/UA was under the control of a controversial chairman whose lack of film marketing experience was legendary. Thus, in the USA *Licence To Kill* opened against fierce com-

demonstrate her ability to handle herself in fist-fights and with heavy-duty weaponry. Additionally, her skills as a pilot play a pivotal role in Bond's defeat of Sanchez. The screenwriters can't resist having her eventually fall madly in love with Bond and Pam's pouting jealousy of 007's involvement with Lupe is the only false note in her characterization. She is excellently played by model/actress Carey Lowell, who brings a refreshing cynicism to her role which ensures that this Bond girl is far more than just an ornament for 007.

LUPE LAMORA (Talisa Soto)

This quiet, intense beauty is the 'kept woman' of Franz Sanchez. Like Domino in *Thunderball*, Lupe is bored with being held a virtual captive in the luxurious surroundings of her lover's estate. In the film's chilling pre-credits sequence, Sanchez catches her in bed with another man and extracts his revenge by having his rival's heart cut out then whipping Lupe mercilessly. Bond uses her vulnerability to his advantage and seduces her in his successful attempt to penetrate Sanchez's organization. Model Talisa Soto gives an impressive performance in what could have been a clichéd,

one-dimensional role. Her beauty is accentuated by costume designer Jodie Tillen's decision to attire her in eye-popping gowns and dresses.

007'S VILLAINS

FRANZ SANCHEZ (Robert Davi)

While *Licence To Kill* may cause controversy between Bond fans, what is not debatable is the effectiveness of Robert Davi's performance. He invests Sanchez with some fascinating character traits, including a warped code of morality, making him a complex and interesting villain. Sanchez is capable of routinely ordering horrific torture for those who cross him. Yet, he is a man who rewards loyalty and keeps his word – even when it costs him millions. Cultured, polite and witty, Sanchez is also brutally ambitious in his

Above: Carey Lowell as Pam Bouvier, with legendary Las Vegas entertainer Wayne Newton in the role of Professor Joe Butcher.

Left: Talisa Soto as Sanchez's reluctant mistress Lupe Lamora.

Robert Davi in action as the vengeful Sanchez.

research vessel the *WaveKrest* – transports drugs and money internationally. Bond convinces Sanchez that Krest has double-crossed him, thus causing Krest to suffer a horrendous death. Anthony Zerbe is well cast as the ill-fated Krest. He doesn't have any redeemable features, but it is difficult not to feel some sympathy for him when Sanchez locks him in a high-pressure chamber until he literally goes out of his head (a sequence trimmed by censors in several countries).

KILLIFER (Everett McGill)

A trusted colleague of Felix Leiter, Killifer betrays his old friend and accepts a bribe from Sanchez whom he allows to escape in a very surprising plot twist. Everett McGill is excellent in the role, making the transformation of the initially likable Killifer into a backstabbing opportunist a very believable development. When Bond arranges for him to fall victim to the same shark that ravaged Leiter, it's difficult to suppress a cheer.

PROFESSOR JOE BUTCHER
(Wayne Newton)

This respected television evangelist routinely cons gullible converts into donating funds to his religious retreat near Isthmus City. In reality, the complex is a massive front for Sanchez's drug processing operation. Butcher uses his broadcasts to signal the daily price of cocaine to international buyers who then bid in the guise of making a charitable donation. The casting of Las Vegas singing sensation Wayne Newton is an unorthodox but highly inspired idea. While his interpretation of Butcher is over the top, viewers of American television will find the character subdued compared to those 'evangelists' who have been exposed as real-life con men.

DARIO (Benicio Del Toro)

A silent and ruthless hit man and former Contra, Dario is employed by Sanchez to carry out gruesome assassinations. It is he who murders Della Leiter and butchers Lupe's lover. In a refreshing change of pace for a henchman, Dario is also competent. He recognizes Bond when 007 infiltrates Sanchez's drug processing plant and immediately exposes him. The part is played with genuine menace by Benecio Del Toro, who has a significant screen presence and the most sinister of smiles.

TRUMAN-LODGE (Anthony Starke)

Truman-Lodge is a yuppie financial wizard who oversees Sanchez's investments with microscopic

goal of heading an international drug cartel. He owns a palatial estate in Isthmus City, where he presides over a puppet government and a virtual army of henchmen. Sanchez is played with remarkable skill by Davi, who emerges as one of the strongest antagonists for 007 in many years.

MILTON KREST (Anthony Zerbe)

Owner of a marine exploration and research company in Florida, Krest is seemingly devoted to finding a method of breeding fish to feed Third World nations. In reality, his company is a massive front for Sanchez's operation. Krest – using his

precision. He can accurately quote the price of heroin at any time and he is used by Sanchez to induce other drug barons to form an international cartel with Sanchez as the leader. Ultimately, Bond manages to have Sanchez (falsely) suspect Truman-Lodge of ripping him off. This, combined with his nervous, panicky personality, upsets boss Sanchez enough to make him terminate the financial mastermind.

HELLER (Don Stroud)

Chief of security for Sanchez, Heller ruthlessly pursues and eliminates anyone who poses a threat to his employer. When Bond plays to Sanchez's paranoia by suggesting Heller is conspiring against him, the security chief is murdered in a rather unique way: he is impaled on a forklift.

007'S ALLIES

Q (Desmond Llewelyn)

The value of Desmond Llewelyn to the Bond franchise was quite apparent in *Licence To Kill* which gave him his biggest and most important role to date. This time, the grumpy gadgets genius signifies his respect for Bond by taking a leave of absence to join him in Isthmus City. Q ignores Bond's repeated admonitions that fieldwork is out

Above: In his largest role to date, Desmond Llewelyn's Q assists Bond 'in the field' in Isthmus City by posing as a chauffeur.

Left: The honeymoon is over for Felix Leiter and his new bride Della – Dario and his confederates are about to carry out Sanchez's plan of revenge.

Timothy Dalton with Frank McRae as Sharkey in a sequence deleted from the final cut.

of his league and even 007 comes to rely on his abilities. Q poses alternately as a chauffeur, crew member aboard a harbour patrol boat and a Mexican gardener – all as part of a successful plan to gain access to Sanchez. Naturally, he would not travel without a few necessities 'for the man on holiday' and provides Bond with any number of hi-tech gadgets. It's refreshing to see Desmond Llewelyn finally get a role that is far more than a cameo. Just as he reminds Bond that he would have been dead long ago if it had not been for Q Branch, so too would the series have suffered noticeably if it were not for the talents of this universally loved actor.

FELIX LEITER (David Hedison)
Although Hedison had not played the role of Leiter since 1973's *Live And Let Die*, bringing him back in *Licence To Kill* was an inspired idea. It's nice to see some recognition that there should be a consistency in the role – even if it took sixteen years to realize it. Although Leiter appears relatively briefly in the film, the character is the catalyst for all the events which occur. The scene in which he is mangled by

a shark and left for Bond to find with a note on him that reads 'He disagreed with something that ate him' actually appeared in the novel *Live And Let Die*. It is a highly emotional moment on-screen. It's also good to see Leiter playing an active role in the action. The only bothersome note is Felix's demeanour at the end of the film – he's a tad too happy for a fellow who lost his wife to a murderer and his leg to a shark.

SHARKEY (Frank McRae)
This likable deep-sea fisherman is a personal friend of Bond and Leiter (as well as a member of Leiter's wedding party). He proves to be a valuable ally to Bond when he pursues Sanchez as a rogue agent and doesn't hesitate to accompany 007 into life-threatening situations – which ultimately leads to his becoming the film's sacrificial lamb when he is murdered by Krest's men. The role is played with considerable understated skill by Frank McRae, so when his character is killed the audience feels sincerely moved.

DELLA LEITER (Priscilla Barnes)
The humorous, outgoing new bride of Felix Leiter, Della learns early that being a CIA agent's wife is no easy task: her fiancé is pursuing Sanchez while she waits impatiently at the church for their

AROUND THE WORLD WITH 007

Because of the escalating cost of shooting a major film in Britain, budgetary concerns convinced the producers to shoot most of the location work in **Key West, Florida** and **Mexico**. Although Eon used **Churubusco Studios** in Mexico City – the largest studio in the nation – location work was hampered by technical and logistical problems ranging from lack of resources to oppressive heat in the outlying areas. In the end, the film cost virtually as much as it would have if the studio work had been shot in England – a frustrating experience for the producers and studio.

wedding to begin. She and Felix present the best man James Bond with an inscribed cigarette lighter which later saves Bond's life. Della also alludes to Bond getting married one day and is mystified by 007's pained reaction. 'He was married once . . . but that was long ago', explains Felix in a nice, understated allusion to Tracy Bond. Della's death at the hands of Dario is depicted offscreen – a tribute to the film-makers who resisted sensationalizing the scene.

M (Robert Brown)

Fittingly, Robert Brown's last appearance as M is his most effective. The sequence in which he orders Bond to resign because he refuses to stop his pursuit of Sanchez has some of the tension of the Sean Connery/Bernard Lee sequences. Although the scene is rather implausible when examined in detail. Why are intelligence agencies using a major tourist attraction – the Hemingway House in Florida – as a base of operations? Why would M post conspicuous guards with machine guns in full view of the public when there are no dangerous criminals anywhere in the vicinity? Nevertheless, the terseness of M towards his top field operative is refreshing and Brown delivers his best performance in his swan song as 007's crusty superior.

MISS MONEYPENNY (Caroline Bliss)

Again, the Moneypenny character is basically superficial and Caroline Bliss – in her second and last appearance in the role – never gets a chance to demonstrate whether she could have excelled in the part Lois Maxwell defined for so long. Here, Moneypenny is relegated to a brief sequence in which she expresses her concern to M about Bond's wellbeing after his dismissal from the service.

KWANG (Cary-Hiroyuki Tagawa)

This sophisticated agent of the Hong Kong narcotics agency successfully infiltrates Sanchez's operation by posing as a drug baron. After years of work, Kwang's plans are disrupted when Bond makes an ill-advised attempt on Sanchez's life. Kwang prevents the assassination and chastises 007 for being a loose cannon. However, moments later they are attacked by Sanchez and his men. Kwang commits suicide rather than be captured. Ironically, Bond is credited as being the man who exposed Kwang to Sanchez and is automatically allowed access to Sanchez's drug processing operation.

VEHICLES

KENWORTH TANKER LORRIES Sanchez uses these vehicles to transport illegal drugs in liquid form as part of petrol shipments. When the deliveries have reached their final destinations, Sanchez provides a process to separate the drugs from the petrol and solidify them for resale. The film's climactic chase sequence finds Bond driving a tanker in pursuit of Sanchez, while ducking Stinger missiles and gunfire. The stuntwork in these scenes is truly impressive, as Bond actually drives a tanker on two wheels. The scene culminates with Bond and Sanchez battling fiercely to the death atop one of the tankers – another well-staged sequence that generates a good deal of suspense.

Bond pursues Sanchez in the spectacularly filmed climactic tanker chase.

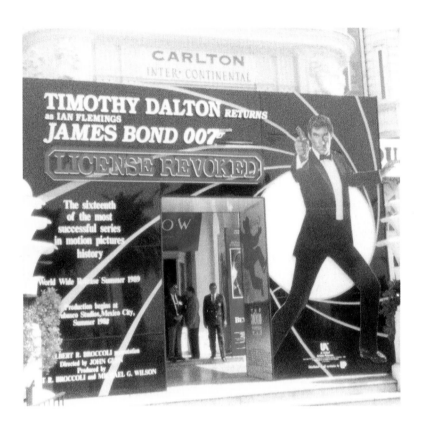

This advance advertisement on the Carlton Hotel in Cannes featured the film's original title.

THE *WAVEKREST* Ostensibly Milton Krest's marine research vessel, the *WaveKrest* is actually a floating drug emporium. From this ship, Krest transacts the sale of illicit narcotics, using a fleet of hi-tech underwater vessels.

GADGETS & WEAPONS

DENTONITE TOOTHPASTE Given to Bond by Q, this ordinary-looking tube of toothpaste is actually the latest in plastic explosives. When used in conjunction with a cigarette packet which acts as a detonator, the combination is deadly. Bond uses both in his ill-fated attempt to kill Sanchez.

EXPLODING ALARM CLOCK As Q points out, this is the only clock guaranteed not to wake up the user. It is an amusing gadget but is not used by Bond in the course of his mission.

LASER CAMERA Pam Bouvier accidentally tries to take Bond's and Q's photograph with this instant camera – and almost succeeds in frying them. The camera actually shoots a red-hot laser beam which destroys anything in its path. As a bonus, the camera also takes X-rays.

TOP SECRET CAST & CREW DOSSIERS

✻ **Pedro Armendariz**, who portrays the corrupt President Lopez, is the son of **Pedro Armendariz** who played the immortal Kerim Bey in *From Russia With Love*.

✻ Stunt supervisor **Paul Weston** had the unenviable job of doubling for Robert Davi for the scene in which Sanchez is engulfed in flames. This required a stunt man's worst nightmare: a full body burn. He emerged unscathed from the tremendous heat, and still maintains that his scariest stunt was the fight on top of a train in *Octopussy*, during which a miscue almost caused him to be decapitated.

SIGNATURE GUN Designed to look like a Hasselblad camera, this actually assembles into a high-velocity rifle which fires .220 calibre bullets. It has an optical palm reader which excludes anyone but the registered owner from using the weapon.

RAPPELLING CUMMERBUND Bond's cummerbund has a purpose beyond vanity: it allows him to rappel down the front of Sanchez's hotel/headquarters to spy on his high-level meeting with other drug barons. (It is not explained, however, how Bond achieves this on the façade in full view of a street teeming with people.)

MANTA RAY COVER Bond wears this unique outfit to swim undetected past the underwater video cameras of the *WaveKrest*. Although seen by Krest's men, he is dismissed as a giant manta ray, which is actually plausible although it sounds unlikely.

RAKE RADIO TRANSMITTER One of the most amusing jokes in *Licence To Kill* finds Q in disguise as a gardener with a rake which contains a hidden two-way radio in the handle. After he reports Bond's whereabouts to Pam, Q – who routinely chastises 007 for his ill-treatment of gadgets – casually tosses the device away. Desmond Llewelyn improvised the sequence, which always gets a chuckle from avid fans.

MUSIC

Michael Kamen provides the very efficient, if unremarkable, score this time. The title song by Gladys Knight harks back to the days when Bond films never used rock bands for music. The song seems rather uninspired at first but with repeated listening it seems to improve. Much more impressive is the song heard over the end credits – 'If You Asked Me To', sung by Patti Labelle. Although ending Bond films with love songs is a questionable practice, this time it works quite well. Ironically, the song became a much bigger hit several years later when Celine Dion released her version.

MARKETING & MERCHANDISING

Trouble began brewing with the marketing campaign for *Licence To Kill* long before its release. The first problem was the film's original title:

License Revoked, which was changed when it was discovered that US audiences associated the term with losing a driving licence! Even the revised title was controversial, as licence is spelled 'license' in the USA. After much debate, it was decided to go with queen and country and the British spelling prevailed.

Cubby Broccoli had authorized the creation of a series of unique teaser posters, some drawn by world-famous artist Bob Peak. Much to his chagrin, the studio bypassed these in favour of a teaser which bore a very close resemblance to the one employed for *The Living Daylights*. The usual release poster was even less inspired. It depicted Bond clad in black shirt and trousers as though this were *Die Hard*. The result was offputting to Bond's most loyal audience. In Europe, a different poster design was almost as uninspired – Bond running amidst a pastiche of awkwardly placed characters from the film.

On the merchandising front, however, things were a bit more exciting. John Gardner adapted the screenplay into novel form. The children's market was exploited with *The James Bond Fact File*, a British book designed for younger fans. *The Making of Licence To Kill* book was a highly informative look at the day-to-day production. Both *The Official James Bond Movie Book* and *The Official James Bond Poster Book* were released in updated editions. Another book, *The James Bond Girls*, was a photographic tribute to 007's onscreen lovers. Domark released the *Licence To Kill* computer game and the film spawned a British souvenir brochure and a comic book adaptation. A special vehicle set was designed by Matchbox and sold exclusively in British Woolworths stores and a well-designed board game was sold in France. In the USA, Martini and Rossi sponsored 007 parties at nightclubs with giveaways including Martini glasses with the film's logo.

THE BOX OFFICE

Released in competition with such heavyweight summer fare as *Batman*, *Lethal Weapon 2* and *Indiana Jones and the Last Crusade*, the US box office for *Licence To Kill* fell considerably from the previous film to $35 million – the lowest grossing 007 film in this market since *The Man With The Golden Gun*. Internationally, however, the film proved more durable, grossing a worldwide total of $156 million, down $35 million from *The Living Daylights* but still marginally ahead of

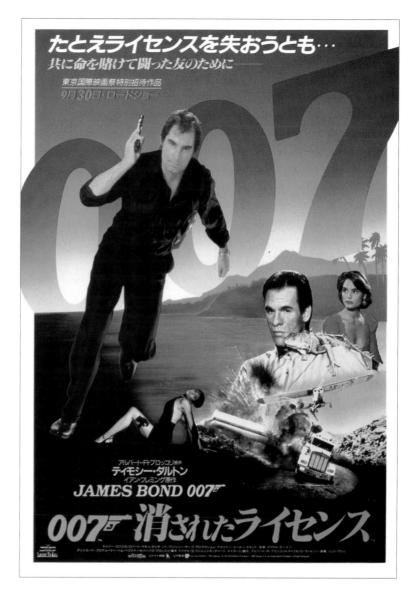

A View To A Kill. Cynics quickly proclaimed the Bond series to be out of touch with audiences and out of steam, ignoring the fact that *Licence to Kill* was still a very sizable hit. ∎

Above: The advertising campaign emphasized the more casual look of Dalton's Bond, as illustrated in this poster.

Left: Diecast vehicles from the *Licence To Kill* toy gift set.

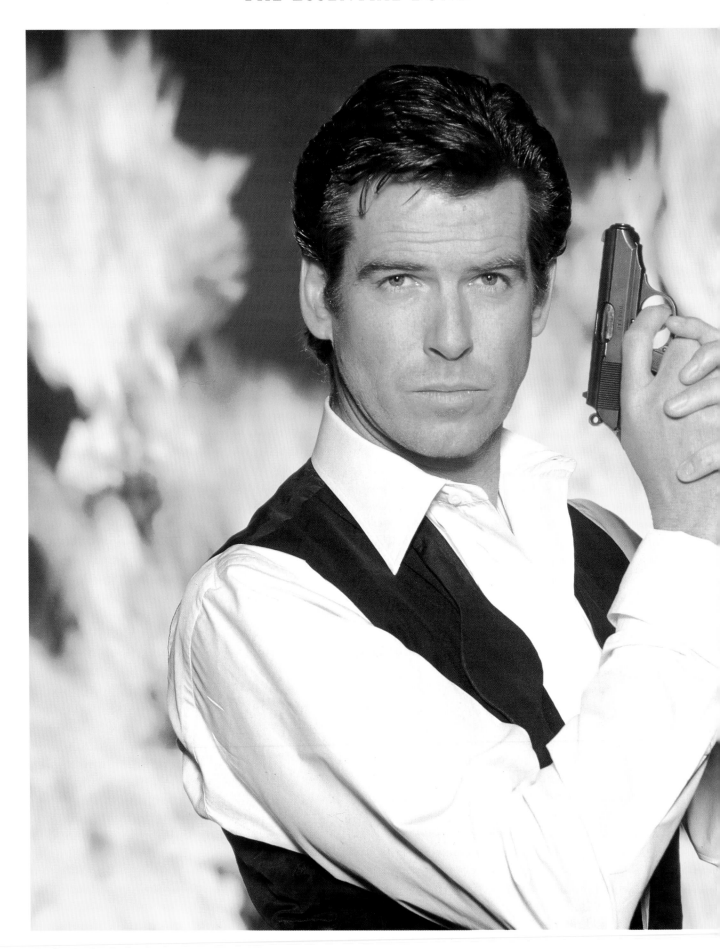

GOLDENEYE

(1995)

Presented by **ALBERT R BROCCOLI** Director **MARTIN CAMPBELL** Producers **MICHAEL G WILSON**
& BARBARA BROCCOLI Screenplay **JEFFREY CAINE & BRUCE FEIRSTEIN**
Story **MICHAEL FRANCE** Director of Photography **PHIL MEHEUX**
Production Designer **PETER LAMONT** Editor **TERRY RAWLINGS** Music **ERIC SERRA**
Release date: UK 21 November 1995, USA 13 November 1995. Running time: 130 minutes

BY LATE 1992, THE LENGTHY LITIGATION THAT HAD
prevented a new James Bond film from going into production had
been resolved between Eon Productions and MGM/UA, which was
now under a new management team. The two companies formed
an aggressive strategy to return Agent 007 to the big screen.
However, the task was not easy. Not the least of considerations was
that in the years following *Licence To Kill* the Soviet empire had
crumbled and the Cold War had come to an end. Conventional
wisdom in the film industry was that it would be futile to attempt
a comeback for James Bond. He was best left as an icon of the past.

Yet, Cubby Broccoli was determined to bring Bond back in a big
way. Although Cubby had passed the torch of day-to-day film production to Barbara Broccoli and Michael G Wilson, he was still very
active in the important decisions made during this period. He had
hired writer Michael France to write and research the story that
would become known as *GoldenEye*. However, a potential crisis
loomed: Timothy Dalton resigned from the role of 007. Despite
rumours to the contrary, the Broccolis had never interviewed any
other actors for the role and Dalton's amicable departure caused a
casting dilemma.

Proof that patience is a virtue came with the selection of Pierce
Brosnan for the new 007. Brosnan, still smarting from his heart-
breaking loss of the role in 1986, was enormously pleased when he
was informed in June 1994 that the part was his. The choice of
Brosnan – a popular one with the public – was inspired as he
represented a complete revitalization of the 007 franchise. A major

press conference was called in London and Brosnan won over the media with his low-key demeanour and self-deprecating sense of humour. Privately, he later admitted, he was extremely nervous about the pressure he would be carrying. Not only was his career on the line as a leading man, but the financial stability of an entire studio rested on his ability to establish himself as a relevant action hero for the 1990s.

The next problem occurred when Pinewood Studios proved unavailable for filming – ironically because it had been taken over by the Sean Connery film *First Knight*. Michael G Wilson and Barbara Broccoli made the dramatic decision to build an entirely new studio at Leavesden, an airfield twenty miles outside London. An abandoned Rolls-Royce factory there could be converted into gigantic sound stages. It fell to production designer Peter Lamont, executive producer Tom Pevsner, associate producer Tony Waye and their crews to construct a state-of-the-art facility in six weeks – a remarkable achievement. Martin Campbell was signed to direct the $50 million film. Immediately prior to production, Eon invited the world media to a spectacular press conference at the new studio, where the entire cast was formally introduced.

Box-office results for *GoldenEye* made true believers out of even the most hardened cynics, with record-breaking grosses posted internation-ally. While *GoldenEye* succeeds in updating 007 for a new millennium, it also boldly retains the classic elements of the series: exotic locations, glamorous wardrobes, women with suggestive names and hi-tech gadgetry. The chief asset of the film is clearly Pierce Brosnan, who in the years since 1986 matured both physically and as an actor. In retrospect, the best thing that could have happened to him was not getting the part in 1986 – he is far more suitable as Bond today, a fact he now willingly acknowledges. Brosnan has a very commanding screen presence and a unique ability to deliver a witticism. Indeed, it can be said that for the first time since the Sean Connery era, it would be difficult to imagine any other contemporary star in the role. Brosnan was fortunate to have an excellent supporting cast chosen on the basis of their abilities, not box-office clout.

GoldenEye is not a perfect film. The script (which eventually had contributions from numerous writers) is often erratic, with individual scenes more engrossing than the main scheme, and the musical score by Eric Serra often works against, rather than enhances, major sequences. Still, the return of James Bond was welcome news for a world which had almost forgotten that an action hero could have style and grace. Even after thirty-five years, nobody did it better than 007.

Below: Due to the unavailability of stage space at Pinewood Studios, Eon Productions created an entirely new and massive studio at an abandoned aircraft factory in Leavesden, England. Production designer Peter Lamont supervised the mammoth undertaking.

Previous spread: Pierce Brosnan set the screen on fire as the new 007.

THE ASSIGNMENT

James Bond and his colleague and close friend Alec Trevelyan (Agent 006) are assigned to destroy a Soviet nerve gas factory during the Cold War. The mission goes awry and Trevelyan is executed by Soviet General Ourumov.

Nine years later, M informs Bond that a secret Russian weapons system called GoldenEye has been stolen, so may be in criminal hands and could cause massive destruction. Bond discovers the weapon may be in the possession of Janus, a mysterious, unseen organized-crime chief operating in the new Russia. Bond is shocked to learn that Janus is actually Trevelyan, who is plotting with Ourumov to financially cripple London electronically then cover up the crime by firing the GoldenEye over the city. Bond – with the help of former Russian computer programmer Natalya Simonova – penetrates Trevelyan's secret lair in Cuba and, in a fierce battle to the death, destroys his former colleague and thwarts his plan to use the GoldenEye for purposes of mass destruction.

007'S WOMEN

NATALYA SIMONOVA
(Izabella Scorupco)
This Russian computer programmer is assigned to the Severnaya weapons facility in Siberia. When Natalya witnesses the destruction of the facility and the theft of the GoldenEye by General Ourumov, she is marked for death. She is a heroine for the 1990s: independent, courageous and cynical and she is played very capably by Izabella Scorupco.

One minor complaint: it is a pity that this very beautiful woman is so drably attired throughout the film. Surely there could have been a scenario introduced in which she would wear a more flattering wardrobe.

XENIA ONATOPP (Famke Janssen)
Refreshingly flying in the face of political correctness, the character of Xenia Onatopp harkens back to the glory days of Bond villainesses. Larger than life and played with enormous zeal by Famke Janssen, Xenia stands out in every respect. A ravishing beauty, she combines her love of kinky, S&M sex with her penchant for murder. Her preferred method of assassination is strangling her lover to death with her thighs. A former Soviet fighter pilot, it falls to her to hijack a hi-tech Tiger helicopter from the French Navy. The scenes

between Xenia and Bond are very well written and feature the type of *double entrendres* that were so much a part of the Connery era. Xenia dresses exotically and has an unusual penchant for cigars – which she smokes in a most suggestive manner.

CAROLINE (Serena Gordon)
An attractive, conservative MI6 agent, Caroline is sent into the field by M to evaluate 007's performance in the south of France. The character exists primarily for panicky reaction shots when she is an unwilling participant in Bond's car chase with Xenia (after which, she is willingly seduced in the Aston Martin DB5). The idea that an agent who has saved the world from destruction so many times would be submitted to being evaluated by a junior bureaucrat is difficult to believe.

007'S VILLAINS

ALEC TREVELYAN (Sean Bean)
Trevelyan is one of the more complex Bond villains, well played in understated fashion by Sean Bean. The unusual twist is making the bad guy a former friend and colleague of Bond. The situation allows for some excellent dialogue, as Bond is constantly berated as being a trusting, naïve fool by his calculating former ally. The

All things come to those who wait: Pierce Brosnan celebrates the announcement of his being cast as 007 with producers Barbara Broccoli and Michael G Wilson.

AROUND THE WORLD WITH 007

In the Bond tradition, locations for *GoldenEye* were extensive and exotic. Most impressive were the locations in **Monte Carlo**, where Bond becomes embroiled in intrigue at the casino and in the port area. The car chase between the Aston Martin and Xenia's Ferrari was filmed on the mountain roads in the south of France. **Russian** locations were confined to second unit work, and were later seamlessly edited into sequences shot at the St Petersburg set built at **Leavesden Studios** in England. For the scenes in Cuba and on the unnamed Caribbean island where Bond romances Natalya, **Puerto Rico** proved to be a suitable locale. The miraculous bungee jump in the pre-credits sequence was shot at a dam in **Locarno**, Switzerland.

trate an elaborate scheme to steal the GoldenEye for their own personal enrichment. Ourumov is a respected and powerful figure in the post-Communist regime and is not suspected of having personally annihilated the staff of the Severnaya weapons centre. For James Bond, he represents a target for revenge, because it is Ourumov whom he witnessed 'executing' Trevelyan during their ill-fated mission to blow up a Soviet nerve gas factory years before. Bond is later astonished to find the two men are actually allies. Ourumov is ultimately killed by Bond in a gunfight aboard Trevelyan's train. The role is very effectively played by Gottfried John, an actor whose intense physical appearance is perfectly suited to the character of Ourumov.

BORIS GRISHENKO (Alan Cumming)

This nerdy computer genius had formed a close friendship with Natalya during their tenure at the Severnaya weapons centre. In fact, Boris is on Trevelyan's payroll and lures Natalya into a death-trap in the aftermath of the Severnaya massacre. Boris has a superiority complex and prides himself on being able to manipulate Trevelyan's massive

Above: Izabella Scorupco as Natalya Simonova. Polish-born, she was a popular actress and singer in Sweden when she was cast in the film.

Right: Famke Janssen as the *femme fatale* Xenia Onatopp, one of the most impressive villainesses of the series.

character of Trevelyan is a strong one and Bean's interaction with Pierce Brosnan provides the film's best moments. (Their meeting in a grave-yard of statues depicting former Soviet icons is genuinely eerie.) Their fight to the death during the climax is one of the best-staged action sequences in recent memory. A minor irritation in the plot is that Trevelyan's motivation for treason is quite shallow. The audience is expected to accept that he has committed treason simply to avenge his late parents' suicide (they were Lienz Cossacks) which was caused by their mistreatment at the hands of the British after the Second World War. Bean is far too young to have been so affected by such political events and it would have been more credible simply to make greed his only motivation for plotting his heinous crime.

GENERAL OURUMOV (Gottfried John)

This traitorous Soviet general sides with Alec Trevelyan at the end of the Cold War to orches-

computer systems to ensure the success of his scheme. Ultimately, it is his ego that leads him to his death. Boris is the weakest character in the film and, despite his considerable screen time, is largely superfluous to the main story. Scottish actor Alan Cumming does a credible job of mastering a Russian accent but the performance – like the character – is too out of sync with the rest of the cast. The death of Boris – frozen solid in a wave of liquid nitrogen – is one of the more ludicrous demises for any Bond villain.

007'S ALLIES

JACK WADE (Joe Don Baker)
A coarse, crude but likable CIA agent assigned to St Petersburg, Russia, where he acts as Bond's contact, Wade is diametrically opposed to 007 in every imaginable way. He dresses like Oscar Madison of *The Odd Couple*, speaks in offensive tones and is content to drive a beaten-up Soviet car. The character of Wade is far more suitable for actor Joe Don Baker's talents than that of the villainous Whitaker, whom he played in *The Living Daylights*. Wade could wear out his welcome with the audience very quickly but the writers wisely limit his screen time and make his brief appearances rather refreshing.

VALENTIN ZUKOVSKY
(Robbie Coltrane)
Zukovsky is the head of the Russian Mafia in St Petersburg and a former enemy of Bond. In an excellently written sequence, Bond asks his help in locating Janus and Zukovsky is not shy about reminding him that he still limps from a gunshot wound inflicted by 007. Nevertheless, the men form an awkward alliance – Bond motivated by Zukovsky's information and Zukovsky motivated by greed. Zukovsky is a potentially fascinating character as played by the charismatic Robbie Coltrane. The only mystery is why he is limited to such little screen time.

DIMITRI MISHKIN (Tcheky Karyo)
Mishkin, the Russian defence minister, initially threatens to execute 007 for the theft of the GoldenEye. When Mishkin learns that Ourumov is the culprit, he is shot dead by the general.

M (Judi Dench)
The announcement that Bond's new superior would be played by a woman made fans sceptical that the decision was merely a nod to political

correctness. After all, how could Bond – the great seducer of otherwise strong-willed women – take orders from a member of the fair sex? With her first scene in *GoldenEye*, Judi Dench quieted the cynics with a dynamic, no-nonsense approach to the role. There is real tension between her and Bond, especially in the superb sequence in which he admits he regards her as a number-crunching bureaucrat, while she responds that he is a 'sexist, misogynist dinosaur – a relic of the Cold War'. In recent years, the Bond/M sequences had become pale shadows of those wonderful scenes with Bernard Lee from the early films. With Dench in the role, the relationship takes on a whole new mystique. There is still mutual respect between the two but it is understated and therefore all the more meaningful.

MISS MONEYPENNY
(Samantha Bond)
As the latest incarnation of Miss Moneypenny, Samantha Bond portrays her as a liberated woman of the 1990s. She enjoys boasting to 007 about her

Sean Bean as the traitorous Agent 006 – one-time best friend of James Bond.

TOP SECRET CAST & CREW DOSSIERS

❊ During production, **Roger Moore** visited the set at Leavesden. He quipped that early tests of Brosnan were not impressive, so the producers had called him back to the role.

❊ While in London to promote the film, **Desmond Llewelyn** was lured into a surprise segment of *This is Your Life* in which he was honoured by old friends and Bond colleagues.

❊ Credit for the spectacular bungee jump goes to stunt co-ordinator **Simon Crane** and stunt man **Wayne Michaels**. Michaels made a mind-boggling 640-foot plunge, accelerating to 100 miles per hour. To prevent him from being slammed into the wall of the dam, the bungee cord was attached to a crane to allow him maximum clearance.

various dates and takes delight in playing somewhat hard to get. The good-natured secondary action is reminiscent of the early Connery/Maxwell days. This Moneypenny still has eyes for 007, but it is obvious she is quite content with their evidently platonic relationship.

Q (Desmond Llewelyn)
Despite the new faces at MI6, the producers wisely retained Desmond Llewelyn as Q – a character so beloved it will probably be more difficult to replace him than Bond. Llewelyn seems to relish having the opportunity to chastise his fifth 007 actor and Brosnan appears honoured to be the recipient of his barbs. Q gives Bond the prerequisite tour of his workshop and introduces him to the BMW Z3 Roadster. He also obtains the biggest laugh in the film when he dramatically grabs what is presumably a gadget disguised as a sandwich from Bond's hands. 'Don't touch that!' he shouts. 'It's my lunch.'

BILL TANNER (Michael Kitchen)
In Fleming's novels the character of Tanner was M's chief of staff and enjoyed a close friendship with 007. His only screen appearance prior to *GoldenEye* was in *For Your Eyes Only*, in which James Villiers was cast in the role as an older, strict authoritarian figure. Tanner appears in yet another guise in this film. Played by Michael Kitchen, he discusses the crisis involving the Russian Severnaya facility with Bond and M. When the latter overhears Tanner refer to her as 'the evil queen of hearts', he is given an embarrassing – and amusing – dressing-down by his boss.

VEHICLES

BMW Z3 ROADSTER This sleek, stylish 1996 convertible sports car was introduced in the film months before it became available to the general public (although advance orders on a limited edition '007' model sold out in one day). Q describes the elaborate gadgets on the car (the ejector seat, parachute braking system, Stinger missiles and radar system) but disappointingly none of them is employed during the course of the film. (This is an obvious concession to budgetary concerns.) In fact, the BMW is barely used at all. It is seen briefly in a sequence in which Bond drives it to a meeting with Jack Wade on a Caribbean island. Nevertheless, the car was promoted with a gigantic cross-promotional campaign and the high number of vehicles sold due to the link with *GoldenEye* became the talk of the marketing world.

ASTON MARTIN DB5 In a welcome return to the series, Bond once again drives his classic 1964 Aston Martin DB5 – although this time few gadgets are in evidence. The car is seen in the wild chase sequence between Bond and Xenia, and 007 later drives it to the casino in Monte Carlo. Brosnan looks very much at home behind the wheel and undoubtedly he is enjoying riding in the same type of car that Sean Connery drove in the first Bond film Brosnan ever saw, *Goldfinger*. A few modest gadgets are used by Bond. There is a fax machine in the dashboard and also a cellular voice communication system. A special feature designed for seducing willing women is a refrigerated drinks compartment containing a rose and a chilled bottle of Bollinger champagne.

TIGER HELICOPTER This state-of-the-art, heavily armed prototype helicopter is designed for use by NATO and about to be demonstrated by the French navy when it is hijacked by Xenia

Moneypenny III – Samantha Bond as the more liberated secretary to M.

Bond's BMW Z3 Roadster premiered in the film long before it was available to an eagerly awaiting public.

Onatopp. The Tiger is used by Xenia and Ourumov in their theft of the GoldenEye from Severnaya. To cover up their crime, the pair activate the GoldenEye weapons system, effectively destroying the entire facility. They escape in the Tiger, which is immune to electronic impulse damage. Later, Trevelyan attempts to get rid of the Tiger – as well as Bond and Natalya – by strapping them into the helicopter and activating heat-seeking missiles which will return to destroy them. However, Bond manages to activate the ejector seat, thus ensuring that he and Natalya escape the blast.

XENIA'S 1995 FERRARI 355 A flashy
red convertible sports car, this Ferrari is driven by Xenia Onatopp in her chase with Bond's Aston Martin DB5 on mountainous roads in the south of France. After wreaking havoc on innocent bystanders, 007 outmanoeuvres the Ferrari, causing it to go into a tailspin.

RUSSIAN TANK For the spectacular chase
scene through the streets of St Petersburg, three actual Soviet tanks were used. Originally, the scene was to be shot on location in Russia. However, producer Barbara Broccoli was concerned about restrictive and incalculable financial demands from local officials, so production designer Peter Lamont built a replica of the city's streets at Leavesden Studios that was accurate down to the last detail. It is virtually impossible to distinguish the second unit footage shot in the real St Petersburg from the St Petersburg set he created. The sequence is technically amazing and

fun to watch but does little to advance the plot until Bond uses the tank to blow up Trevelyan's train.

CAGIVA MOTORCYCLE Bond 'confis-
cates' this motorcycle from a Soviet soldier during the film's extremely exciting pre-credits sequence in which 007 drives it off a cliff then skydives into a plunging plane.

TREVELYAN'S TRAIN The criminal mas-
termind owns a discarded ICBM carrier once used by the Soviet Army and converts it into his

The Aston Martin DB5 (seen here on location in the south of France) was brought out of retirement for the chase sequence with Xenia's Ferrari.

Trevelyan's ominous-looking train was an adapted British diesel engine. Built at Leavesden Studios, the engine was transported by road to the Peterborough location some 100 miles away.

employ the system to destroy the Severnaya control station and abscond with the disc. Trevelyan intends to wreak havoc with the GoldenEye and reduce London to 'the Stone Age'. Ultimately, the GoldenEye is destroyed by Bond and Natalya, who reconfigure Trevelyan's computer system in a highly entertaining finale.

PARKER PEN Q gives this deadly implement, which contains a class four grenade, to Bond and it saves the day at the end of the mission. Bond arms it by clicking the pen three times in rapid succession and disarms it by clicking it three more times. When Boris toys with the pen, Bond loses track of whether it is armed or unarmed in a sequence that is full of suspense.

RAPPELLING BELT An ordinary-looking leather belt, this converts into a rappelling device with seventy-five feet of steel-reinforced cord designed to hold Bond's body weight. It also has an explosive piton in the buckle.

CODE-CRACKING DEVICE This electronic keypad adheres to a lock and automatically calculates all possible combinations in a matter of seconds. It is used by Bond to gain access to the Archangel Soviet nerve gas facility.

mobile lair. He fits the train out with such unique options as armour plating, closed-circuit television and a removable roof that conceals a heliport for his personal helicopter. The foreboding look of the coal-black train is reinforced by the bizarre design of the engine.

GADGETS & WEAPONS

GOLDENEYE This is the top-secret Russian weapons system. The GoldenEye is actually a disc which generates access codes to two satellites which then convert into offensive weapons. The satellites set off an electromagnetic pulse over a specified area and cause any object that works on an electrical circuit to fail. Ourumov and Xenia

PITON LASER GUN In the pre-credits sequence, Bond makes a spectacular bungee jump from the top of a dam. As he falls, he uses this gun to fire a piton and rope into the rock below, thus allowing him to be lowered to the ground. The gun also serves as a laser cutter to allow 007 entry through a hatch. The bungee jump, accomplished by stunt man Wayne Michaels at a dam in Locarno, Switzerland, set a world record of 640 feet. The extremely dangerous stunt (Michaels could easily have been slammed into the concrete wall) is beautifully shot and makes one of the most breathtaking sequences ever to appear in a Bond film.

OMEGA SEAMASTER LASER WATCH This professional diver's watch features a laser beam which helps Bond to escape a deathtrap when locked in Trevelyan's train.

Q'S GADGETS Among the novel items found in Q's workshop are a phone box with a concealed air bag which virtually suffocates the victim, an X-ray document scanner disguised as a tray and, most amusingly, Q's leg cast, which fools even Bond into thinking he is recuperating from an

Producer Michael G Wilson oversees the hectic shooting schedule.

accident. From his wheelchair, however, Q activates a device which fires a missile from within the cast, making an explosive introduction for Desmond Llewelyn.

MUSIC

The attempt to have composer Eric Serra provide an avant-garde score for *GoldenEye* had unsatisfactory results. His experimental themes are largely out of place in a Bond movie. Reaction to his score was universally negative among critics and fans. Even those themes that are more mainstream and pleasant are used in the wrong sequences. For example, Serra provides a distracting romantic theme which undermines the witty banter during the sequence in which Bond encounters Xenia at the casino. Even more misguided is his choice of a song to end the film, 'The Experience of Love', a bland and forgettable tune warbled by Serra himself. It ends an otherwise exciting film on a very downbeat note. Much more successful is the film's title song written by Bono and The Edge and superbly performed by Tina Turner. However, as the writers did not collaborate on the score, the song is not evident again in the course of the film.

MARKETING & MERCHANDISING

'You know the name. You know the number' read the inspired tag line on the teaser poster, which featured a striking photograph of Pierce Brosnan in a typical Bond pose. In case anyone did need an introduction, a superbly edited teaser trailer was shown in cinemas in the summer of 1994. Reaction to it was so strong that the media carried news stories that audiences were loudly cheering the return of 007. In New York City, a gala premiere was held at Radio City Music Hall to a sell-out crowd of 6,000, followed by a party for cast and crew at the Museum of Modern Art. In London, the social event of the season was the royal premiere and a black-tie party held at the Imperial War Museum, which was decorated with the Soviet icons from the film. 'Red

This rare publicity photograph shows that the Bond of the 1990s had returned with the traditional emphasis on style.

Army guards' stood watch outside, and inside Russian folk bands and a full orchestra entertained an eclectic gathering of show business celebrities ranging from Bono to Martin Scorsese.

On UK television Jonathan Ross hosted an excellent, light-hearted documentary entitled *In Search of James Bond* while in the USA Elizabeth Hurley did the same with *The World of 007*. BMW launched a massive marketing tie-in with the Z3 Roadster, starting with a press conference at Central Park in New York City with Pierce Brosnan, Desmond Llewelyn and Izabella Scorupco. Later, journalists were wined and dined at the famous Rainbow Room then driven in their own Z3 to the premiere at Radio City. The company even issued intricately detailed 1:18 scale commemoratives of the car and demand was so high that they were made available commercially.

There were many notable merchandising and publishing tie-ins. John Gardner adapted the screenplay into a novel. *The Making of GoldenEye* was published in the UK. An updated edition of *The Incredible World of 007* was available in the USA, Britain and Japan. Seemingly every country had either a souvenir brochure or a commemorative magazine. In Germany, *Playboy* devoted an entire issue to Agent 007 and saw it become an instant collectors' item selling for up to £50. Corgi produced a replica of Bond's Aston Martin DB5 in *GoldenEye* packaging, along with Xenia's Ferrari. Sohni-Wicke made a toy Walther PPK and accompanying accessories for the boys' market. Other collectables included *GoldenEye* trading cards, a resin statue of Pierce Brosnan and commemorative watches and crew jackets.

THE BOX OFFICE

GoldenEye proved to be a box-office powerhouse which defied the conventional wisdom that big-budget action films suffer if released in the winter. The film smashed box-office records internationally and went on to gross a staggering $351 million worldwide, making this by far the biggest Bond film of all in terms of generating revenue (although *Thunderball* still stands as the record holder in terms of the number of paid admissions). ∎

TOMORROW NEVER DIES

(1997)

Director **ROGER SPOTTISWOODE** Producers **MICHAEL G WILSON & BARBARA BROCCOLI**
Screenplay **BRUCE FEIRSTEIN** Director of Photography **ROBERT ELSWIT** Editors **DOMINIQUE FORTIN &
MICHEL ARCAND** Production Designer **ALLAN CAMERON** Music **DAVID ARNOLD**
Release date: UK 9 Decemer 1997, USA 19 December 1997. Running time: 123 minutes

Bemfore *GOLDENEYE* HAD EVEN BEEN RELEASED,
MGM/UA began preparations for the next Bond epic, *Tomorrow
Never Dies*, with the firm intention to premiere the film by early
December 1997. The deadline left producers Michael G Wilson and
Barbara Broccoli with the shortest period ever for pre-production
work on a Bond film. Indeed, for many months it seemed as though
bad luck was the order of the day. For example, the Leavesden
Studios, which Eon built for *GoldenEye*, were not available due to
pre-production work on the *Star Wars* prequels and Pinewood
Studios could not allocate enough space to accommodate the entire
production. Consequently Eon had to build yet another studio from
scratch. The producers settled on an abandoned grocery warehouse
in Hertfordshire in England, and line producer Anthony Waye and
production designer Allan Cameron set about converting this into
the state-of-the-art Eon Studios. Other key scenes would be shot
at Pinewood, thirty miles away, creating a logistical nightmare for
the producers.

The wide-ranging location work on the film hit a potentially
devastating snag at the last minute when the government of
Vietnam rescinded permission to shoot extensive sequences inside
the country. Director Roger Spottiswoode and other crew members
were literally about to board planes to Vietnam when they received
the news. Incredibly, they almost instantly found suitable locations

Above: Bond averts nuclear disaster by mere seconds when he commandeers a terrorist plane.

Previous spread: Power-crazed media magnate Elliot Carver with his sadistic security chief Stamper.

in Thailand which could double for Vietnam. Constant changes to writer Bruce Feirstein's script also demanded that he stay on location in Thailand, where he found himself in the unenviable position of rapidly rewriting key sequences, staying only hours ahead of production. Then another potential catastrophe loomed when Pierce Brosnan received a rather severe cut during a fight sequence. In true Bondian style, however, the actor minimized any delays and jumped back into the fray very quickly. By the time the hectic production had been completed, the budget exceeded $100 million – a record for a Bond film but an indication of the studio's confidence in the franchise.

Tomorrow Never Dies is superior to *GoldenEye* in many respects. It continued the approach which proved so popular with the previous film: a modern, hi-tech look for the 1990s combined with traditional elements of the earlier classics including larger-than-life girls, gadgets and villains. The film looks expensive and Michael G Wilson and Barbara Broccoli successfully continued Cubby's mission to put every penny on the screen. The use of exotic locations is far more impressive than had been the case with *GoldenEye*.

There are some wonderful and memorable elements in *Tomorrow Never Dies*, among them an outstanding cast. Even the supporting characters are played by a diverse group of highly talented actors. Pierce Brosnan is even more impressive this time round and seems far more comfortable in the role of 007. He also looks better, having put on a bit of weight and obviously benefited from an intensive exercise regime. The film is beautifully photographed by Robert Elswit, with one scene standing out particularly: Bond is sitting sombrely in a chair in his hotel room awaiting the arrival of an unknown assassin. The image of Brosnan, clad in white shirt and shoulder holster, seems intentionally to recall the sequence in *Dr. No* in which Bond awaits the arrival of Professor Dent. It is little touches like these which make *Tomorrow Never Dies* a 007 aficionado's delight.

While there is real spectacle which had been lacking from the last several Bond films, *Tomorrow Never Dies* is not without a few errors. For example, the attention paid to character and detail in the first two-thirds of the story is all but lost with Bond's arrival in Vietnam. The film begins to concentrate almost solely on action sequences at the expense of the wonderful dialogue that is prevalent earlier. The motorcycle chase is spectacular, but a bit too long – as is the climactic finale, in which Bond runs about shooting machine guns in *The Terminator* mode. Nevertheless *Tomorrow Never Dies* is a classy,

007's WOMEN

WAI LIN (Michelle Yeoh)

A Red Chinese agent of The People's External Security Force, Wai Lin is assigned to investigate the activities of Elliot Carver. Circumstances lead to Wai Lin and 007 encountering each other several times during the course of their respective missions, and although Bond suggests they team up she prefers to go it alone. Ultimately, they become partners but Wai Lin remains immune to 007's seductive charm until after the mission is over. Wai Lin is very much a Bond heroine for the 1990s in that she is completely independent, fearless and perfectly capable of defending herself (she is a martial arts expert). She is played with considerable charm by Michelle Yeoh, one of the Orient's biggest box-office sensations. She performed an amazing array of stunts for the film, has a quiet, unassuming demeanour and commands the screen in the action sequences.

Left: Michelle Yeoh as the fearless Wai Lin.

Below: Brosnan and Michelle Yeoh in a promotional photograph for the BMW R1200 motorcycle.

exotic entry in the series and can proudly rank as one of the best Bond films in many years. It does, however, have the bittersweet distinction of being the first 007 epic produced since Cubby Broccoli's death in 1996. Fittingly, his name still appears in the credits and the film is 'lovingly' dedicated to his memory.

THE ASSIGNMENT

British media magnate Elliot Carver has a unique strategy to ensure the success of his new cable news network: he will secretly instigate international catastrophes with the assurance that his television and radio stations, as well as his newspaper *Tomorrow*, will be the first outlets on the scene to provide coverage. In this way, he intends to create a worldwide monopoly of the news industry. Carver's initial scheme is an audacious one. He uses his technology to bring the UK and China to the brink of nuclear war, after which his henchmen will seize control of the Chinese government. James Bond races against time, as the UK and China prepare for war. Forming a partnership with Chinese agent Wai Lin, Bond pursues Carver to his headquarters in Vietnam and meets him and his men in a spectacular and highly explosive confrontation. Bond and Wai Lin prevent nuclear war and ensure that Carver falls victim to his own technology.

Paris Carver – who re-ignites a love affair with Bond and pays with her life.

Teri Hatcher is truly an inspired choice for the limited but very important role of the tragic Paris. She looks absolutely stunning and is attired in glamorous outfits which accentuate the sensuality of her scenes with Brosnan. Their love scene, in which Bond tenderly disrobes her, is one of the most truly erotic sequences in any of the films, aided by the fact that Bond genuinely cares for this woman. His despair over discovering her body is an unusually moving moment and accentuates his compassion in a very emotional way. Paris is one of the more tragic of Bond's women because it is solely because of his actions that she is murdered.

007'S VILLAINS

ELLIOTT CARVER (Jonathan Pryce)
This world-famous, power-crazed media magnate seeks a virtual monopoly on the international news reporting industry. His slogan is 'There's no news like bad news'. Carver is cultured, intellectual and possesses a sarcastic sense of humour. He is a cold-blooded murderer who orders the assassination of his own wife when he suspects she has betrayed him. Unlike most Bond bad guys of recent years, Carver is an unabashed megalomaniac who realizes that in today's society power is not expressed merely in terms of finance but, rather, through influencing the media.

Carver is brilliantly portrayed by Jonathan Pryce, who dominates the screen in all of his scenes. They say a Bond film's strength is usually measured by the quality of its villain. The character of Elliott Carver is the best Bond antagonist since Christopher Lee's Scaramanga.

HENRY GUPTA (Ricky Jay)
An international techno-terrorist, Gupta is in charge of orchestrating the scientific aspects of Carver's plan to initiate a war between China and the UK. He has a unique ability to secure the most lethal, top-secret weapons in the world and use them for criminal purposes. Gupta meets his death when Carver shoots him.

PARIS CARVER (Teri Hatcher)
Paris is a former lover of James Bond and present-day wife of Elliot Carver. Bond rekindles their affair in the hope of getting inside information about Carver. However, Paris is on to Bond immediately and makes it clear that his habit of using women for one-night stands will preclude her from helping him. Ultimately, she relents – a decision which costs her her life as the film's sacrificial lamb.

STAMPER (Gotz Otto)
This Aryan muscleman serves as chief of security to Carver and carries out his murderous assignments with relish. Tall, blond and handsome, Stamper brings back memories of Red Grant, but only on a superficial level – the character is never fully defined or fleshed out, although Gotz Otto plays the role with consider-

Left: Stamper lets off some steam by murdering British sailors.

Below: The evil assassin Dr Kaufman is brilliantly played by Vincent Schiavelli.

able menace. The one insight given into his psyche is amusing: he describes his apprenticeship to the torturer Dr Kaufman as though he has studied with a great humanitarian.

DR KAUFMAN (Vincent Schiavelli)
One of the most amusing and memorable characters ever to appear in a Bond film, Kaufman is a world-famous assassin who confronts Bond after having murdered Paris Carver. He politely brags about his prowess as a murderer and torturer but dismisses the latter skill as merely a 'hobby'. The sequence is superbly written and Vincent Schiavelli – ordinarily an odd choice of casting for a Bond movie – is hilarious in the role. When Bond shoots him dead, we wish we had seen a bit more of him, although on an artistic level, it's better that the producers did not overextend his welcome.

007'S ALLIES

JACK WADE (Joe Don Baker)
Wade was eccentric and amusing in *GoldenEye*, but in *Tomorrow Never Dies* he is a buffoon and it is no longer believable that he could possibly be working for the CIA. Clad in a pretentiously ugly loud Hawaiian shirt and silly hat, his appearances are fortunately kept to a bare minimum – thus

Above: Dame Judi Dench reprises her role as M.

Below: Posing as an Avis car rental representative, Q greets Bond at the airport in Hamburg.

allowing the character narrowly to avoid making Sheriff Pepper look like King Lear.

M (Judi Dench)

Dench's encore performance as M is as impressive as her debut in *GoldenEye*. M argues against the British strategy of using a military strike against the Chinese. She is given forty-eight hours to get to the bottom of the crisis and she assigns Bond to

the job. Although she normally disapproves of his womanizing, ironically she orders him to seduce Paris Carver and pump her for information. There is a brief, but wonderfully written, scene in which Bond and M have a no-nonsense conversation while speeding through London in her limousine. Dench plays the role with enormous skill and makes the part her own, despite the indelible image of Bernard Lee.

MISS MONEYPENNY (Samantha Bond)

As in *GoldenEye*, Moneypenny has been reinvigorated by good writing and an appealing performance by Samantha Bond, who is perfect in the role. Although Moneypenny appears only briefly, she gets the film's biggest laugh. This occurs when she calls Bond and interrupts his erotic encounter with a gorgeous Danish professor, Inga Bergstrom. After Bond explains that he is merely 'brushing up on a little Danish', Moneypenny replies, 'You always were a cunning linguist, James.'

Q (Desmond Llewelyn)

The seemingly immortal Llewelyn makes an amusing appearance when Q turns up at the airport in Hamburg, posing as an Avis car rental employee. In a highly amusing sequence, he goes through the motions of asking Bond if he needs

various types of accident insurance. Bond takes sadistic pleasure in sarcastically reminding him that he needs maximum coverage because 'accidents do happen'. Q then takes Bond to a hangar to introduce him to the BMW 750iL's remote-control steering system. Bond takes over and brings the speeding car to a stop literally inches in front of a horrified Q.

ADMIRAL ROEBUCK (Geoffrey Palmer)
This temperamental, hard-headed commander of the UK fleet is at odds with M over what type of response to make to the Chinese threat. Roebuck's hastiness in urging a military response almost leads to disaster on two occasions: when his firing of a missile almost causes a nuclear disaster in the film's thrilling pre-credits sequence, and later when he brings the UK and China to the brink of war. When Roebuck accuses M of not having 'the balls' for her job, she responds, 'Perhaps. But the advantage is, I don't always have to think with them,' thus ensuring a huge laugh from the audience.

ROBINSON (Colin Salmon)
The MI6 staff becomes ethnically diverse with the inclusion of Robinson, a black agent who is now M's chief of staff. (Actor Michael Kitchen who played the role of Tanner in *GoldenEye* was unavailable for *Tomorrow Never Dies*.) The handsome Salmon possesses a baritone voice which commands attention and his no-nonsense approach to the role complements Judi Dench's similar style of playing M.

VEHICLES

BMW 750iL This car is a virtual arsenal on wheels and counts among its gadgets: rockets hidden in the sunroof, re-inflatable tyres, a retractable chain cutter which rises from the bonnet, bullet-proof glass and body, an electronic defence system capable of emitting a 20,000-volt shock to would-be carjackers, magnetic flash grenades, a tear-gas mechanism, a metal spike dispenser (an obvious tribute to the unused nail dispenser on the old Aston Martin DB5) and a hidden safe which slides out from the glove compartment. Most ingeniously, the car can be driven by remote control via an Ericsson cellular phone, which provides a

Even the licence plate is identical! A miniature BMW is prepared for filming.

Above: The spectacular motorcycle jump. Note the absence of helicopter blades – they were optically added in post-production.

Right: Original storyboards for the sequence.

closed-circuit monitor which allows Bond to steer from the back seat. Virtually all the aforementioned gadgets are employed in the spectacularly staged and highly entertaining chase scene in a car park. In reality, seventeen BMWs were on hand for the sequence, which was shot at Brent Cross Shopping Centre in London. Although some of the cars remained as back-ups, others had certain specific gadgets and functions.

BMW R1200 MOTORCYCLE In a complicated and action-packed chase sequence which dominates the middle of the film, Bond and Wai Lin commandeer the 1170cc motorcycle when they are pursued by cars and a helicopter through the crowded streets of Saigon. The scene climaxes with the film's most aggressive stunt when Bond (actually stunt driver Jean Pierre Goy) races the vehicle from one rooftop to another over the whirling blades of the chopper. Goy used a wooden ramp and drove the BMW at 60mph to clear the forty-four-foot drop and land on a virtual mountain of cardboard boxes. To the relief of the cast and crew, this amazing feat was accomplished in one take.

STEALTH SHIP This is the armour-plated floating HQ of Elliott Carver. The stealth ship, based on an actual naval vessel, cannot be

detected by radar. Thus Carver plays havoc with the UK and Chinese forces, launching missile attacks on both so that each side will think the other is responsible. The climax of the film takes place on the stealth ship when Bond and Wai Lin wreak havoc in an all-out battle against Carver and his henchmen. The exterior design of the ship is somewhat disappointing – it appears to be a largely indistinguishable and nondescript floating pile of steel. However, production designer Allan Cameron does a very creditable job of making the interior live up to Bondian standards with the pre-requisite hi-tech look originally introduced to the series by Ken Adam.

ASTON MARTIN DB5
Bond's traditional vehicle of choice makes a very brief, but welcome, appearance in *Tomorrow Never Dies* when he is seen driving it to M's office. No gadgets this time, however, as the BMW 750iL has so many onboard.

GADGETS & WEAPONS

ERICSSON CELLULAR PHONE
In addition to enabling Bond to call willing women, the Ericsson cellular phone boasts an amazing number of extras. It has a device that allows the operator to scan someone else's fingerprints, which Bond uses to gain access to Carver's safe. It also emits a laser beam capable of cutting through steel and the detachable antenna serves as a lock pick. Most importantly, the phone has a pad which allows Bond to operate his BMW 750iL by remote control. The phone opens to reveal a closed-circuit television monitor which lets 007 see where the car is going – even if he is not driving. A touchpad allows him to control the vehicle's direction and a warning system in the car politely alerts him to impending hazards, such as missile attacks. Additionally, the phone activates a 20,000-volt security system which can be used as a defensive weapon (as the unfortunate Dr Kaufman finds out).

WALTHER P99
Bond gets a new Walther in *Tomorrow Never Dies*, but via Wai Lin not Q. The sleek and deadly 9mm weapon has a magazine capacity of up to sixteen rounds (nine more than Bond's traditional Walther PPK 7.65).

WAI LIN'S GADGETS
Wai Lin may be an agent of a Communist government but when it comes to hi-tech gadgetry she gives the capitalist 007 a run for his money. When Bond visits her

seemingly nondescript office located in a Saigon marketplace, he is surprised to see a veritable 'Q Branch' of hidden gadgets and weaponry including: computerized maps pinpointing any location in the world, a flame-thrower disguised as a statue of a dragon, sliding walls which reveal dozens of lethal weapons neatly displayed and an Omega Seamaster wristwatch which also acts as a detonator. Earlier Wai Lin, dressed in her sleek black catsuit, uses a wrist device that fires a rope and piton, allowing her to walk vertically down walls.

GPS ENCODER
This top-secret CIA device sends navigational instructions to satellites which, in turn, transmit the orders to military ships. When Henry Gupta delivers a stolen encoder to Carver, the media mogul gains the ability to misdirect a UK warship into Chinese

This highly unusual and stylish teaser advertisement was used in the Japanese market.

Welcome back, Commander Bond. For the first time in twenty years, we see 007 in full dress uniform as a Royal Navy commander. We've seen him so attired only twice before: in *You Only Live Twice* (1967) and *The Spy Who Loved Me* (1977).

territorial waters, thus setting in motion what he hopes will be a prelude to a nuclear war between China and the UK.

MUSIC

Bond fans rejoiced upon hearing the score for *Tomorrow Never Dies*, which was composed by David Arnold. Barry was originally planning to score the film but could not come to terms with the studio. However, he gave Arnold his hearty endorsement. Arnold lived up to all expectations, providing an energetic and highly atmospheric score which is one of the best heard in recent years. He also pays homage to Barry with some themes which intentionally recall those from the early Bond films. Arnold, a long-time avowed fan of

Barry's Bond music, had simultaneously produced a very well-received 007 music tribute entitled 'Shaken and Stirred', which featured alternative rock performers' intriguing versions of classic Bond music. *Tomorrow Never Dies* also features two very strong songs: 'Tomorrow Never Dies' by Sheryl Crow and 'Surrender' by k d lang. Both are outstanding efforts, and the main title track received a Golden Globe nomination. Either song – along with Arnold's score – should, in many people's view, have been nominated for an Oscar.

MARKETING & MERCHANDISING

Tomorrow Never Dies was so heavily promoted through marketing tie-ins that many critics joked James Bond had acquired a 'Licence to Sell'. In fact, die-hard fans seemed to love the fact that 007 was virtually everywhere, as radio, television and print advertisements extolled the new film with promotional tie-ins to BMW, Ericsson phones, Bollinger champagne, Omega watches, Brioni clothing, Avis rental cars, Golden Wonder potato crisps and many other manufacturers. Visa hired Pierce Brosnan and Desmond Llewelyn to appear in character in a big-budget, hi-tech commercial

were devoted almost solely to the 007 phenomenon and featured a stunning pictorial of actress Daphne Deckers, who appears as Carver's spokeswoman in the film. Author Raymond Benson wrote a novel of the screenplay and there was the excellent and highly candid *The Making of Tomorrow Never Dies* from Boxtree. Souvenir magazines were released in the USA, Japan and Britain. Ironically, one of the biggest marketing successes connected to 007 was for the previous film. The *GoldenEye* Nintendo 64 became the toy sensation of the year, as supplies quickly sold out internationally before Christmas and could not be replenished until the new year. As usual, the London premiere (this time benefiting the King George's Fund for Sailors) was the social event of the season. The cast, producers and director appeared onstage at the Odeon Theatre to welcome the black-tie crowd. After the film, a virtual city was erected under large tents in central London where party guests danced to live orchestras and gourmet food was served.

THE BOX OFFICE

Even after the film-makers breathed a sigh of relief that their incredible efforts had ensured that *Tomorrow Never Dies* would be ready in time for its projected Christmas release, another crisis loomed. Director James Cameron's highly anticipated *Titanic* – delayed from its summer premiere date – would open in the USA on the same day as *Tomorrow Never Dies*. In international markets, both films would also open within weeks of each other. There was plenty of speculation that *Titanic* would act as an iceberg and sink Bond at the box office. However, the much-vaunted 'Battle of the Blockbusters' proved to be a non-event. While *Titanic* went on to become the biggest moneymaker of all time, Bond proved his durability by grossing a very sizable $334 million – only slightly less than *GoldenEye*, which did not have this type of competition. In the USA, *Tomorrow Never Dies* became the top-grossing Bond film, with a box-office take of $124 million ($19 million more than *GoldenEye*). With all due respect to Mr Cameron, Agent 007's grosses were, relatively speaking, also titanic. ■

which was aired extensively in the USA. In London, Christmas 1997 resembled the *Thunderball* mania of Christmas 1965, with Bond promotions more numerous than decorated trees. The department store Dickins & Jones went as far as to devote over two dozen display windows to promote the new film. On television, British specials detailed *The Making of Tomorrow Never Dies* and there was a superb documentary focusing on the history of Bond music. In the USA, *The Secret Files of 007* celebrated the series via interviews with alumni of the series and there was ample coverage of the new film as well.

In terms of merchandise and publishing, Bond was also very visible. Corgi Toys released the *Tomorrow Never Dies* Aston Martin DB5, while BMW issued collectable versions of the 750iL and R1200 motorcycle (both limited editions). Sohni-Wicke produced a toy replica of Bond's Walther P99 and accompanying accessories. In the USA, Exclusive Toy Products manufactured six-and-a-half-inch dolls of Bond, Wai Lin and Carver. Inkworks published a commemorative trading card set based on the film. Fans could get a 'date' with 007 with the *Tomorrow Never Dies* wall calendar by te Neues. *Playboy* kept their tradition of Bond coverage going strong, as European issues

AROUND THE WORLD WITH 007

The film-makers endured a head-spinning schedule of location photography in **Bangkok** (and more remote locales not far from the island of **Phuket** where *The Man With The Golden Gun* had been filmed), **Hamburg**, the **Pyrenees** in France (doubling for the Khyber Pass) and **Baja Studios** in Mexico (where the sinking of the *Devonshire* was staged in the same enormous tank built for *Titanic*). Extensive location work was done throughout the UK, with studio sequences shot at **Eon Studios** at **Frogmore** in Hertfordshire and on the '007 Stage' at **Pinewood Studios**, as well as that studio's tank (which figured prominently in Bond films dating back to *Dr. No*). For the sequence in which Bond encounters Paris Carver in his Hamburg hotel room, the producers used the famous **Stoke Poges Golf Club** in Buckinghamshire – site of the classic golf game in *Goldfinger*. For the *Tomorrow Never Dies* sequence, the ballroom was modified and became 007's hotel suite.

THE LITERARY 007

JAMES BOND WAS 'BORN' IN 1953 WITHIN the pages of *Casino Royale*, Ian Lancaster Fleming's first novel. No one – Fleming included – could have predicted that the modestly pro- moted thriller would be the catalyst for an international literary and cinematic phenomenon. Perhaps the reason for the success of James Bond was the fact that Fleming had many traits in common with the hero he created. Both were daring men of action, both had an almost fanati- cal determination to indulge in fine food and drink and exotic travel. Not the least of their common traits was a shared interest in beautiful women. In dreary post-war Britain, Fleming's writings gave

the public a much-needed escape into a world most would never experience personally. Additionally, as the British Empire continued to shrink, at least in the pages of Fleming's novels time stood still and a lone Englishman could be counted on to save the world from dire threats.

Fleming was born on 28 May 1908 in London. The son of a distinguished, upper-class hero of the First World War who perished in battle, he was educated at Eton where he excelled at athletics. However, he became embroiled in an incident over a girl and left early. He later tried his hand as a journalist for Reuters and gained a degree of fame for his insightful coverage of a spy trial in

Russia during the 1930s. He then became a successful banker but, despite the monetary rewards, did not want to be confined to an office. Instead, he returned to journalism and took a position with *The Times* in London. He was sent to Russia ostensibly to cover news, but in reality was serving as a spy for the British foreign office.

Fleming's desire to avoid the mundane things in life eventually led to his joining British naval intelligence in 1939. During the Second World War, he distinguished himself and rose to the level of commander, reporting to England's master spy Admiral John Godfrey. He later headed a clandestine commando squadron which carried out a number of high-profile missions that Fleming had planned. It was during the war that he first visited Jamaica – and immediately fell in love with the island. Following his career in the navy, Fleming bought a residence on the island and named the modest house Goldeneye. It was here that he lived with his wife, the former Lady Ann Rothermere. (Fleming had married at the age of forty-four when Rothermere became pregnant with his child. Complicating matters was the fact that she first had to divorce her husband.)

Living in Jamaica stimulated Fleming's creativity. Although he had never written a novel before, he had enough confidence to purchase a gold-plated typewriter on which he embarked on his literary journey to create a thriller. The result, *Casino Royale*, was a modest success when published in the UK in 1953. Sales in the USA were poor, however, and the book was retitled *You Asked For It* with equally ineffective results. Nonetheless, it was the hero of Fleming's adventurous tale who eventually began to catch on with readers. James Bond was named after the author of a book entitled *Birds of the West Indies*, which Fleming used extensively in Jamaica. From this modest beginning, sales of the Bond novels eventually grew until, by the late 1950s, he had developed a loyal international following. When President Kennedy named *From Russia, With Love* as one of his ten favourite books of all time, sales of Bond books reached phenomenal levels.

Fortunately, Fleming lived to see the success of the first two Bond movies. Although not a fan of the cinema, he seemed quite pleased with

Broccoli and Saltzman's film adaptations of his works. Tragically, he died on 12 August 1964, one month before the premiere of *Goldfinger* – the film which brought the series to a level of popularity not even Fleming could have hoped for. Bond's literary father was only fifty-six, a victim of a life of high living, hard drinking and smoking. Yet, his life reflected his fitting epitaph: 'I shall not waste my days in trying to prolong them. I shall use my time.'

The twelfth and last of Ian Fleming's full-length James Bond novels, *The Man With The Golden Gun*, was published in 1965, several months after his death. *The Living Daylights* and *Octopussy*, two short stories he had written in 1961 and 1962, were published in 1966, and the Pan paperback edition of the book featured another 007 short story, *The Property of a Lady*.

Two years later, author Kingsley Amis (writing under the name Robert Markham) published the first officially authorized, non-Fleming Bond novel: *Colonel Sun*. Although it was well received by the public and critics, Amis did not attempt an encore. Plans to have a variety of well-known writers create Bond stories never materialized and it was not until 1981 that 007 reappeared in the literary world with the publication of UK author John Gardner's *Licence Renewed*. Initially, Gardner's Bond novels – although controversial among fans – became best sellers. Eventually, however, Gardner seemed to tire of the character. In 1996, he published the last of his thirteen 007 novels, *Cold*.

In 1997, American author Raymond Benson (who had previously written the acclaimed analysis of the 007 phenomenon *The James Bond Bedside Companion*) was chosen to continue the literary adventures of Agent 007. His first published effort relating to Bond was a short story in *Playboy* magazine. His debut novel, *Zero Minus Ten*, was published in mid-1997 and was praised by fans for his determination to bring back the details and descriptive prose which were such important aspects of Ian Fleming's novels. Benson wrote the novelization of *Tomorrow Never Dies* and a year later had his second original Bond novel, *The Facts of Death*, published in the summer of 1998. ■

THE JAMES BOND FAMILY

THERE ARE FAR TOO MANY PEOPLE TO acknowledge individually when it comes to citing those responsible for the success of the James Bond films. Suffice to say that over the course of the decades, Eon Productions has worked with a 'stock company' of directors, writers, technicians, stunt men and administrative talent. Many of these individuals have been associated with the series for many years, and their names are familiar to fans who study every aspect of the films. This extended 'family' is legendary in the motion picture business and the tradition continues to this day. What follows is an abbreviated 'Who's Who' of those individuals who have made multiple contributions to the Bond films.

THE BROCCOLI FAMILY

ALBERT R 'CUBBY' BROCCOLI Along with Harry Saltzman, Cubby was the patriarch of the Bond films. In the 1950s, he and his partner, Irving Allen, formed Warwick Films and the pair produced a series of very successful motion pictures. Broccoli tried to convince Allen to purchase the screen rights to the James Bond novels but his partner was not interested. After the duo disbanded their partnership, Cubby formed Eon Productions with Saltzman, who already had an option on the screen rights to the Bond novels, and secured a one-million-dollar deal with Arthur Krim, president of United Artists, to make the first 007 movie. The rest is history. Cubby would become one of the most respected and honoured producers ever. In 1982, he was given the prestigious Irving G Thalberg Award by the Motion Picture Academy of Arts and Sciences – an event he considered to be the greatest achievement of his career.

Because the Bond films were so time-consuming, Cubby produced only two non-007 films after

The Men with the Midas touch: Harry Saltzman and Cubby Broccoli review costume designs for *Goldfinger* with Honor Blackman in 1964.

1962: *Call Me Bwana* and the children's classic *Chitty Chitty Bang Bang*. The beloved, larger-than-life producer died in 1996 but his legacy will endure as long as great films are honoured.

DANA BROCCOLI Although her name does not appear on the credits of the Bond films, as the wife of Cubby Broccoli Dana has always had an important influence behind the scenes. In fact, Cubby always credited his spouse with persuading him to cast Sean Connery in the role of 007. Dana, a talented screenwriter and playwright, now serves as the head of Eon Productions' affiliated corporation, Danjaq.

MICHAEL G WILSON Although the stepson of Cubby Broccoli and son of Dana, Michael G Wilson never intended to join the Bond film team (his closest association in the earlier days was doubling for a Korean guard in *Goldfinger*). He became a successful lawyer specializing in tax cases. Ironically, it was these talents that led Cubby to ask him to lend his knowledge temporarily to the running of Eon Productions. Wilson became actively involved when Cubby and Harry Saltzman split in the mid-1970s. He later took an active interest in the making of the films, and served as assistant to the producer on *The Spy Who Loved Me*. Then he became executive producer on *Moonraker*, *For Your Eyes Only* and *Octopussy*. Starting with *A View To A Kill*, Michael would be Cubby's full partner as producer, a role he would carry on with for *The Living Daylights* and *Licence To Kill*. Wilson would later produce subsequent Bond films with Barbara Broccoli. As 007 fans know, his talents also extend into the field of writing, as Michael has coauthored (with Richard Maibaum) the screenplays for *For Your Eyes Only*, *Octopussy*, *A View To A Kill*, *The Living Daylights* and *Licence To Kill*. His temporary assignment at Eon had become a permanent career.

BARBARA BROCCOLI James Bond has always been an important part of Barbara's life and career. She

Above: Director Terence Young with Claudine Auger at the after-premiere dinner party for *Thunderball* in London.

Below: Composer John Barry with director Lewis Gilbert at a scoring session for *You Only Live Twice*.

could hardly escape him as the daughter of Cubby and Dana Broccoli. A graduate of Loyola University in Los Angeles, where she gained a degree in motion picture and television communications, Barbara has been a long-time contributor to the 007 series. A popular presence on the set, she has earned a reputation for taking her responsibilities very seriously and for accepting the most challenging assignments. She served as assistant director on *Octopussy* and *A View To A Kill* and as associate producer on *The Living Daylights* and *Licence To Kill* (for which she oversaw the incredible tanker lorry chase sequence). She and Michael G Wilson produced *GoldenEye* and *Tomorrow Never Dies*.

Additionally, Barbara serves as head of development for Danjaq. She also has her own independent production company, Astoria Productions, which recently made the highly acclaimed HBO film *Crime of the Century*, which detailed the notorious kidnapping case involving Charles Lindbergh's baby.

PRODUCERS, DIRECTORS & EDITORS

HARRY SALTZMAN The Canadian producer had an unusual start in show business: booking acts in vaudeville. He later emigrated to France where he brought this talent to the music hall and circus circuit. Following a stint in the Royal Canadian Air Force in the Second World War, Saltzman established himself as a producer of successful television series. He was later one of the co-founders of Woodfall Productions, and under this banner produced such highly acclaimed British films as *The Entertainer*, *Look Back in Anger* and *Saturday Night and Sunday Morning*. Harry eventually obtained an option on the Bond novels but could not find financing until he became allied with Cubby Broccoli. While Cubby was content overseeing the Bond phenomenon, Saltzman was more restless. He later produced the popular Harry Palmer films with Michael Caine, *Chimes at Midnight* and the epic *Battle of Britain*. He was also a major investor in Technicolor, but he eventually lost heavily on that gamble. Saltzman and Broccoli always had a tenuous relationship at best and Harry eventually sold his share of the Bond films to United Artists. *The Man With The Golden Gun* would be his final 007 producing credit. He remained marginally active in film and stage production until his death in 1994.

TERENCE YOUNG The influential British director of *Dr. No*, *From Russia With Love* and *Thunderball*, by all accounts Young helped form the popular conception of the screen hero. He groomed Sean Connery for the role and remained close friends with the actor over the years. Young had also worked previously for Cubby Broccoli's Warwick Films but it was the success of his Bond films that catapulted him into the ranks of internationally recognized directors. He died in 1994.

GUY HAMILTON Hamilton introduced a more overt brand of humour into the Bond series, starting with his first 007 film *Goldfinger*. He would later direct *Diamonds Are Forever*, *Live And Let Die* and *The Man With The Golden Gun*.

LEWIS GILBERT Gilbert was director of three of the biggest Bond spectacles: *You Only Live Twice*, *The Spy Who Loved Me* and *Moonraker*.

JOHN GLEN A former editor on the Bond films, Glen eventually rose to the rank of director and to date has directed the most entries in the series: *For Your Eyes Only*, *Octopussy*, *A View To A Kill*, *The Living Daylights* and *Licence To Kill*. As editor and second unit director, Glen worked on *On Her Majesty's Secret Service*, *The Spy Who Loved Me* and *Moonraker*.

PETER HUNT Hunt joined the Bond films as editor of *Dr. No*, and then went on to edit *From Russia With Love*, *Goldfinger* and *Thunderball*. His innovative style of lightning-fast editing techniques has influenced virtually all action adventure films since. He also served

Above: John Glen with Roger Moore, 'clowning' on the set of *Octopussy*.

Below: Aerial photographer (left) Johnny Jordan on location in Switzerland for *On Her Majesty's Secret Service.*

as second unit director for *You Only Live Twice*. With *On Her Majesty's Secret Service*, he made an impressive debut as director and launched a successful career in that capacity.

TOM PEVSNER Pevsner was associate producer on *For Your Eyes Only*, *Octopussy*, *A View To A Kill*, *The Living Daylights* and *Licence To Kill*. He took over the role of executive producer for *GoldenEye*.

ANTHONY WAYE Waye was the first assistant director on *For Your Eyes Only* and *Octopussy*, production supervisor on *A View To A Kill*, *The Living Daylights* and *Licence To Kill* and line producer for *Tomorrow Never Dies*.

JOHN GROVER Grover was assistant editor on *The Spy Who Loved Me* and *Moonraker* and editor on *For Your Eyes Only*, *Octopussy*, *The Living Daylights* and *Licence To Kill*.

WRITERS

RICHARD MAIBAUM Maibaum played a major role in the definition of the Bond character. With his innovative screenplays, he successfully integrated a hip sense of humour into the violent proceedings. A veteran of Cubby Broccoli's Warwick Films, Maibaum would either author or co-author the screenplays for every Bond film except *You Only Live Twice*, *Live And Let Die* and *Moonraker* until his death in 1991. Starting with *For Your Eyes Only*, he collaborated on the scripts with Michael G Wilson.

DIRECTORS OF PHOTOGRAPHY & CAMERAMEN

TED MOORE Moore was director of photography on *Dr. No*, *From Russia With Love*, *Goldfinger*, *Thunderball*, *Diamonds Are Forever*, *Live And Let Die* and *The Man With The Golden Gun* (with Oswald Morris).

ALEC MILLS The camera operator on *On Her Majesty's Secret Service*, *The Spy Who Loved Me* and

Octopussy, Mills went on to be the director of photography on *The Living Daylights* and *Licence To Kill*.

JOHNNY JORDAN Jordan was the aerial photographer who lost a foot filming the spectacular Little Nellie air battle in *You Only Live Twice*. He returned for *On Her Majesty's Secret Service* and shot exciting footage of the ski chases while suspended in a harness beneath a helicopter. The valiant Jordan died the next year in an accident while filming *Catch 22*.

ALAN HUME Hume was director of photography on *For Your Eyes Only*, *Octopussy* and *A View To A Kill*.

WILLY BOGNER JR Former Olympic skier from Germany and acclaimed film-maker, Bogner specializes in filming seemingly impossible action sequences set on snow or ice. His speciality is holding a hand-held camera while skiing backwards. Bogner worked on *On Her Majesty's Secret Service*, *The Spy Who Loved Me*, *For Your Eyes Only* and *A View To A Kill*.

STUNT MEN

BOB SIMMONS One of the key players in the success of the Bond action sequences, Simmons was a long-time stunt man on the films and eventually progressed to stunt coordinator. His flair for staging realistic and imaginative fight sequences has seldom been equalled. He also doubled for Sean Connery in many films and it is he, not Connery, who appears in the opening gun barrel of the first three Bond movies. Simmons' last film prior to his death was *A View To A Kill*. He had also published his autobiography, entitled *Nobody Does It Better*.

GEORGE LEECH This stunt man extraordinaire appeared in numerous Bond films. Leech was one of the crew members of the Disco Volante in *Thunderball*, doubled as Q's luckless assistant who tests a bullet-proof coat in *Goldfinger*, performed Bond's escape from Piz Gloria via a

Above: Bob Simmons with Roger Moore on location for *Octopussy*.

Below: Maurice Binder with Roger Moore on the set of *For Your Eyes Only*. Binder's brilliant main title sequences became an integral part of the Bond phenomenon.

cable car in *On Her Majesty's Secret Service* and was devoured by a shark in *For Your Eyes Only*.

PAUL WESTON This talented stunt man was seen in *Moonraker*, *Octopussy*, *The Living Daylights* and *Licence To Kill*.

B J WORTH Worth is a specialist in performing incredible aerial stunts, including the free fall in *Moonraker*, the Eiffel Tower jump in *A View To A Kill*, the HALO jump in *Tomorrow Never Dies* and the amazing fight on a net dangling from a cargo plane in *The Living Daylights*. He also worked on *Octopussy* and *GoldenEye*.

SIMON CRANE Crane was a stunt man in *A View To A Kill*, *The Living Daylights* and *Licence To Kill* and then stunt co-ordinator for *GoldenEye*.

THE MEN BEHIND THE TITLES

MAURICE BINDER Binder became legendary in the film industry for his highly innovative main title sequences, which would become a trademark of the Bond series. His penchant for using nude women in silhouette amidst hi-tech special effects became synonymous with the 007 films. Binder provided the main titles for every film up to and including *Licence To Kill*, with the exception of *From Russia With Love* and *Goldfinger*.

ROBERT BROWNJOHN As British advertising art director, he created the highly sensual title sequence for *From Russia With Love* and *Goldfinger*.

DANIEL KLEINMAN Following in the footsteps of the late Maurice Binder, Kleinman has proved that he is more than up to the job. The former director of Bond music videos provided the titles for *GoldenEye* – a superbly designed sequence featuring Soviet icons falling in ruins. His work on *Tomorrow Never Dies* is no less impressive.

SPECIAL EFFECTS

JOHN STEARS The only person to date to be awarded the Oscar for visual effects on a Bond film (*Thunderball*), Stears is the man who can be credited with providing some of the most inspired action scenes in the series, and was the person with enough audacity to cut up a new Aston Martin DB5 to install the gadgets for *Goldfinger*. Stears, an Oscar winner for *Star Wars*, worked on all the Bond films up to and including *On Her Majesty's Secret Service* as well as *The Man With The Golden Gun*.

DEREK MEDDINGS Famous for his superlative work with miniatures, Meddings – who won the Oscar for *Superman* – worked on *Live And Let Die*, *The Man With The Golden Gun*, *The Spy Who Loved Me*, *Moonraker* (for which he was nominated for an Oscar), *For Your Eyes Only* and *GoldenEye*. He died during the final days of production on the last film and it was dedicated to his memory.

JOHN RICHARDSON A veteran of the Bond films, Richardson worked closely with Derek Meddings. An Oscar winner for *Aliens*, he provided many of the miniature special effects for *Moonraker*, *Octopussy*, *A View To A Kill*, *The Living Daylights*, *Licence To Kill* and *Tomorrow Never Dies*.

CHRIS CORBOULD Courbould was the special-effects supervisor for *GoldenEye* and *Tomorrow Never Dies*. He had previously worked as technician and second unit supervisor on *Moonraker*, *For Your Eyes Only*, *A View To A Kill*, *The Living Daylights* and *Licence To Kill*.

PRODUCTION DESIGNERS

KEN ADAM Probably the first production designer to become a celebrity in his own right, Adam raised the art to new heights with

Above: Production designer Peter Lamont is seen here talking to fans at Pinewood Studios.

Below: A light moment between production designer Ken Adam and Sean Connery on the set of *Diamonds Are Forever* at Pinewood Studios.

his spectacular and highly acclaimed sets for the Bond films. His work on the '007 Stage' for *The Spy Who Loved Me* (with Peter Lamont) and the volcano set for *You Only Live Twice* were examples of production design at its most impressive. Adam, who won Oscars for *Barry Lyndon* and *The Madness of King George*, was never thus honoured for his work on the Bond films. He served as production designer for *Dr. No*, *Goldfinger*, *Thunderball*, *You Only Live Twice*, *Diamonds Are Forever*, *The Spy Who Loved Me* and *Moonraker*.

PETER LAMONT Lamont's association with the Bond series dates back to *Goldfinger* when he served as a draughtsman working with Ken Adam. He subsequently worked on many of the early Bonds and finally graduated to production designer with *For Your Eyes Only*, *Octopussy*, *A View To A Kill*, *The Living Daylights*, *Licence To Kill* and *GoldenEye*. Lamont also gained critical praise for his work with James Cameron, serving as production designer on *True Lies*. His superbly detailed re-creation of Cameron's *Titanic* earned him a well-deserved Oscar.

PETER MURTON Murton was art director for *Goldfinger* and *Thunderball* and production designer for *The Man With The Golden Gun*.

SYD CAIN A multi-talented veteran of the Bond series, the acclaimed Cain worked on the art direction of *Dr. No* and eventually progressed to production designer for *From Russia With Love*, *On Her Majesty's Secret Service* and *Live And Let Die*. More recently, he worked on storyboards for the creation of the *GoldenEye* weapons system and other key sequences in the film. ∎

AGENT 007 AND POPULAR CULTURE

Few cinematic heroes have had as influential an impact on popular culture as James Bond. Although the success of the Bond novels in the mid-1950s spawned an avalanche of imitators in the literary world, the most glaring example of the 007 influence came with the success of the films. By the mid-1960s, virtually every actor in the world had a spy film or television series in development. Some were quite inspired, such as the 1965 film version of John le Carré's *The Spy Who Came in From the Cold* (with an Oscar-nominated performance by Richard Burton). Others were low-budget potboilers, such as *Spy in Your Eye*, *Secret Agent Fireball* and *Bang! Bang! You're Dead!* So desperate were producers to get on the Bond bandwagon that they even convinced Sean Connery's brother Neil (at the time a plasterer) to star in the notorious exploitation film *Operation Kid Brother*. This second-rate Italian 'epic' also featured a host of alumni from the Bond films including Lois Maxwell, Bernard Lee, Anthony Dawson, Adolfo Celi and Daniela Bianchi. Nevertheless, the spy boom of the 1960s did produce some worthy spin-offs of the Bond phenomenon.

THE MAN FROM U.N.C.L.E.

This classic series actually had input from Ian Fleming, who originally gave advice to producer Norman Felton about development of the show. When Broccoli and Saltzman protested that Fleming was helping to undermine the Bond films, the author sheepishly withdrew – although he did create the name of the show's hero, Napoleon Solo. The series starred Robert Vaughn as the dapper Solo, David McCallum as his mysterious and sombre Russian fellow agent Ilya Kuryakin, and Leo G Carroll as their dignified, if somewhat eccentric, superior Alexander Waverly. U.N.C.L.E. stood for the United Network Command for Law and Enforcement and each week the secret agency battled the evil forces of the SPECTRE-like organization THRUSH. The

The Man From U.N.C.L.E. proved so popular that it spawned a series of feature films. The first – *To Trap a Spy* – co-starred *Thunderball*'s Luciana Paluzzi.

show, which premiered in September 1964, was successful because it did not take itself too seriously. The lead actors were marvellously talented and Vaughn and McCallum became international teen idols. Before the series was taken off air in early 1968, the show had inspired a number of feature-length films which consisted of two-part

James Coburn as *Our Man Flint* (1966), the first of his two appearances in the role.

episodes combined with limited original footage generally featuring *femme fatales* designed to spice up box-office potential. On a return-on-investment ratio, these low-budget features were among the most successful films of their time. In 1983, Vaughn and McCallum repeated their roles in the well-received television film *Return of the Man From U.N.C.L.E.*, which also featured George Lazenby.

MATT HELM

In the 1950s, Cubby Broccoli's producing partner Irving Allen declined to take up Cubby's suggestion to purchase the screen rights to the Bond novels with him. Trying to make the best of a bad decision, Allen tried to exploit his own spy franchise, starting in 1966 with the Matt Helm films, based on author Donald Hamilton's novels. Hamilton fans were horrified when Allen cast Dean Martin as the playboy spy from the organization ICE. They correctly feared this would turn the series into an outrageous spoof. Artistically, the Helm films were a case of diminishing returns. The four films produced between 1966 and 1969 had shoddy production values and plots. Still, Martin was charismatic enough to make these romps enjoyable and they were considerable

box-office successes. The best of the lot was the initial film, *The Silencers* (1966). It was followed by *Murderer's Row* (1966), *The Ambushers* (1967) and *The Wrecking Crew* (1969).

DEREK FLINT

James Coburn made only two films as the super-spy Derek Flint, but they are still well regarded among spy-film aficionados. Flint was an intentionally over-the-top parody of Bond and Hugh Hefner – a seemingly immortal superman who lived in a luxurious penthouse with an array of beautiful women. Always reluctant to disturb his elaborate lifestyle, Flint had to be cajoled into saving the world by the crusty boss wonderfully played by Lee J Cobb. Flint worked alone and used only one hi-tech gadget – a cigarette lighter that contained over eighty secret weapons. Coburn was terrific in the title role, making two appearances in *Our Man Flint* (1966) and *In Like Flint* (1967).

I SPY

The most intelligent and highly acclaimed of the Bond-inspired television series, *I Spy* (which ran from 1965 to 1968) was never more than a moderate success in the ratings. Filmed on a large budget, the series was unique in that it was shot in exotic locations all round the world. The show starred Robert Culp as Kelly Robinson, a tennis professional who was actually a secret agent for the US government. Bill Cosby shot to stardom as his colleague and trainer Alexander Scott. Cosby became the first black actor to star in a successful dramatic series and he won several Emmys for his work. He and Culp enjoyed a genuine chemistry and made *I Spy* one of the best of the secret agent series. They repeated their roles in 1995 for *I Spy Returns*, but the television film caused little fanfare because the plot mistakenly centred on the spy's son and daughter.

HARRY PALMER

A gritty look at the espionage world, the Harry Palmer films stripped the glamour from the life of a spy during the Cold War era. The series, based on the novels by Len Deighton and produced by Harry Saltzman, presented Michael Caine as a reluctant, world-weary MI6 agent who would rather bed willing women than help save the West from Communism. The first film of the series, *The Ipcress File* (1965), was a critically acclaimed box-office hit. *Funeral in Berlin* (1966) followed with impressive results. The third film, *Billion*

Dollar Brain (1967), was an attempt to bring in Bond-like spectacle but by then the bloom was off the rose. Caine replayed the role of Palmer in the 1996 television film *Bullet to Beijing*.

GET SMART!

Created by Mel Brooks and Buck Henry, this situation comedy, which made its debut in 1965, spoofed the Bond genre in a broad way and became a classic series. Don Adams starred as bumbling Agent '86' of CONTROL, an organization which battled the evil forces of KAOS. Smart was assisted by the beautiful Agent '99', played by Barbara Feldon, along with a strange assortment of hilarious supporting characters including Edward Platt as the chief and Dick Gautier as Hymie the robot. The series was so popular that it spawned several famous tag lines, including Smart's trademark 'Sorry about that, Chief ...' and 'Would you believe ...'. Adams revived the role (sans Feldon) in the 1980 feature film *The Nude Bomb* and with Feldon for the 1990 television film *Get Smart Again!* A revival of the television series in the early 1990s was not successful, largely because of uninspired writing and the fact that Adams had been relegated to a supporting role.

THE WILD, WILD WEST

Premiering in 1965, this series was an unabashed version of 007 set in the American West. Robert Conrad starred as James West, a government agent who travelled in a luxurious train which concealed a virtual Q Branch of incredible weapons and gadgets. He was assisted by partner Artemus Gordon, a master of disguise played by Ross Martin. The series was quite clever and proved to be a hit in the USA. The show spawned two television reunion films in the 1970s and 80s, but both were far too camp to capture the feel of the original series.

MISSION: IMPOSSIBLE

This was an ingeniously scripted series which initially starred Steven Hill as the leader of the IMF (Impossible Mission Force), a group of highly diverse secret agents each with their own unique talents. When Hill left the show in the first season he was replaced by Peter Graves, who is most closely identified with the series. The plots were incredible, but so well written that the scenarios always seemed plausible. The charismatic cast included Martin Landau, Barbara Bain, Greg Morris, Peter Graves and, later, Leonard Nimoy. The series was a sizable hit and ran for many

Even Sean Connery's brother Neil joined the spy craze with this Italian 007 rip-off, which also starred Bond actors.

years. It was (unsuccessfully) revived with Graves in the 1990s, but the big-screen 1995 adaptation starring Tom Cruise was a box-office smash (although purists correctly argued that it had little of the flavour of the series).

DANGER MAN

Patrick McGoohan starred as John Drake in this real-world look at Cold War espionage. Although Drake had remarkable abilities, he did not resemble Bond in any overt way. He did not womanize, was subject to making costly mistakes and disdained the use of guns, preferring to use his wits to stay alive. The series, known as *Danger Man* in the UK, was expanded to an hour and exported to the USA where it was successful under the title *Secret Agent* (aided immeasurably by a hit title song by Johnny Rivers). McGoohan, who maintains a cult following, may have used the character of Drake as the inspiration for his classic 1967 series *The Prisoner*, one of the greatest series on television.

OTHER SHOWS

Other notable shows that were eventually influenced by the Bond films (but did not necessarily owe their existence to them) were *The Avengers* and *The Persuaders*, the latter starring Roger Moore. ∎

THE OTHER JAMES BONDS

Peter Sellers and Ursula Andress in an out-take from the 1967 satirical version of *Casino Royale*.

AS MOST BOND FANS KNOW, SEAN Connery was not the first actor to play Agent 007. That distinction fell to American actor Barry Nelson, who played Bond in the one-hour, 1954 US live television adaptation of *Casino Royale*. The show is regarded as high camp now, with a crewcut Nelson known as 'Card Sense Jimmy Bond'. However, this was a noble attempt to retain the flavour of Ian Fleming's first Bond novel, and Peter Lorre was memorable as the villainous Le Chiffre. The show was largely unseen, but in recent years has popped up in various incarnations on home video. (Fans beware: all versions on video are missing the climax of the show except for *Casino Royale: The Collector's Edition* which is available from The Ian Fleming Foundation.)

In 1967, Charles K Feldman, who had the screen rights to *Casino Royale*, decided he could not compete with the Broccoli and Saltzman franchise. Instead, he opted to adapt Fleming's novel into a bloated, big-budget madcap comedy starring an impressive selection of big names in the film business. Among those caught up in this glorious mess were Peter Sellers, Ursula Andress, David Niven, Woody Allen, William Holden, John Huston and many others. The film went instantly over budget and any semblance of a plot was tossed out to make way for spectacular comedy set-pieces. It took five directors to bring this disjointed epic to the screen. However, ignoring the fact that it is a terrible waste of a wonderful novel, the film has many highlights. Its sheer goofiness

STRIP CARTOON BOND

In the late 1950s, *The Daily Express* brought the comic strip rights to serialize the James Bond novels. Written by a staff writer, they were drawn by John McLusky. The strips appeared only on weekdays and ran for 139 days. Although some three years before the film of *Dr. No*, the similarity of McLusky's Bond to that of Connery is uncanny. The first strip was *Casino Royale*, followed by *Live And Let Die*, *Diamonds Are Forever*, *From Russia, With Love*, *Dr. No*, *Goldfinger*, *Risico*, *From A View To A Kill*, *For Your Eyes Only* and *You Only Live Twice* which were adapted from the novels by Henry Gammidge.

After a twelve-year absence, Sean Connery returned to the role of 007 in *Never Say Never Again*, a 1983 remake of *Thunderball*.

is infectious and there are many moments of truly inspired comedy. Contrary to popular belief, it was also a critical and box-office success.

The most interesting development in terms of a rival Bond film was Sean Connery's return to the role, after a twelve-year absence, in 1983's *Never Say Never Again*, a remake of *Thunderball* which derived from producer Kevin McClory's court settlement with Ian Fleming in the early 1960s. McClory had originally hired Connery to co-author a script (with Len Deighton) entitled *James Bond of the Secret Service* in the mid-1970s. However, the threat of legal challenges from Eon prevented him from obtaining financing. Ultimately, producer/lawyer Jack Schwartzman succeeded in bringing the project to the screen almost a decade later with Connery in the role of Bond and Irvin Kershner as director.

The film was a commercial success, although on an artistic level fans argue its merits. While all agree that Connery gave a terrific performance as a world-weary Bond, many 007 purists felt the film lacked the polished look of an Eon production. It did boast an impressive cast, with Kim Basinger in a star-making turn as Domino, Klaus Maria Brandauer wonderfully charismatic as Largo and Barbara Carrera superb as the villainous Fatima Blush. Max Von Sydow portrayed Blofeld, but his scenes are far too limited to have any real impact. This was a troubled production to get off the ground and the final cut suffers from erratic editing and a weak climax. However, there are many memorable sequences and the fact that Connery returned once more to the role was

enough for most fans. *Never Say Never Again* was a sizable hit.

The next incarnation of James Bond was by far the most unusual – *James Bond Jr*, an animated series which premiered in 1992. The show centred on the adventures of Bond's nephew and his assortment of eccentric colleagues, such as IQ (the gadget-creating nephew of Q). Although 007 himself never appeared in the short-lived series, the animated heroes did battle with hi-tech versions of Bond bad guys like Oddjob and Jaws. ■

THE 007 PHENOMENON

Above: Pierce Brosnan (with co-stars Desmond Llewelyn and Izabella Scorupco) at the launch of the BMW Z3 in New York.

Right: Authors Lee Pfeiffer (left) and Dave Worrall with Sean Connery in New York City, 1997.

JAMES BOND FANS HAVE TRADITIONALLY been very active and creative in the ways they pay homage to Agent 007. In recent years, many high-profile international events have provided a forum for aficionados to 'bond' with other fans and collectors as well as alumni from the films. In 1993, Spy Guise made an early attempt at organizing Bond fans with the 'Spy-Fi Convention' in New Jersey. The event attracted fans from around the world as well as celebrity guest Lois Maxwell. In 1994, Creation Entertainment held the first official James Bond Convention in Los Angeles. Hundreds of fans turned out for an elaborate display of rare film props and dozens of dealers' tables selling 007 collectables. Celebrities who appeared included George Lazenby, Martine Beswick, Lynn-Holly Johnson, Peter Hunt, Gloria Hendry, Richard Kiel, Bruce Glover, Bill Conti and others. The highlight was the first 'Goldeneye Award', which was given to Cubby Broccoli by

The Ian Fleming Foundation. Pierce Brosnan was seen on film presenting the award, which Michael G Wilson accepted on behalf of Cubby (who was ailing). This was followed by a glorious thirtieth anniversary screening of *Goldfinger* at the prestigious Academy Theater.

In 1995, Creation held another Bond convention in New York City to commemorate the premiere of *GoldenEye*. To the delight of fans, the guest list included Pierce Brosnan, Michael G Wilson, Martin Campbell, writer Bruce Feirstein, Izabella Scorupco, Famke Janssen and Desmond Llewelyn – each of whom graciously answered questions from the audience. The following evening, thousands of fans joined the cast and crew for the star-studded premiere of the film at Radio City Music Hall.

In 1996, Event Media hosted 'The Official James Bond 007 Jamaican Festival' on the lush Caribbean island. Ursula Andress attended, returning to Jamaica for the first time since *Dr. No*. Other celebrities included Lois Maxwell, George Lazenby, Richard Kiel, Maud Adams, John Stears, Jay Milligan, Michael France, John Glen and others. Highlights included exclusive tours of Fleming's home, Goldeneye, entertainment by the Byron Lee Band (who appeared in *Dr. No*), panel

AROUND THE NET WITH 007

Bond fans and collectors satisfy themselves by holding informal collectors' events throughout the world, often sponsored by Bond-related fan magazines. Additionally, they keep up-to-date with the latest news on high-profile websites. Among the more notable are:

❋ MGM/UA'S Official 007 Website **http://www.mgm.com/bond/** This website has the latest official news on the world of Bond as well as updates on films in production. There are also sites for the most recent 007 films.

❋ NUV'S 007 Shrine **http://www.nuvs.com/jbond/** This web magazine features the latest news, tours, interviews and other aspects of interest to fans of Bond and other classic spy films. The site also links to **www.spyguise.com**, the world's largest on-line catalogue of licensed and vintage 007 collectables and memorabilia. Fans can also subscribe to *Collecting 007* magazine.

❋ Kimberly Last's 007 Site **http://www.mcs.net/~klast/www/bond.html** One of the most acclaimed sites, it features up-to-date information about the Bond films and the actors who have played 007.

❋ The Ian Fleming Foundation **www.ianfleming.org** A non-profit organization, the foundation preserves and promotes Ian Fleming's works. The website allows fans to keep up with the latest Bond news and to subscribe to *Goldeneye* magazine.

discussions, contests and endless parties – as well as an opportunity to view rare collectables and props. At a black-tie dinner, celebrities were given awards by the government of Jamaica.

Pinewood Studios has also been the site of many notable Bond-related events. The James Bond Fan Club has held Christmas luncheons in the lavish dining-hall which are attended by celebrities from the series. In 1995, TWINE Entertainment brought many alumni of the films to the studio to shoot the documentary *The Making of Goldfinger and Thunderball* for MGM/UA and Eon Productions. More recently, the 'Let's Bond in Britain' tours of James Bond film sites have made Pinewood a highlight of the programme. The studio, which is out-of-bounds to the public, has allowed Dave Worrall to lead attendees on extensive tours of the areas in which the Bond films were shot, including the famed '007 Stage'. Other stops on the one-week itinerary have included Stoke Poges Golf Club, Shrublands health spa from *Thunderball*, and the graveyard from *For Your Eyes Only*. The group has also attended pre-premiere screenings of the latest Bond films in London (courtesy of Eon Productions, UIP and MGM/UA) and have held parties in the 'Bond Room' at London's Planet Hollywood. Celebrity attendees have included Desmond Llewelyn, Lois Maxwell and production designer Syd Cain. ∎

Above left: Christopher Lee at the James Bond Fan Club's Christmas luncheon at Pinewood Studios, November 1996.

Above right: George Lazenby enjoying himself at 'The Official James Bond Jamaica Festival' at the Jamaican Grand Hotel, October 1996.

Left: Members of the 'Let's Bond in Britain' annual tour of film sites visit Stoke Poges, where the classic golf game in *Goldfinger* was filmed, December 1997.

Their world was not enough...